Creative Visualization
FOR
DUMMIES®

by Robin Nixon

WILEY

A John Wiley and Sons, Ltd, Publication

Creative Visualization For Dummies®

Published by
John Wiley & Sons, Ltd
The Atrium
Southern Gate
Chichester
West Sussex
PO19 8SQ
England

Email (for orders and customer service enquiries): cs-books@wiley.co.uk

Visit our Home Page on www.wiley.com

For general information on our other products and services, please contact our Customer Care Department within the U.S. at 877-762-2974, outside the U.S. at 317-572-3993, or fax 317-572-4002.

For technical support, please visit www.wiley.com/techsupport.

Wiley also publishes its books in a variety of electronic formats and by print-on-demand. Some content that appears in standard print versions of this book may not be available in other formats. For more information about Wiley products, visit us at www.wiley.com.

British Library Cataloguing in Publication Data: A catalogue record for this book is available from the British Library

ISBN: 978-1-119-99264-6 (paperback), 978-1-119-99342-1 (ebook), 978-1-119-99421-3 (ebook), 978-1-119-99420-6 (ebook)

Printed and bound in Great Britain by TJ International Ltd, Padstow, Cornwall

10 9 8 7 6 5 4 3 2 1

WILEY

About the Author

Robin Nixon is a technology and motivational author who has written books for McGraw-Hill and O'Reilly, as well as publishing over 500 articles on topics including technology, self help and the environment. He has been the director of Internet and software development companies in both the UK and US, as well as running hotel and dining businesses in both countries. For the last 25 years Robin has practiced creative visualization on a daily basis in both his personal and business lives. This is Robin's 9th book.

Dedication

For Julie

Author's Acknowledgements

I would like to thank Nicole Hermitage for commissioning this book, Kerry Laundon, Jo Jones, Mike Bryant, Andy Finch, Carrie Burchfield, Jennifer Bingham and Charlie Wilson for helping me to bring it to completion, and everyone else who has helped to create this book, and without whom it would not be the same.

Publisher's Acknowledgements

We're proud of this book; please send us your comments through our Dummies online registration form located at www.dummies.com/register/.

Some of the people who helped bring this book to market include the following:

Commissioning, Editorial, and Media Development

Development Editors: Jo Jones and Charlie Wilson

Commissioning Editors: Nicole Hermitage and Kerry Laundon

Assistant Editor: Ben Kemble

Copy Editor: Andy Finch

Technical Editor: Mike Bryant

Proofreader: David Price

Publisher: David Palmer

Production Manager: Daniel Mersey

Cover Photos: © iStock / Dmitry Melnikov

Cartoons: Rich Tennant (www.the5thwave.com)

Composition Services

Project Coordinator: Kristie Rees

Layout and Graphics: Cheryl Grubbs, Kim Tabor

Proofreaders: Broccoli Information Management

Indexer: BIM Indexing & Proofreading Services

Special Help

Brand Reviewers: Carrie Burchfield and Jennifer Bingham

Publishing and Editorial for Consumer Dummies

Kathleen Nebenhaus, Vice President and Executive Publisher

Kristin Ferguson-Wagstaffe, Product Development Director

Ensley Eikenburg, Associate Publisher, Travel

Kelly Regan, Editorial Director, Travel

Publishing for Technology Dummies

Andy Cummings, Vice President and Publisher

Composition Services

Debbie Stailey, Director of Composition Services

Contents at a Glance

Table of Contents

Introduction

· ·

*P*eople have known that creative visualization works for thousands of years, but only recently have they named the practice and put it through studies to prove its efficacy. *Creative visualization* is based on the simple observation that when you imagine something, such as a goal in life you wish to attain, you're then able to bring that desire to fruition. In fact, often only by first visualizing something can you develop the idea or ignite the creative spurt that goes off in your brain like a light bulb.

But creative visualization isn't just useful for being creative; it's also a powerful personal development tool you can use to modify traits that are making you unhappy, increase your levels of energy and stamina, become more confident, and enjoy life more fully.

Almost without knowing it, we all use visualization on a daily basis when daydreaming, or thinking about people, places, and things. Visualizing is something we do naturally, which creative visualization simply harnesses into a more structured form.

Furthermore, creative visualization can help you to achieve goals in life that you've otherwise found hard to achieve. Using powerful visualizations you can clearly focus on your aims, set the right goals, and imagine attaining them. By doing so you bring forth the desire and commitment to overcome obstacles and stick with your ambitions until you achieve them.

This book also shows you how to use creative visualization to overcome anxiety and phobias, increase your mental and physical wellbeing, improve your sleeping patterns, revise for exams more efficiently, overcome procrastination, and much, much more.

With such a range of benefits resulting from bringing creative visualization into your life, reading this book and trying the exercises can open up a whole new way of thinking and living, and can help you make the changes you want in your life.

About This Book

Unlike other personal improvement systems you may have tried, I believe that creative visualization is the most natural and easy means of achieving the changes in your life that you desire. After you get the hang of creative visualization, the techniques are so obvious that you may wonder why you never used them before. And you also begin to see results very quickly, which in turn spurs you on to keep going and use creative visualization even more in your life.

And making creative visualization part of your life is so easy! After you've practised visualizing a few times, you barely notice that you're visualizing because the techniques become entirely embedded in your regular routine and merge into your way of life. More than that, though, because you can make the visualizations as beautiful as you like, they're a joy to use and you enhance your life simply by practising them.

This book's main aim is to get you started on the road to bringing creative visualization into your life. The practice has worked wonders for me and thousands of other people, and I know that once you get these techniques under your belt, your enjoyment of life and sense of fulfilment is going to be greater than ever.

Please note, however, that wherever I mention the ability of creative visualization to help with your personal health – for example, by assisting you to become more relaxed and lower your blood pressure – I'm not suggesting that you ignore medical advice in preference to these techniques. Far from it, in fact. Modern medicine has a tremendous ability to help with all manner of illnesses and ailments, so always consult a doctor or licensed practitioner when you first notice any health problem. Always think of creative visualization as an enhancement that helps increase the effectiveness of everything you undertake – including professional medical treatment – and not a replacement for it.

Conventions Used in This Book

To help maximise the clarity of information in this book I adopt a few conventions:

- ✔ *Italics* are used for emphasis and to highlight new words or define terms.
- ✔ **Boldface** is used to indicate the key concept in a list.
- ✔ A `monofont` is used for web and email addresses.

Also, when I refer to the psychological concept of the *unconscious mind,* if you prefer you can read this as the better-known term *subconscious mind.* Either term refers to a sort of consciousness bubbling underneath your main consciousness and which remains alert and active at all times. You may also choose to think of this mind as the soul.

Within each chapter you find a set of mental flash cards, which you're more than welcome to replace with your own, and I encourage you to do so. The best visualizations are the ones that you create for yourself because you may find them easier to remember and may work better for you.

What You're Not to Read

To make this book as interesting as possible. I include anecdotes and simple mental flash card visualizations throughout. You can choose to ignore these sections if you prefer because they serve merely to augment the main text of the book.

Foolish Assumptions

In writing this book, I make the following assumptions about you; I hope they aren't too presumptuous:

- ✔ You're a human being, the same as me and everyone else on Earth.
- ✔ You have aspects of your life that you want to change.
- ✔ You may have tried other personal improvement systems, perhaps with less than satisfactory results.
- ✔ You're ready to move on to a new level in your life.
- ✔ You want to be a happier, more confident, and more fulfilled person.

How This Book Is Organised

This book is divided into five parts, which include 21 chapters. The table of contents lists all the headings, allowing you to find the bits that interest you easily and quickly. Following is an overview of the major sections.

Part I: Introducing Creative Visualization

In this part of the book, I introduce creative visualization, explain how and why it works, and detail some of the things it can help you to attain or achieve. I also describe how you can prepare yourself so the visualizations provided in later sections have the maximum benefit.

Part II: Discovering How to Visualize

This part of the book covers the main types of visualizations, including unguided, guided, audio, visual, and written visualizations, as well as the power and purpose of positive affirmations. It also shows you how to start making changes in your life to reach your desired goals and how to choose the best times and locations to practise your visualizations.

Part III: Visualization Exercises for a Happier, Healthier Life

In this part, I get down to the nitty-gritty and provide numerous exercises you can practise to improve your outlook on life, achieve success, and feel and express a wider range of emotions. I explain how to limit the effects of stress, anxiety, and negative emotions, how to increase your levels of energy and stamina, how to quit unwanted bad habits, and how to rid yourself of fears and phobias. I also provide many exercises to help improve your relationships with others.

Part IV: Using Creative Visualization to Achieve Success

This part of the book concentrates on helping you to set and achieve goals, from improving the way you present yourself to others, managing public speaking, being a good leader, and motivating people, to improving your physical prowess in sport and enhancing your physique. I also deal with improving your results in education, getting a good job, and attaining promotions and pay rises. And I reveal several exercises you can practise to enhance your creativity.

Part V: The Part of Tens

This part of the book provides four chapters containing a selection of simple visualizations you can use to bring about positive changes; tips on top places to visualize; books, blogs, websites, and videos you can use to find out more about the subject; and ten of the best benefits of using creative visualization.

Icons Used in This Book

This book contains icons to indicate particularly useful pieces of information:

Under this icon, I provide practical advice for using.

This icon indicates a visualization exercise you can try for yourself.

Note these sections of text, because they contain ideas that are worth remembering.

This icon highlights some pitfalls and errors that you want to avoid so that your change programme proceeds as smoothly as possible.

I hope that the real-life stories I include under this icon prove useful and inspiring.

I often include specific examples to help illustrate visualizations or techniques; tailor them as necessary to help yourself attain your personal goals.

Where to Go From Here

If you want to discover everything I know about creative visualization, by all means read this book conventionally from start to finish. But, as with all *For Dummies* books, the chapters are also self-contained so you can dive straight in wherever you like (although if you're new to visualization, Part I provides an invaluable grounding in the subject).

So, if you just can't wait or you're already comfortable with the basics of creative visualization, go straight to the relevant chapter. For instance, if stopping smoking is your concern, leap to Chapter 10, and if you're keen to work on your shyness, Chapter 12 is the one for you.

Simply use the table of contents or the index to find the right chapter or section, and start solving your problems and improving your life.

After you've read this book, I believe that you're going to realise better than ever that the world is truly your oyster and that you can achieve your goals when you put your mind to it.

So please continue to practise the creative visualization techniques because they can help you through all parts of your life. And show others how to use the techniques too, so they can also benefit from the remarkable results creative visualization brings. Now go out and enjoy life to the full!

Part I

Introducing Creative Visualization

In this part . . .

You'll learn all about what creative visualization is and how powerful a tool it is for changing many aspects of your life. You'll see how the mind and body are closely connected so that simply through visualizing you can develop your personality and emotions, as well as your body. You'll also learn how creative visualization can help you to accomplish your goals in life, and even help rid yourself of bad habits and phobias.

Chapter 1

Unlocking the Power of Your Mind: Introducing Creative Visualization

In This Chapter

▶ Understanding how visualization works

▶ Considering the power of creative visualization

▶ Examining the connection between body and mind

*O*ver the years many techniques have been invented to help people with their personal development, including activities such as meditation, relaxation, hypnotism (and self-hypnosis), Neuro-Linguistic Programming (NLP) and many, many more. But all these different techniques have one major thing in common: they require the use of imagination, generally through visualizing yourself in particular ways or situations.

Without referring to 'creative visualization' by name, developers and proponents of personal development programs have always understood that (when suitably directed) the mind contains the power to help make dramatic changes in a person's life. Only recently, however, has creative visualization become a technique in its own right, fully equal to (and some say even more effective than) many other personal development systems. This chapter talks you through the power of the mind and how you can use it to visualize creatively.

Discovering How Creative Visualization Works

Creative visualization is the basic technique underlying positive thinking. It is used to bring changes you desire into your life, such as achieving goals you set, modifying unwanted behaviours (for example quitting smoking) and enhancing feelings and emotions (for example becoming happier and more self-confident). It is also a good tool for improving physical performance (as used by many top athletes) and enhancing your physique.

Creative visualization is something you probably do quite often (to one extent or another) without even realising it. For example, when was the last time you daydreamed? If you're like most people, it was probably today (perhaps within the last hour or so), because daydreaming is one of the most common human activities – but daydreaming is really nothing more than unguided or unstructured visualization.

When you daydream, your thoughts tend to flit about, resting on one idea after another, in a similar way to dreaming when asleep. Often, if something is on your mind, your daydreams keep returning to whatever that thing is and then drift off again before later coming back to that subject. Usually the flitting is guided by connections between ideas with each new thought reminding you of something else, so you follow a thread of thought.

Daydreaming allows you to achieve many things because you're generally relaxed when you do it: when you're waiting for a bus, taking a coffee break, being a passenger in a car, and so on, you distance yourself from your thoughts and let them take their own journey. And in doing so, in your mind's eye you see (or visualize) these daydreams, noticing the faces of people you think about, places you've been, and things you've done, like little mental movies.

It is believed that the purpose of daydreaming is to help people make better sense of the world as they encounter it. Unlike sleep dreams, daydreams tend to be somewhat more logical in their flow and based around actual people, things, and events. By running them through your mind over and again you sort your experiences, saving them in your memory in such a way that the important details are more easily recallable.

We can harness this natural pastime to our own ends by learning to replace unguided daydreaming with guided creative visualization. By doing this we have much greater control over our visualizations, the effects they'll have, and how effective they'll be at bringing changes we want into our lives.

Humans are very good at pattern recognition and quickly notice (and make a mental note) when things are somehow related to each other. For example, have you noticed how often you see a new actor in a movie and think to yourself 'that person is just like so and so'? This sensation is your mind automatically recognising similarities between the two people, and daydreaming is one of the times when this type of recognition occurs. With daydreaming you build a better understanding of the relationship between things in the world. Pattern recognition is used in creative visualization to connect two or more ideas, people or emotions together in order to bring about changes you desire.

Using the power of affirmations

One of the simplest personal development techniques and a superb companion to creative visualization is using positive affirmations. Affirmations repeated daily have helped numerous people, due to the fact that people's *unconscious* is always listening and likes to believe what it hears (another reason to try to be always positive).

The term *unconscious mind* was coined by Sigmund Freud and is used in psychology to refer to the thoughts we have that are out of reach of our consciousness. However, outside of psychological circles the phrase *subconscious mind* is often used in its place, probably because it has connotations of greater awareness than the former term. Therefore wherever I use the word 'unconscious' in this book, please feel free to exchange it with the word 'subconscious' if you prefer.

Researchers found that in meetings just one person repeating his opinion twice is sufficient for participants to later recall that person's point of view as the main agenda or theme of the meeting – often without remembering who brought that subject up. That's something worth remembering next time you're in a meeting and have an important issue to discuss!

If you take the time to re-affirm your ambitions and desires every day, you start to believe every word you say and your unconscious mind helps to slightly reform your personality so that the beliefs, emotions or intents behind the affirmations become a part of your personality, helping your goals to become actualised. This happens because your mindset changes each time you use your affirmations so that you become more motivated and more confident that you can make the changes you desire, and so you put more effort into and spend more time working on these goals.

Setting, re-affirming, and achieving goals

Creative visualization allows you to start taking control over aspects of your own life that you want to develop or modify, such as your emotions, actions, habits, phobias, and so on. You do so by choosing specific goals that you re-affirm continually through visualizations and affirmations, until you begin to achieve them. If you choose to try and conquer your fear of heights, for example, you need to hold positive visualizations in your mind when going to a high location, so that your fears are minimised. When you do this over time you become desensitised to the fear and the positive visualizations have an ever greater effect. Chapter 11 explains more about how this works and provides several visualization exercises.

Don't worry if you believe that you have difficulty in visualizing because anyone can visualize. For example, what colour is your front door? And how many rooms are there in your house? In order to answer these questions, almost without realising it you visualize your house and take a good look at it with your imagination. This is the process used in creative visualization, in which common things and experiences you can easily recall or imagine are used as seeds and then expanded upon.

One of the keys to using visualization successfully is to understand that you aren't trying to become someone else, or to change other people. Instead your aim is to focus on yourself and your psychological makeup, and then to develop your own personality in order to have a richer and more fulfilled life. By doing so, your relationships with others and interactions with the world prosper.

If you don't currently have any specific goals in mind, use an exercise to help you locate aspects of your life that you want to change. Take a look at Figure 1-1, the Cartwheel of Life. This tool helps give you a quick overview of the extent of your personal development to date.

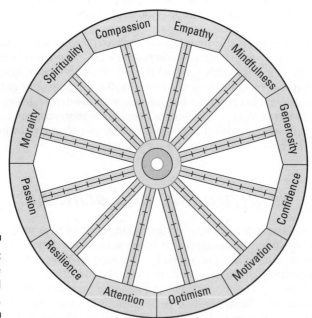

Figure 1-1:
The Cartwheel of Life.

Imagine that the cartwheel represents how you travel through life. It comprises a central axle with 12 spokes attached, each of which represents a different aspect of your psychological makeup. Each spoke is divided into eight parts. The farther along a spoke a particular attribute extends from the axle, the more complete that quality is in your personality.

Ideally, to travel as far as you can in life you want each of these qualities to reach to the wheel's rim, because if only one or two of them make it to the edge, the rim falls off, the wheel breaks, and you aren't going anywhere. On the other hand, with three or four attributes extending to the rim you can progress through life (although somewhat carefully), but any bumps in the road that you encounter may well cause the wheel to break and bring you to a crashing halt.

For example, without sufficient resilience you may give up too quickly when you encounter difficulties. Without optimism you may be less likely to set out on difficult projects. And without motivation you may find it hard to achieve your goals. The same goes for all the various qualities in the wheel. Although they are all emotional or psychological traits, they are all needed not only for your emotional wellbeing, but also for you to succeed materially in life.

If you can get half a dozen or more of these qualities sufficiently matured in your life to reach the cartwheel's rim, the wheel is much stronger and better able to travel over rough roads. As you progress through life's journey and invest the time into extending more spokes towards the rim, you find that you can travel faster, farther, and through far more rugged terrain.

Certainly it would be a very rare person indeed who had all 12 cartwheel spokes reaching to the rim – like most people I'm probably only halfway there. But the point is that this metaphor allows you to get a feel for how far you've come, and how far you've yet to go.

Spend a few minutes examining the cartwheel and, if you can, make a copy of it and shade in each spoke with a pen or pencil up to the point at which you feel you've progressed so far. After completing all the spokes, you have a basic diagram of your current personal development, which you may want to retain so you can refer to it in the future and see how you've progressed. You also now have a very good idea of areas in your life that you may like to work on, and for which you may want to set goals.

Improving skills with mental practice

Most people have effective imaginations and their daydreams often branch out into 'what if?' scenarios in which they visualize things that they want to experience. If you have something negative on your mind, sometimes your daydreams revolve too much around these thoughts and you can become anxious or depressed. Negative thoughts can predominate because whatever is current in your life tends to get the most attention and analysis, which shows just one reason why thinking positively as much as possible is so important.

By following the thread of thought in a daydream, you tend to analyse the ideas, events, or people you think about and, each time you move your attention to a related new thought, the connection between these thoughts is reinforced in your mind. As you can see in the later section 'Connecting your brain with your body', this reinforcement and the connections made between your thoughts are stored physically in your brain.

Creative visualization aims to replace unguided daydreaming with structured visualizations to build new connections or neural pathways – but only those you want to create. In essence, when you use creative visualization techniques, you're consciously reprogramming parts of your brain, creating new connections where you want them (or reinforcing existing ones) and allowing unwanted connections to wither. This is the process that occurs in our brains throughout life as we learn things in the normal course of living. But with creative visualization we can harness the process to learn new behaviours and modify emotions.

Minimising and removing negative emotions

When you're mastering creative visualization, your life is a 'glass half full' kind of life. For example, when you focus on what you don't want, like being less fat, you're still thinking about the concept of fatness, and as a result your unconscious focuses in on it. Instead, visualize being thinner so your unconscious thinks about thinness. In the same way, for example, the cartwheel exercise in the earlier section 'Setting, re-affirming, and achieving goals' works best when you use it to consider how far you've progressed in each area of your life, not how little.

Whenever you find yourself tempted to think negative thoughts, try to visualize something positive instead. If you feel sad, remember a happy time and think about it. If you're angry, visualize something peaceful, such as relaxing on a deckchair at the beach. Or if you're susceptible to feelings of low self-worth, remember one of your positive achievements and dwell on that.

Your own psyche is also helped if you don't have negative thoughts about other people. Yes, I know, everyone loves a good gossip, but speaking or thinking negatively about someone else just sends negative messages to your unconscious, and in the long run you feel worse not better. Therefore the old saying 'If you have nothing good to say about someone, say nothing', makes a lot of sense.

Engendering a positive and motivating attitude

You can reduce negative thoughts and emotions by building an automatic response so each time you notice an unwanted thought you take the time to deal with it. Of course, it's not always that easy. For example, if I say to you 'Don't think about chocolate', that's going to be the only thing you think about!

Instead you have to be sneaky to get past your unconscious and the best technique to do so is to acknowledge your negative thought or emotion, accept it, and let it go without acting on it. Go to Chapter 8 for exercises on letting go of negative thoughts.

At the same time, remind yourself that this thought isn't the real you (or the you that you want to be) thinking, and use your affirmations, which soon become your new way of thinking. Your attitude then markedly improves over time. You'll notice it, and so will other people who may even remark on your improved outlook or change in demeanour.

Ordering the cosmos

The idea behind cosmic ordering is that you harness the power of positive thinking and the creative energy of your thoughts in order to manifest whatever you desire. Followers believe that there are no limits and you can ask for absolutely anything you desire, such as a new love or a new house, money or wealth, health or healing.

You may have read that UK TV personality Noel Edmonds attributes his extraordinary career resurgence to something called 'cosmic ordering'. In my view, the more likely explanation for his comeback success is that he used to be a famous TV personality (already a big help). With the help of his reflexologist, however, who recommended the practice, he regained his self-confidence by putting his faith in cosmic ordering and writing down his hopes for the future. Now this is a well-known positive thinking reinforcement technique that psychologists have understood for many years, and the likelihood is that it did help boost his confidence and so he probably presented very well with TV bosses who then rehired him – but whether the cosmos granted his wishes is a matter for debate.

No scientific evidence exists for cosmic ordering, but the techniques used are certainly the same as those in positive thinking and creative visualization. Therefore, psychologists and biologists tend to look for a mental or physical process that achieves the attained results in their scientifically controlled studies.

Making Changes in Your Life with Creative Visualization

The changes you desire may include becoming a calmer and happier person, overcoming procrastination, increasing your motivation, and so on. Or they can be physical changes such as losing weight, reducing aches and pains, or increasing stamina.

Before you use creative visualization, decide to make real changes that can be measured in terms of results in your own life (seen both by you and others) and in terms of performance, whether academic, physical, or otherwise. That way you can attain the most benefit and, when you come to look back at the results, you know for certain that the visualizations worked (and can continue to do so).

Listening to your inner self

The best way to start making changes in your life is to listen to your inner self. By this I mean try to understand what it is that you truly desire from life, and the things you do and don't like about yourself and how you interact with the world. To do so, you want to achieve a calm and detached state of mind so any painful thoughts can be considered without too much discomfort, and to avoid being overly swayed by strong emotions. Chapter 3 includes advice on how you can quickly relax yourself and provides techniques for reducing stress and anxiety to help with this.

The first few times you visualize you may have difficulty getting started because thoughts are racing through your mind and your concentration wavers. If you experience this problem, try the following simple relaxation exercise:

1. **Take a few deep breaths and then clench all the muscles in your body.** Include your face through your body to your arms, legs, hands, and feet.

2. **Hold this position for a few seconds and then slowly exhale.** As you do so think to yourself 'toes relax, toes relax', and then 'feet relax, feet relax', and feel your feet become light and comfortable.

3. **Proceed slowly with 'calves relax, calves relax', followed by 'knees relax, knees relax', and 'thighs relax, thighs relax'.** Carry on until your legs and feet feel pretty good.

4. **Continue through your pelvis, stomach, chest, shoulders, neck, mouth, eyes, forehead, and mind, in that order.** Each time, think the relaxation command twice while all the time breathing gently and steadily.

Looking at the history of creative visualization

Although the power of positive thinking has been known about for thousands of years, the technique became established only in the last hundred years or so, after a number of books were published on the subject. Therefore, the subject of creative visualization as a personal development technique is relatively new and still developing.

The world at large was first introduced to the techniques used in creative visualization with the work of Wallace Wattles, who wrote *The Science of Getting Rich*. In the book, which was published in 1910, Wattles discusses the importance of maintaining 'a certain way of thinking' in order to achieve financial success, by using mind-training techniques to attain a state of positivity and self-affirmation'.

This book was followed in 1916 by *The Master Key System* by Charles F. Haanel, who was an American entrepreneur, author, and millionaire, and has been claimed to be the inspiration behind Bill Gates' success at Microsoft. Gates is said to have discovered the book while still a student at Harvard, and was apparently so impressed by it that he dropped out of college to form the world-famous company.

Within a couple of decades the power of visualization became even more widely known when the blockbuster title *Think and Grow Rich* by Napoleon Hill was published in 1937. This book was founded on Hill's earlier 1928 work *The Law of Success*, which was commissioned by Andrew Carnegie (a billionaire and firm proponent of writing down your goals), and was based on interviews of around 500 American millionaires over 20 years.

One of the earlier book's 16 creeds is: 'You must have imagination in creating your definite purpose and in building the plans with which to transform that purpose into reality and put your plans into action.'

Think and Grow Rich further distilled his creeds into 13 'steps toward riches', some of which are desire, faith, auto-suggestion, imagination, and persistence.

This exercise is very effective when you feel highly strung and you can also use it when you have difficulties getting to sleep at night. Properly performed the process takes up to five minutes, after which (if you still aren't relaxed) you can repeat it again if necessary.

Setting goals that you want to achieve

When you're relaxed, you can use this state of mind to accomplish many things. To start with you're in the best frame of mind to start choosing the goals that you want to visualize about. Try thinking about things in your life that you want to change, whether relationships, finances, health, or something else, and then try to narrow these down to a handful of goals. Go to Chapter 2 for more information on identifying areas in your life that you want to modify.

I can't tell you specifically what these goals should be because everyone is different, but the numerous visualization exercises in this book cover a very wide range of typical goals and ambitions. If you're still having difficulty deciding exactly what to change, have a browse through the book – whatever stands out to you is likely to be something that deep down you have an interest in; so go ahead and explore it.

When you've come up with a handful of goals that every time you consider them seem more important to you, you're ready to start. Any goals that seem to get less important are either already being achieved or not really of that much interest to you, so you can ignore them.

Changing unwanted behaviours to desired ones

No doubt you have behaviours that you're unhappy about. For instance you may have decided that you shout at the kids too often when they misbehave and would rather reduce that knee-jerk reaction. Or maybe you're in the habit of having a bowl of ice cream each evening while watching TV, which isn't helping your weight, and so on.

Behaviours such as these tend to start simply and then over time become habits that you find hard to break. Humans are creatures of habit, and forming habits is something everyone does. So the answer isn't simply to stop doing the behaviour, because most people find that next to impossible. Instead you need to establish new habits to replace the old ones.

One of the more powerful visualization techniques is the *interrupt* – also known by psychologists as a pattern interrupt – in which a new pattern replaces the old one. For example, to shout less at the kids you would visualize a situation in which this happens, such as one of them kicking a football into a window and smashing it (which would make most parents angry).

To discover and develop the interrupt technique, imagine a scenario that makes you so angry that you'd shout at someone. Visualize this event right up to the point at which you begin to shout, but instead see yourself exhaling as rapidly and deeply as you can, followed by counting slowly to ten. Now repeat the visualization over and over again, each time breaking away from the point at which you would shout into the breathing routine. After a few run-throughs this interrupt becomes natural and fast and you're ready to imagine another circumstance that makes you shout, with which you can also visualize the interrupt and switch to deep breathing.

After you've visualized a number of these situations, you'll find that any new scenario that you think up has you going straight to the breathing without even considering the shouting. Practised over time you can find that you do indeed shout less and less. And the same goes for breaking the ice cream habit, teaching yourself to swear less, or any other behaviour you want to change. Visualize an interrupt, in which you do something else, just before (and replacing) the behaviour; the interrupt can be as simple as having a glass of water or blowing your nose.

Achieving goals you previously thought impossible

As long as you're realistic and keep your goals within the realms of possibility, you can find that creative visualization helps you to achieve even the most seemingly impossible ambitions.

A quick search of Google reveals that the range of people using creative visualization to achieve amazing results is huge, which goes to show that everyone can use the same techniques to achieve major changes in their lives.

For example, Arnold Schwarzenegger used visualization techniques to become a seven-times Mr Universe, a movie star, and Governor of California. He says:

> *I visualized myself being and having what it was I wanted… Before I won my first Mr Universe title, I walked around the tournament like I owned it… I had won it so many times in my mind that there was no doubt I would win it. Then when I moved on to the movies, the same thing. I visualized myself being a famous actor and earning big money… I just knew it would happen.*

The more frequently you visualize something that may appear impossible to achieve, and the more you increase your positive expectations of attaining it, the greater the chance you have of doing so. Only by consistently focusing on the positive outcome you desire, and strongly believing you'll obtain it, will every fibre of your being work towards this outcome, so that you'll be ready to seize any and all opportunities that come your way, and even make your own. The point is to never give up as giving up is the only way of confirming to yourself that you'll never be able to achieve your goal.

A vestige of visualization

Roger Bannister, the first man to run a sub-four-minute mile, says he used creative visualizations of breaking the record many times before the race. In golf, Tiger Woods also uses visualizations to help him compete at the highest levels, as does Jack Nicklaus, who says his secret to success is '10 per cent technique, 40 per cent position, and 50 per cent creative visualization – a mental picture of a successful shot'.

The list continues in science and technology. At the age of 16 Albert Einstein used creative visualization 'thought experiments' to discover that the speed of light is constant, by visualizing himself sitting on a cart chasing a point of light.

He said: 'Words or language do not seem to play any role in my mechanism of thought. My elements of thought are images.' And Thomas Edison and his great rival Nikola Tesla also visualized, the latter claiming that he 'did not need drawings of any kind in the design process'.

In the arts, Chopin was a well known visualizer and Beethoven, who went totally deaf, had to imagine all his later compositions as he composed them. Walt Disney was a great visualizer, though he called the process 'imagineering'. Popular UK entertainer and hypnotist Derren Brown uses visualization for many of his 'tricks', such as his astounding memory feats.

Exploring the Mind/Body Connection

Although much of the human nervous system is under automatic control – for example, controlling of the heartbeat, regularity of breathing, core temperature, and so on – the body is also highly connected with the brain. You can therefore communicate with your physical body using creative visualization, to help improve fitness, combat fatigue and illness, and decrease pain.

Connecting your brain with your body

Reflexologists say that the soles of your feet have different parts (or zones) corresponding to various organs in your bodies (and that hands have similar zones too). Acupuncturists take this idea further, claiming that hundreds of points on your body (when stimulated with needles) have effects on other parts of the body. Certainly, all nerve endings lead directly to the brain via long connections and therefore all parts of the body are connected via the brain to all other parts of the body.

In several studies, patients undergoing treatment who have been asked to visualize, have become healthier far more quickly than those patients who only received treatment. Examples of visualizations that have been tried include imagining your white blood cells as being warriors being set loose on cancerous cells to destroy them, or imagining healing nutrients being sent via the blood directly to a wound to help it heal more quickly.

Now I would never advocate using creative visualization in place of following prompt and professional medical advice. But used in conjunction with the latest medicines and treatments, creative visualization has been shown to enhance the results and speed up healing.

So considering your whole self when using creative visualization makes good sense. And if your goal is to feel happier, achieving this state benefits your mind and body; after all, depression can lead to aches and pains and bad posture, resulting in other physical ailments.

 Adopting an upright posture and a smile while visualizing does wonders for increasing the results and your general feeling of wellbeing. This approach is known as *positive biofeedback*. Check out the later section 'Using biofeedback to change your emotions' to find out more about positive biofeedback.

Getting to know neurons

All human organs are connected to the spine and brain – and therefore to each other – via synapses, which are junctions that permit neurons (nerve cells) to pass an electrical or chemical signal to other cells. Neurons join with each other using these synapses to create new pathways that allow electrical signals to pass along them, transporting information around your brain (and other parts of the body).

The human brain has about a hundred billion neurons, with each one connected to an average of a thousand others, making for a massively interconnected system.

When a neuron receives signals it decides whether to act upon them by determining whether they're strong enough to be passed onto other neurons. If a neuron receives a signal from only a few other neurons it may well perceive this signal as random noise, much like the fuzzy screen and hissy audio you used to get on older, untuned television sets. And it doesn't activate its own mechanism to retransmit the signal to other neurons. But if lots of other neurons send it a signal, the neuron activates and the signal is passed on.

The connections between neurons aren't fixed. Babies have relatively few connections, but as they develop and learn, neurons continuously sprout new links to other neurons. When the result makes sense and (for example) helps to pick up an object, the connection remains and is reinforced by many nearby neurons also connecting to form additional pathways, so that people get better and better at picking things up. On the other hand, when a connection turns out to be useless because it didn't help, it isn't reinforced.

This constant rebuilding of pathways is known as *neuroplasticity*, a theory that focuses on how the brain can rewire itself to forge new connections and break cycles of negative thinking and acting.

Thinking with your heart as well as your mind

Looking more deeply into the mind/body connection, if you ask someone where he feels sadness, he very often points to his heart, as people do when asked about where joyful feelings come from. You rarely see people point to their head unless they have a headache.

This behaviour is easily explained, because a universally accepted sign for love is the heart, because people often feel emotions deep within their bodies, not inside their heads. When you're in love your heart goes all a-flutter, and when afraid you can feel sick to the pit of your stomach. Emotions have a real physical effect as well as a mental one.

Therefore when visualizing you'll substantially enhance your results by imagining that you're physically feeling and engaged with the visualization, and not merely performing a mental exercise.

This is understood in several personal improvement techniques. For example, there's a concept in Cognitive Behavioural Therapy called the 'ABC Model' which states that our thoughts and actions create our emotions, which result in our behaviours – both wanted and unwanted. First comes an activating event, which is interpreted according to our beliefs, resulting in a given set of consequences. An example of this could be as follows:

- ✔ **Activating event**: Your boss asks whether you've completed a piece of work.

- ✔ **Beliefs**: You may think: 'My boss thinks I'm not working hard enough and is trying to catch me out.'

- ✔ **Consequences**: You say defensively, 'I have nearly finished', although you still have a lot more to do. This results in you feeling annoyed and resentful, which causes stress.

In this instance it's most likely your boss simply needs the piece of work and has not formed any conclusion about your work ethics. With a different set of beliefs you can understand this and not end up feeling accused and stressed out.

Using biofeedback to change your emotions

Biofeedback is the process of becoming aware of physiological functions with the aim of being able to manipulate them at will. Processes that can be controlled include brainwaves, muscle tone, skin conductance, heart rate, and pain perception, and biofeedback may be used to improve health and physical, mental or emotional performance, with changes often occurring both physically and to thoughts, emotions, and behavior.

Because your body and mind are so closely intertwined, your creative visualization is always more effective if you use as many of your senses as you can. The techniques in this book often suggest that you imagine touching or smelling something, perhaps even tasting it too, and you're often asked to look around and listen as well, making full use of the five classical senses (see Figure 1-2).

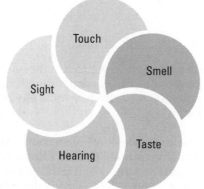

Figure 1-2: The five classical senses.

But did you know that you have more than five senses? In fact, another five are generally recognised, as shown in Figure 1-3:

- ✔ **Balance and acceleration** are sensed using a maze-like structure in the inner ear called the labyrinth, which contains an intricate system of loops and pouches within which liquid sloshes about as you move. By detecting where the liquid goes you can tell whether you're tipping over or your body is accelerating or decelerating.

- ✔ **Pain and temperature** are sensed via nerve endings all over your body and are considered different from simple touch sensations.

- ✔ **Position** (also known as *kinaesthesia*) is your ability to know where parts of your body are with respect to others.

Each of your ten senses brings information into your mind, telling you something about your surroundings and the world around you. In fact they are the only way you perceive the world. Therefore, to make your experience of life as rich as possible, try to use as many senses as you can – whatever you're doing. For example, when you look at something, take a moment to really look. Listen intently rather than just hear, and touch things the way you did as a child, feeling their texture. If you're missing any of these senses or they're limited, make up for this by using the senses that are available to you even more.

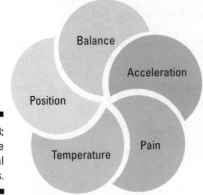

Figure 1-3:
The five additional senses.

The aim of personal development is to improve yourself in the future, but when you get to the future it's going to be your present. If you have difficulty fully appreciating your present now, you may also have difficulty enjoying your future when it becomes your present.

Appreciating your senses here and now makes achieving your goals through creative visualization easier, because your brain connects neurons to each other (thus 'programming' your mind) according to the things you learn and the experiences you have. Therefore by providing as many different types of input to your brain as you can when visualizing, you'll increase the number of connections relating to the subject at hand, creating neural pathways for the types of thinking, emotional responses, or whatever you wish to reinforce.

Why not try and sharpen some of your additional senses by testing them out?

- You can test the position sense by touching your finger to your nose while your eyes are shut – see how easy it is?

- To test for balance you need a friend and a seesaw. One of you closes his eyes and sits right in the middle of the seesaw, over the pivot, with the seesaw parallel to the ground. The other person quietly tips the seesaw from one end, whilst the person with his eyes closed tries to determine the direction he is being tipped.

- To detect acceleration and deceleration try closing your eyes when riding as a passenger in a vehicle. Try and feel for when you're slowing down or speeding up.

- You most probably already know what pain feels like but have you ever tried filling a few bowls of water with different combinations of hot (but not too hot!) and cold water and dipping your hand into them? Have a go at sorting them in to order of warmth using your sense of temperature.

Practising biofeedback visualizations

A *biofeedback visualization* is one in which you use your mind and body together, enhancing your visualization because many more neural pathways are created in your brain by doing so than if you merely imagine something without incorporating your senses. For example, if you particularly enjoy a certain fragrance such as lavender, you can introduce that into your visualization exercises by imagining its smell – having just mentioned lavender to you, you should have easily recalled its smell because the neurons that govern smell are linked to all other parts of your brain, including memory.

So if you'd like to strengthen a visualization about becoming more relaxed and you find the smell of lavender relaxing, try to imagine that smell during the visualization. If you find that you can't do it at the same time, that's all right: you can imagine the smell immediately before or after visualizing and it will still be linked to the visualization.

Likewise, when visualizing while walking in the park you can touch flowers, trees, fences, or any other objects to provide tactile feedback that will provide additional memories and create extra neural pathways to enhance the effectiveness of the visualization.

Biofeedback becomes particularly useful when you use your body to help achieve an emotion or feeling. When you're happy you naturally smile. But the inverse is also true; by smiling you make yourself happier. Wherever your emotions have an effect on your body, you can reverse this reaction by making your body do the action (or take on the posture) associated with the emotion or feeling, and your mind follows suit.

Believing that a technique is going to work: The placebo effect

A placebo is an inert substance given to a patient who is informed that it's actually a medicine. Although creative visualization is not directly related to placebos, the fact that placebos work gives a clue as to how creative visualization works, and the connection is positivity.

When a physician hands you a couple of pills and tells you they'll do something, you have a general positive expectation that this person knows a lot more than you do and you accept what you're told and believe they'll work.

With creative visualization you're using the knowledge that positive thinking brings positive results to formulate a visualization on which you concentrate in order to emphasise your desires to your unconscious mind.

The brain is a mysterious and still only partially understood organ. The mind itself can have a powerful effect on the body and create deep changes, as demonstrated in hypnotherapy, for example, in which the way you use your mind can directly influence your central nervous system.

The placebo effect is enhanced greatly when people start visualizing a desired change. At first, they don't always believe that the change is going to happen, although they know that it may. As they visualize more and more they come to embody the change they desire, and the belief and the positive effect increases.

By 'embody' I mean that the desire to change becomes so entrenched that it transitions from being just a desire into being a part of you. For example, as Chapter 13 discusses, someone who is shy but strongly desires to become more confident, and who practises visualizations and affirmations around this wish on a regular basis, will find that the aim gradually becomes realised. Over time he'll move from thinking, 'I wish I were more confident of my abilities in this area', to 'I am more confident than I was', and finally, 'I now feel completely confident'.

This is particularly noticeable when accompanied by affirmations in which you regularly repeat a phrase such as, 'I am a confident person'. At first you may not feel this way, but after a few days you'll feel that maybe you're a little more confident and that what you're saying has some truth to it. Eventually, when you repeat the affirmation, you may follow it by remarking to yourself, 'Yes, I truly believe I am now a confident person.' And at this point your goal has been accomplished.

Knowing that losing belief can diminish results

Every possibility exists that an *anti-placebo* effect can be experienced, where a hitherto effective medicine may cease to be effective if a patient loses faith in its abilities. For example, in 2010 a published study claimed that a popular health supplement (used to treat joint pain and arthritis) appeared to have no statistically positive benefit after all. As a result, sales of the product plummeted, with tens of thousands of people who had previously been absolutely certain that it was helping them now believing the opposite.

When my household heard this story, we thought we'd try an experiment because both my wife and I have trouble with our joints. So we also stopped taking the supplement to see if we noticed any change. If the study was correct we shouldn't have noticed any difference. But we both felt our symptoms deteriorate and quite quickly too.

However, we knew that placebos can work even when known to be placebos, and so we resumed taking the supplements and after a few days we both felt much better. So does this supplement work, or is it simply a placebo? The answer to that question doesn't matter to us – because (perhaps due to adopting the right frame of mind) we both find it helps, and that's good enough.

Remember that stopping a prescribed medication without being told to do so by a physician could seriously damage your health. Never stop taking any medicines or supplements you have been prescribed by a qualified professional without first discussing this with him and being given his approval.

If you believe that something is going to help you, the chances are that it will. Even if you lose your belief in the specific medicine, as long as you know that placebos can work anyway, you can still continue to benefit. That's the power of positive thinking.

Chapter 2

Laying the Groundwork for Visualization

. . . .

. . . .

*W*hen you're laying the groundwork for visualization, the object is to explore every aspect of your goals from start to finish. Your aim is to see how you can begin on the path to achieving goals, what steps to take while doing so, what obstacles may get in your way (so you can overcome them), how to attain the goal, what happens after that, and all the stages in between.

People are different, and so you need to tailor the visualizations in this chapter and throughout this book to your own personality and situation. When you do so, try to be as imaginative and creative as you can. The more wonderful and powerful you make your visualizations, the stronger and more effective they're going to be.

In this chapter I explain how you can choose the right goals to match your general ambitions in life, and explain the importance of having a positive expectation for all your goals. By understanding right from the start that you're free to tailor the exercises in this book to match your personal circumstances (to make them as effective as possible for you), you approach them from a more active point of view, more as tools you can use in the way that suits you best, rather than exercises to follow rigidly.

In the process of laying the groundwork for visualization this chapter provides an array of techniques to help you decide on your goals, build your confidence and visualize achieving success – the common aspects of creative visualization (set a goal, believe you can achieve it, then see it achieved).

Deciding What You Want to Achieve

In order for your visualizations to be effective, you need to have a very clear idea of exactly what you want to achieve. For example, instead of having a vague desire to 'be happier' (which is too large a subject to tackle with a single visualization), concentrate on smaller parts of your life that lead to the larger overall change.

In addition, to achieve a major goal in life such as landing the job you always wanted (as opposed to more minor goals like passing an exam or writing a report) you need to decide what's preventing you from realizing that goal or holding you back. Determining your major goals may take some thinking about because you may never have put them into words before.

You can best uncover your goals by thinking of the most important things you would like to be, have or do in the best of all possible worlds. Ignore things that seem unachievable right now. What remains will be major goals that you think you have a chance of realising.

Once you have one or more major goals in your mind you'll be able to see what is standing in your way of achieving these goals. Most likely these impediments are a combination of things and in the next section 'Making a mind movie' I present a useful visualization technique you can use to uncover them.

Making a mind movie

A mind movie is a visualization where you imagine filming a scene or a series of scenes in your mind's eye, which you can then review as if you're watching a movie. Imaginary fast forward and rewind buttons allow you to quickly skip sections so you can focus on the most important events. Once created, mind movies are invaluable for examining things in your life from a more neutral perspective, so you can more clearly identify things you'd like to change and how to do so.

 To use this technique, have a pen and paper ready; or you can use a computer or mobile phone to make notes. The idea is to remember the most outstanding things that occur to you from the visualization and use them in the later section 'Reviewing your movie'.

The creation of your mind movie acts as a refresher; it helps to get your memory in gear and allows you to see your life more objectively.

Follow these steps:

1. **Ensure that you can sit somewhere quiet and uninterrupted for about 30 minutes.**

2. **Sit back, relax and slowly view a typical weekday in your mind, mentally noting anything of interest.**

3. **Take your time and pace yourself so that you complete shooting this mind movie in five to ten minutes.**

4. **Make sure that you film all the important parts of a typical 16-hour day; if anything is missing, shoot these scenes and get your mind to insert them into the right part of the movie.**

Locate your view (your imaginary camera) somewhere other than in the same place as your eyes – in the same way that most movies are shot from different viewpoints. Perhaps start with the camera looking over one shoulder, so it's close by but also a little removed from you.

Experienced visualizers often move the camera (and therefore their view) to different places, sometimes hovering above and looking down, sometimes looking from another person's point of view, sometimes zooming in or circling, and so on. (Check out Chapter 17 for more ways of being innovative in your visualizations). Your weekends are probably quite different to your weekdays and so you can turn your movie into a double feature, with a typical weekday in Part 1 and a typical weekend day in Part 2. If all days are usually quite different for you, choose to film a typical week instead. For example, here's how a typical day of yours may begin:

Your alarm clock rings. You open your eyes and see light at the windows. You get out of bed and visit the bathroom. You get dressed, make coffee and watch television. You wake up the children. You make breakfast and call the children to the table. You read the paper. You put on your shoes and coat. You take the children to school. You drive to work. And so on.

Although this may seem mundane to you, try to go through a completely typical day in your mind from morning until night, but recording only the more important things (if you miss any don't worry, you can always go back and edit them in later). For example, if you have children and have daily battles with them to get them up and out of bed, that's something to film. If you sometimes have arguments with your spouse or any other family members, film that. If you typically weigh yourself in the mornings and aren't happy with what you see, film that too.

If you commute to work, film the journey. Is it OK or too long? Do you enjoy commuting or hate it? Film how you feel about your journey each day. Maybe you'll discover that you prefer not to drive and will decide to try public transport for a change. You never know what you may come up with when you review the movie later on, so film everything that seems to have meaning or cause an emotional feeling.

If you work, try to film all the things you like and dislike in a typical day. Your interactions with colleagues, the types of work you typically have to do, the people outside the organisation you get to talk with or meet and so on. All of these may later lead to unexpected insights when you review your mind movie, so record them all. Remember, if you have a job it probably takes up about half your day, so do your mind movie justice. Or, if you're a student, film the typical type of day you experience at school, college or university.

If you have any difficulty with this exercise, put it off for a couple of days and spend your time until then making mental (or real) notes about what you do in a typical day.

Reviewing your movie

When you've filmed the movie, you need to appraise what you've seen, just as you would after seeing a thought-provoking film at the cinema, because the whole point of this exercise is to be able to view your life as if you're viewing someone else's. It provides an element of detachment that allows you to see things you may otherwise not notice, because as you live your life you often can't see the wood for the trees.

1. **Rewind your movie to the beginning and start to review it.** You may choose to see the movie played back on the large projection screen of a personal cinema, you may simply see the movie being filmed all over again, or you may even see it from different angles each time you review it. It makes no difference at all how you do this, it's purely a matter of personal choice.

2. **When you've discovered the best viewing position for you, watch your movie.** Pause it at the end of each new scene so you can soak in what you just saw.

3. **Decide whether what's happening in that scene is in any way connected with the area of life that you want to change, or the main goal that you're preparing to visualize about.** If the event is connected, ask yourself whether the scene has a positive, negative or no impact on this goal. You need to decide this because positive or negative impacts indicate possible areas you may wish to either remedy or reinforce.

Picking out the positives

If you've already created a mind movie following the advice in the section 'Making a mind movie' and have begun to review it, you need to start extracting scenes from it that either make a positive or negative contribution to your life. Each time you encounter a positive scene, write it down with two '+' symbols before it. When you encounter a negative scene, simply write it down without any symbol preceding it.

The reason for using a double plus (and no minus signs) is to give each positive scene two points. When you get to analysing a negative scene, your job is to find two positive things about it, from which you can turn the negative impact of that scene into something positive.

So work through your mind movie and proceed in one of the two following ways:

1. If you feel that the events or people in your mind movie make a positive contribution to your goal or your life in general, write down or type two + symbols (a double plus) followed by a one-sentence description of the scene, as in the following example:

    ++ Enjoyable breakfast with the kids.

2. If you think that a scene has a negative impact, write down a single sentence scene description (without the double plus), like this:

    Rushed breakfast with the kids.

Here the breakfast wasn't enjoyable because it was rushed. So now you need to turn this negative into a double plus. To do so, choose two things you want to change about the activity, or two positive outcomes you want to happen.

When you've decided on these items, write or type them underneath the scene description, with one per line, each prefaced with a single + symbol and slightly indented, as follows:

    Rushed breakfast with the kids.

    + I want to spend more time as a family.

    + I want the mornings to be less stressful with fewer arguments.

With creative visualization, always try to reinforce the positive and minimise the negative. That's why I don't place minus symbols in front of the negative scene description, and also why you need *two* positive outcomes or changes for each negative scene. Your double plus scenes and the pairs of single plus desires or goals are the things you're going to build visualizations around to achieve your overall desire or goal.

Never visualize negatively: for example, that you *don't want* to be unhappy. Instead, visualize that you *do want* to be happier. The reason for this approach is that your unconscious mind tends to ignore the 'don't want' and focuses only on the word or concept of 'unhappiness'.

Enhancing the positives

Using double pluses helps to indicate that a lot of potential exists to move you nearer to your goals. For example, you can use your mind movie to see whether the rest of the family want to slow down over breakfast and create a more positive start to the day, along with overall improved relationships.

The two single plus statements reveal positive desires that you can use to develop a visualization. Even simply imagining spending quality time together over a meal, with each person listening to the other without arguing, strongly helps you to move towards this particular goal of improving family interaction.

As soon as you start putting together your mind movie analysis, ideas begin popping into your brain as you change from suffering passively from a problem to looking actively for solutions. Things slowly start to click into place, and when you start to practise the visualizations, the speed of change quickens.

Although you may not realise it as a newcomer to creative visualization, when you look back on the time when you took the first small steps, and compare that time with how things are later, you'll see that the changes you needed began immediately, progressed rapidly, and resolved in far better ways than you imagined. (See the later section 'Imagining Yourself Having Achieved' for more info.)

Using the wheel of emotion

Creative visualization is capable of helping you to modify emotions. It can increase or diminish their intensity and the frequency at which you feel them. As discussed in Chapter 1, it is known in techniques such the Cognitive Behavioural Therapy ABC model that emotions can shape our thoughts and our thoughts can change our emotions. This means that the right visualizations can have a positive effect in many areas of your life.

You can experience so many different emotions when you're depressed or something doesn't feel right that deciding exactly what's up can be difficult. But you can use one technique to find out quickly why you feel bad (if you don't already know); it's called 'spinning the wheel' and is ready for you to use to start visualizing creatively.

Figure 2-1 shows the basis for the 'spinning the wheel' technique, with 32 different emotions and 'love' at the very top.

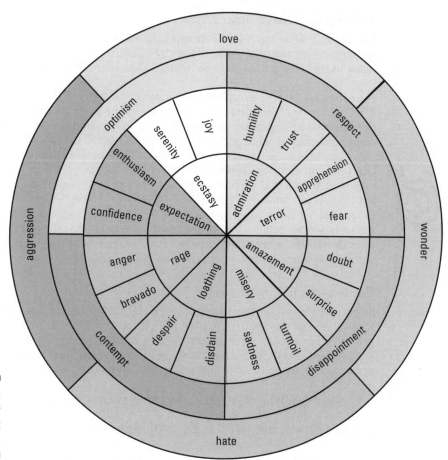

Figure 2-1:
A wheel of
32 different
emotions.

Reading the inner circle

The inner circle of the wheel in Figure 2-1 consists of eight emotions, each of which is the opposite of the emotion on the other side, and the emotions that are next to each other are somewhat related, albeit quite loosely. For example, ecstasy is the opposite of misery, and loathing is the opposite of admiration, while ecstasy and admiration are more similar to each other than they are different.

These inner emotions are known as the *basic* emotions because they're some of the simplest to recognise, but in fact they're often created by a combination of other more complex emotions, as shown in the second circle.

Reading the second inner circle

The second circle contains 16 more complex emotions, each of which has an opposite on the other side of the circle, with emotions next to each other being more closely related to each other than those in the inner circle.

For example, joy is the opposite of sadness and anger is the opposite of fear. Also, each pair of emotions that touches a single inner circle emotion usually combines to form that inner basic emotion. For example, fear and apprehension create terror, while joy and serenity can lead to ecstasy.

Don't see the emotions too narrowly. You may be thinking that some of the emotions shown in the wheel look like rather strange opposites. If you're fearful, is anger what you need? Well, the answer is maybe. Perhaps a wrong exists that needs righting, one about which you need to get a bit angry to help motivate you to deal with it. Or if something is making you apprehensive, perhaps developing a sense of bravado (a sort of false bravery you present to the world) may begin to help you to deal with that fear.

Reading the two outer circles

As you progress from the centre of the wheel to the outside, the emotions shown become ever more complex, so that those in the outer two circles comprise the four second circle emotions contained within their arc of the circle. For example, love comprises a combination of serenity, joy, humility and trust, while aggression comprises bravado, anger, confidence and enthusiasm.

Again, as with all the emotions in the wheel, each of the two outer circle emotions has a roughly opposite emotion on the other side, so that love is the opposite of hate, and optimism can be the opposite of disappointment.

If you compare the emotions in the two outer circles with those in the inner circle, you see that at times a combination of rage and misplaced expectation can cause aggression, while wonder can arise from a mix of terror and amazement. Any emotion that touches another on the wheel is more similar to it than different. The general area of the wheel you look at is a related group of emotions, and its opposite area features a related collection of opposite emotions.

Bearing these relationships in mind, use the following technique to analyse your current emotional makeup in order to identify the feeling or emotion you most want to change:

1. **Relax and try to clear your head of all thoughts.**

2. **Cast your eyes slowly around the wheel illustrated in Figure 2-1.** As you do so keep reading the emotions until you start to feel drawn to a certain section.

3. **After a while, make a decision and place your finger on the exact spot you feel your mind is at right now.**

4. **When you've chosen your place on the wheel, look at all the emotions at or touching that point.**

If you end up pointing at anger, you have a tool to help you analyse why you feel this way. In this case, you're also very likely to be affected by one or more of the surrounding emotions (rage, bravado, contempt and confidence) and some of the other nearby ones (such as aggression and despair) may also be a problem.

Armed with this information about your current emotional state you're better prepared to tailor the visualizations in this book towards altering your particular mood and feelings. For example, if you select the sadness area of the wheel, your objective is to minimise those emotions near to it that you dislike the most, and to increase those on the exact opposite side of the wheel (joy and the emotions surrounding it) that you most want to feel.

Of course, if you select a positive emotion section of the wheel that you're happy with, great! But the wheel is still useful to you in that you can see exactly what types of positive emotions you're feeling right now, and you can decide whether you want to work on increasing any other positive emotions nearby.

Don't take the specific emotions shown completely literally when using and interpreting the wheel, because the idea of this technique is to examine the general areas around the point on the wheel you choose, and the general opposite locations. Considering a combination of the emotions surrounding each location (and its opposites) helps you put your emotional life into deeper perspective.

In other words, because there are far too many subtly different emotions to create a comprehensive yet manageable wheel of emotion, only a subset is included. Therefore consider what a particular word that you've been drawn to on the wheel means to you and how it relates to the words nearby.

If you spin the wheel on different days, or even at different times of the same day, you may well choose a different place on the wheel, but after you've carried out this exercise a few times over a few days, you're likely to find that on average the spot you point at is in the same general area. Therefore, perform this technique more than once at different times to see how your emotional makeup is developing.

Modifying a behaviour: Stopping a bad habit or starting a good one

You may decide that you wish to change a behaviour because it is negatively affecting you or people around you, or simply because you know it isn't good for you (for example drinking to excess, smoking or not exercising).

Changing a behaviour always seems very hard because people are creatures of habit and really get quite uncomfortable when they have to change a routine or something they're used to. But that's exactly the human quality you can use to modify a behaviour, because when you change something for long enough, the new behaviour replaces the old and you become accustomed to it.

This fundamental fact of human behaviour is the power and beauty of creative visualization, because you start off without changing the behaviour and just visualize the new behaviour a number of times before you make the actual change. And these visualizations count towards the number of times of performing the new habit that are required to instil it as a normal routine, therefore speeding up the process of changing.

For example, suppose you've always wanted to learn to play the guitar. Perhaps, like many people, you've purchased an instrument but it mostly rests in the corner of the room because you never seem to find the time to get around to practising. Well, you still don't have to find that time with creative visualization as long as you imagine that you've done so.

Just visualize that, for example, it is the evening. Nothing particularly interesting is on television. All your jobs for the day are done. Your children (if you have any) are quietly doing their homework and you have the opportunity to pick up the guitar and start strumming some chords.

You see, what is happening is a thing called acclimatisation, in which you're becoming used to a new habit. But instead of instilling a new habit by doing that habit, you need only to spend a few minutes imagining doing it, which turns out to be equally as powerful on the mind.

Experts provide differing values for the length of time it takes to establish a new habit, generally between about three and eight weeks. On the whole, though, I have found that changing or forming a new a habit takes about a month to become sufficiently entrenched for you to maintain it. So, if you first visualize the change for two weeks before having to make it, you have to be uncomfortable for only a couple of weeks (rather than a month) as you establish the new habit with action.

Believing That You Can Achieve Change

One of the most fundamental parts of preparing for visualization is that you need to believe that what you're imagining can happen. If you don't believe this, you can't visualize properly, your unconscious mind 'knows' that you're lying to yourself, and nothing can come of your efforts.

Visualizing attaining a goal

Creative visualization is primarily about setting goals; it's a technique for achieving a required result. Whether you want to improve your confidence, lose weight or get better grades in exams, whatever you desire, if you visualize the goal, you can achieve it much more easily than if you don't.

Many top sports coaches use visualization for sports from A to Z, from athletics to zorbing (yes, that is a sport – in which players roll downhill in a large transparent orb).

When you practise something in your mind over and over again, and visualize it happening again and again, you begin to discover how to make it happen. For example, the neurons in your brain that control your muscles rearrange to provide better guidance to them to help you achieve the goal, whether physical or something mental like performing well in an exam. This is the case with all learning (whether mental or physical), which is ultimately stored in the arrangement of neural connections in the brain. The patterns of connections these neurons make defines our ability do anything. The more precise the connections governing a skill, the better we are at it.

You can try an experiment for yourself at home or for part of your lunch break at work. All you need is an empty box or other container such as a waste paper bin, which you place at the far end of a room, and some rolled up balls of paper:

1. **Spend ten minutes throwing the balls of paper into the box and calculate your average number of goals scored as follows: divide the number scored by the number thrown, and multiply by 100.**

   For example, if you make 60 throws and score 9 times, your average is 9 ÷ 60 - 100, the result being a 15 per cent average.

2. **Now put down the balls of paper and spend ten minutes a day for the next week visualizing throwing imaginary paper balls into the box instead of throwing real ones.**

   Play every part of the throw through in your mind, feeling your muscles, noting what your eyes are doing, and seeing the paper ball fall straight into the box, time after time.

3. **After a week of visualizing, spend another ten minutes throwing real paper balls into the box, and then work out your new scoring percentage.**

   Most people who do this see a marked improvement in their average. For example, if you score a 15 per cent average before and an 18 per cent average after visualizing, you've seen a 20 per cent improvement, but I wouldn't be surprised if you saw a far greater improvement than that.

The great thing is that you can use this technique to achieve any of your goals that require practice to improve, not just sporting ones (Chapter 15 covers excelling in sports in detail though). Simply visualize your goal being successfully achieved over and over again and you're sure to improve steadily.

Keeping goals realistic

Unfortunately, odds don't lie: for example, not everyone can win the lottery. Even if thousands of people visualize winning, only one person or at most a very few people can have the winning numbers. And if everyone visualizing did win, the prize fund would be divided among so many people that the individual amounts would be very small for each person anyway.

So be realistic with your goals: they have to be something that you can achieve. When this is the case, you start to believe that you can really attain them.

Am I visualizing about this book? You bet I am, in a number of ways. But am I visualizing about it becoming the bestselling *For Dummies* book ever? Well, that would be a rather tall order, and not too realistic – so, no. But I'm happy to reveal my two goals for this book:

- ✔ I intend to put all the most useful things I've discovered about creative visualization into this book, in order to help as many people as possible.

- ✔ I intend to make this book as interesting and helpful as I can, so good reviews and word of mouth enable it to sell well.

I believe that these aims are reasonable, realistic and achievable.

Dividing large goals into lots of smaller ones

If the result that you're aiming for is complicated or time-consuming, one way to keep your goals realistic is to break the overall aim down into smaller, more manageable parts.

If you want to write a book or complete a large project, break it down into chapters or sections and visualize working on and completing each of these individual parts, instead of focusing exclusively on finishing the whole project.

Don't forget to imagine completing the whole task from time to time as well, especially when you pass the halfway mark, which is the point at which many projects falter and you need a second wind.

Even something as simple as a college assignment can be broken down into parts, perhaps a beginning, middle and end. Many students procrastinate and leave assignments until the very last minute, with their grades consequently suffering. And this procrastination isn't always because they're partying all the time! It can often be because the task seems monumental. But by breaking it down into smaller and smaller segments (until each part looks easily accomplished), you can set aside an hour at a time to work on it and find the job far easier to complete.

But you don't have to go straight into that first hour of work. Spend five minutes visualizing yourself working highly productively on the assignment for an hour and completing the segment, and you soon feel the motivation to put pen to paper (or finger to keyboard).

Keep visualizing completing sections, and the time needed and information required often comes to mind, making completing the work far easier, and the grades received higher than for work handed in at the last minute.

Limiting your number of goals

Beginners to creative visualization are often so impressed by the results that they straightaway start setting several more goals.

Make sure that you don't choose too many goals to manage sensibly, because visualizations can begin to run into each other. When this happens things can get confusing rather quickly.

Limiting the number of goals you choose allows you to set aside the time to work on them. (After all, visualization isn't a replacement for doing the work or practice, but a way to make that work more effective.) Keep a maximum of three goals running at any time, until you've been visualizing for some months. I've used creative visualization for over 25 years, and I currently have seven goals running – rarely if ever have I had as many as ten.

When you've achieved one goal, you can replace it with another and so limiting your number of goals needn't be too restrictive. There's also a handy acronym you can use when selecting your goals: remember the word SMART, each letter of which is the first letter of each of these words:

- ✔ **Specific** Choose specific aims such as 'I wish to increase my salary'. This sets the goal clearly in your mind.

- ✔ **Measureable** Make your goal measurable, for example 'I wish to increase my salary by ten per cent'. That way you can be sure that it has been attained.

- ✔ **Attainable** Ensure that the goal you choose can be achieved. In the case of the salary example, are any other equivalent jobs in your organisation being paid at your current pay scale plus ten per cent? If so then your goal is more easily attainable than otherwise.

- ✔ **Realistic** Looking again at the salary example, it is probably too unrealistic to aim for a hundred per cent pay rise, or even a fifty per cent one. Setting an unrealistic goal can set you back because it is much harder to achieve and you may therefore be disappointed and give up trying.

> ✔ **Timely** Don't set your goal too far in the future or you may simply forget about it. In the salary example you can choose the goal 'I wish to increase my salary by ten per cent in time for the New Year'. This defines a specific and easily trackable time frame, during which you're less likely to lose sight of your goal.

Making positive affirmations

If you choose realistic goals (and not too many), but still have doubts about your ability to achieve them, start working on positive affirmations such as the famous phrase: 'Every day, in every way, I'm getting better and better'. This affirmation has been used repeatedly over the years because its sheer simplicity helps to prepare you for becoming more positive in your outlook.

Affirmations can prepare you for using creative visualization by setting the psychological mood needed in order to obtain the best results.

Affirmations are most effective when they're specific to your goals, and so use one or more of the following (placing your personal aim in the square brackets) and repeat them at least once a day:

> ✔ I'm fully capable of attaining [goal].

> ✔ Reaching [desire] is part of my destiny.

> ✔ Achieving [aim] is simply the next rung on the ladder.

> ✔ I'm already well on the way to attaining [ambition].

> ✔ I will use [achievement] for the good of others.

Repeating positive affirmations allows you to internalise effectively the achievement of your goal. Over time it becomes part of your psyche that you believe is most certainly achievable, and you'll wonder why you ever doubted it!

What's more, you start to see the steps you need to take to realise the result you want. Opportunities that previously went unnoticed become apparent to you and your feeling of confidence about the matter increases as you see the goal getting closer.

For example, if you have a child who is diagnosed with dyslexia, and you look it up in a dictionary or on the Internet, you may also come across a number of other terms such as 'learning disability', 'reading disability', 'attention deficit hyperactivity disorder', 'language impairment', and so on. Then whenever you encounter any of these terms on a website, in a television programme or magazine article, you'll automatically pay attention because it may contain information of use to you and your child.

The same goes with affirmations and creative visualizations. Once you place them firmly in your mind, whenever anything related to them comes to your attention, your mind will be drawn to whatever it is because there may be some information or news of use to you.

Until you put yourself into a goal-setting frame of mind, these types of things may pass below your radar. But when you have a goal to attain, your radar will be finely tuned to anything that might help you accomplish it.

Overcoming obstacles

Sometimes you can run up against a brick wall and your goal appears unachievable. Perhaps you've been visualizing about getting a rise or promotion at work and an obstructive boss, who you think has no interest in your future, repeatedly turns you down. Or a bank refuses to grant the loan you require, or a planning department denies permission for an extension to your house.

Be aware that even when you visualize, life will still try to present you with these roadblocks. Don't worry, it's quite normal and all part of the process of attaining goals that you set – simply stay firm in your belief that you'll realise your ambitions, and be prepared to be flexible.

Whatever the obstacle, don't panic and never give up. Instead, change your visualizations. Roadblocks exist to stop other people, not you! Whatever the obstacle, visualize it diminishing or you getting round it as creatively as you can. You may have to work at it, but as long as you keep visualizing ways round, over or under the obstacle, ideas will come to mind to help you.

Spend some time going over the obstacle in your mind in as many different ways as you can. Ask yourself whether the obstacle can somehow be avoided. Can it be ignored? Can its impact on you be diminished? Will it go away on its own after a period of time? Can it be diverted to another course? Mull over all these things and try to be creative. For example, if the obstacle is a person blocking your progress, imagining them as a thing (perhaps a stubborn elephant blocking the road ahead) makes the person less personal and easier to visualize about.

For the example of seeking a promotion, start to imagine that the boss is no longer working in your office. In your visualizations perhaps she gets promoted to another department, or leaves for a different company. Maybe imagine that a new position comes up that only you can fill, or visualize an even more senior boss taking an interest in your work. Or be really creative and imagine that the boss is a big pile of rocks and mud in the middle of a road on the side of a mountain being weathered away by a rainstorm, and is gradually disappearing down the mountain.

You don't mean any harm to the boss, of course; it's simply *creative* visualization, which lets your unconscious mind perceive the obstacle as smaller than you do currently, and as one that's diminishing.

Curiously, when you do start to change your visualizations, the thing in your way can sometimes appear less of a problem. You may see other opportunities and end up deciding to go in an entirely different direction, and discover that you weren't meant to pass through that particular roadblock in the first place.

The results of visualizations aren't always what you imagine they're going to be. Unexpected things often happen, which at first you may find off-putting or unusual. But with hindsight you come to see that they led to you attaining the goal in a completely different and usually better way.

A few years ago I chose the goal of reducing my alcohol intake to help with losing weight – being out of shape was an obstacle. Although cutting down on my alcohol consumption had the desired result and helped me lose quite a few pounds, it had the secondary effect of leaving my thoughts unclouded in the evenings as I drank less. As a result I soon found myself doing more writing, playing more music, attending to the garden more, and spending more quality time with my family. All positive benefits that I didn't initially have in mind.

Even when obstacles are in your way, keep believing that you're going to achieve your goals, and keep visualizing. You'll be glad that you did.

Imagining Yourself Having Achieved

An important part of preparing for creative visualization is seeing the result of having achieved your goals. Not only does this technique help you to become more focused on your goals, but also it prompts your unconscious to feel as if you've already succeeded.

Even when you break down a goal into smaller component parts to aid visualization (as I explain in the earlier section 'Dividing large goals into many smaller ones'), seeing yourself completing a larger project can still sometimes be difficult. This section provides some suggestions for getting back on track.

Focusing and concentrating on the results of achieving your goal, as well as visualizing the process of attaining it, helps to ensure that you're less likely to become bogged down in the detail and puts the task back into perspective.

When you create your visualizations, take the time to add the benefits of realising your aims and imagining the reward of all your effort.

When you've done something once, repeating that task a second and third time is much easier. Visualization uses this reality, and when you visualize that you've already attained a goal, afterwards when you visualize on the goal again you can feel as if you're working on that goal for the second time. This is because seeing the goal achieved and the impact it has, puts your unconscious in the same frame of mind as if you've already completed the task successfully before, and so you feel as if you already know what to do and how to achieve the result you want.

And if you're going for a goal for a second time in reality, visualizing the result should be even easier and further enforce your ability to attain it again.

Taking ownership of the changes you want to make

Psychology uses an idea known as *ownership*, which means that when people possess something they take ownership of it. Several studies show that if, for example, you give someone one of two items, such as a free red pen, and then offer to swap it for (say) a blue pen, most of the time people decline the offer because the recipient has instantly taken ownership over the item.

In the real world this concept often occurs when we decide to sell something we own. Due to our taking ownership of the particular item, we tend to value it as worth more than someone who doesn't own it, and so buyers and sellers often have to haggle. For example, imagine that you have a lawnmower for sale which cost you a certain amount. Because you spent that amount of money you're loath to let it go for much less and don't want to sell for less than, say, two thirds of what you paid. On the other hand, a prospective purchaser will look at the wear and tear and may only want to spend perhaps a third.

The ownership experiment has been tried with many different items such as stuffed animals, T-shirts and so on, and the result is usually the same; when people take ownership of something, they feel that it's a part of them and don't want to let it go. The same logic applies to visualizations. When you start to imagine something such as a change in habit, you begin to take ownership of the change much more quickly than if you simply make the change and try to stick with it.

If one of your goals is to get into shape, you can imagine yourself swimming every day in the local public swimming pool, traversing a few lengths each time, feeling the splash of water, the breaths you take between strokes, the wetness of your hair, how you kick your legs and so on, including showering and changing afterwards, to complete the picture.

If you visualize in this way for a few minutes each day you start to take ownership of this new behaviour and begin to feel that you want to perform this exercise for real, and after a few more visualizations you'll find yourself heading off in the direction of the local pool because you're really motivated to swim.

The technique of visualizing and ownership is so powerful that you can use it to help stop smoking or drinking, or to motivate you to exercise more; all changes that people find painful to make unaided. For details on how to manage these habits and more, check out Chapter 10.

Taking ownership of the changes you want to make in your life results in these changes feeling a part of you, often before you've even made the change. You therefore have an emotional reason for not wanting to let go of the change which is very useful for holding onto positive traits, habits and emotions.

Picturing feeling proud of yourself

Whatever the specifics of your goal, you always have a general reason to achieve it: that is, you want to enjoy the benefits obtained by doing so. So, spend time in your visualizations enjoying the feeling of how things are going to be when you've achieved your goal.

What are the general rather than specific benefits and results of achieving a goal? Well, one of the main ones is surely pride. Not the kind of arrogant, puffed-up pride that 'comes before the fall' (better known as hubris), but the pride of a job well done, and the satisfaction of having successfully completed a task.

Imagine that your goal is to carve a fabulous wooden statue. One of your visualizations associated with this aim can be to see it finished, perfectly smoothed and varnished; to feel it with your fingers and notice all the little pieces you lovingly carved out. Visualize the piece as a work of art that's amazingly enjoyable to hold and picture other people appreciating it, too. If you want to go professional, imagine a collector purchasing it for a good price and then visualize spending the money.

If the aim is less tactile than carving and more practical, such as giving up smoking, visualize yourself running up and down stairs without becoming out of breath. Imagine smelling clean and fresh morning air, tasting great food without the hint of smoke in it, seeing the inside of your lungs clean and tar free, and living a long, healthy and fulfilling life.

Focusing on flashbacks and flashforwards

To explore and help fulfil your aims, you can use flashbacks of before the change and flashforwards of having achieved your goal. Visualize yourself before starting out on the path to your goal, and then imagine yourself afterwards. Look at what's different and better when the goal's reached.

Flip back and forth between the two images or scenes that come to mind and examine all the improvements you notice. Each one of these improved images is a positive of which you start to take ownership and can incorporate into your psyche. Over time, they become part of you and strengthen your determination to succeed.

If you want to quit smoking, for example, try switching between images of yourself before and after giving up the habit. In the before image you're struggling for breath and coughing after having climbed the stairs. In the after image you've run up the stairs quite easily without any problems whatsoever. Flicking between these two images emphasizes the differences between the two states and further signifies to you the importance of attaining your goal.

Think about how popular the home makeover shows are on TV. People just love to see the improvements that can be made to a house. And the climatic 'reveal' at the end, where the home owner is shown the results, is the part everyone waits for.

You can use this popular concept to create your own mental reveal by concentrating fully on your 'before' image or scene and then putting on a mental blindfold. Wait a few seconds while you change the scene to afterwards, and then surprise yourself when you mentally take the blindfold off, and suddenly see the changes in your life that the attained goal brings. Enjoying the feeling of success in advance encourages you to strive towards it. You can use this technique a few times before it stops becoming a surprise to you; and by the time the effect begins to lessen you should already be seeing some (if not many, or even all) of the changes you desire as the visualization is doing its job.

Considering what you're going to do next

When visualizing it's important to continually consider what you'll do next. Life is like a journey, and so you'll find it is with creative visualization too. The more you use it and see the results, the more you want to use it. So considering your future from time to time is fun and an important part of preparing yourself firstly for enjoying the changes you've brought into your life, and secondly for deciding what to change next.

When you've imagined feeling proud about achieving a goal, and you've examined the differences between before and after getting there (as I describe in the two preceding sections), you can think about where else this achievement is going to lead your life.

If your goal is getting a degree, after visualizing congratulating yourself and looking at the before and after scenes, start visualizing the graduation party you're going to have. Imagine taking up the job or further education opportunity you gain as a result of the degree. See how this brings you more responsibility, money or whatever other positive things you desire.

Chapter 3

Reaping the Benefits of Creative Visualization

In This Chapter

▶ Experiencing the mental benefits

▶ Understanding why you feel better

▶ Noticing how you benefit physically

Creative visualization is a personal development technique that achieves real results – as documented in many biographies and scientific studies. But just what benefits can you hope to gain?

Practising creative visualization helps you to achieve a huge range of goals that you set for yourself, as long as they're realistic and you're prepared to work towards realising them. But the more realistically achievable you believe your goals to be, the more you believe in them, and the more you believe, the more motivated you are to be successful.

If you keep achievability firmly in mind while practising creative visualization, you're bound to attain your desired goals. Personal goals are the ones most easily and quickly achieved through creative visualization, because you have far greater control over your inner self than you do over external events and other people. Sometimes the results may take a while, and sometimes they come amazingly quickly. But regardless of when you notice changes, continuing to practise the techniques is of utmost importance. As long as you keep up the exercises, positive changes do take place, each moving you a step nearer to your goals.

In this chapter, I look at some of the conscious, unconscious, and physical benefits you can expect to attain through creative visualization. You also discover how these benefits can make you feel better, and how you can best appreciate and use them.

Discovering the Conscious Benefits

After you've been practising creative visualization for a while, you're likely to become conscious of certain benefits. They're evident in your mood, habits, actions, and interactions with other people.

One of the most common first goals to set using visualization is to be happier or more contented (exercises for which I describe in Chapter 7): you want to be more relaxed and less stressed out. The word 'contented' is useful here, because although most people express a desire to be 'happier', that's not necessarily what they mean in practice.

The state of happiness is something that comes from enjoying friends or family, watching a film, or enjoying a good meal. On the other hand, when you're trying to concentrate, for example while working hard on a project, being happy can be a distraction and cause you to lose focus. In fact, what you so often crave is being contented (that is, not anxious or unduly worried about things) – in other words, you seek a more restful mind.

When your mind is more rested, and you're content, you're less distracted and better able to focus on things you want to do. You can also more easily reflect on your needs and desires. For example, if you go shopping when you're hungry you're likely to buy far more food that you need. But if you go when your stomach is full you think much more clearly and purchase only the food you need.

Feeling better about yourself

If you have feelings of low self-worth or depression, one of the first things you can do to help is remove negative thoughts that may be holding you back. So often when you don't feel good inside you tend to dwell on it and get stuck in a vicious circle of ever declining morale.

But by breaking the circle using creative visualization you can interrupt the downward spiral and leave room to start injecting some positivity or at least some constructiveness into your thoughts. After visualizing for just a few minutes you may well notice that you start to feel better, even when you've started off in a good mood!

Not only is feeling better about life a benefit in itself, it helps improve your interactions with other people and makes your whole outlook seem a lot more positive. You find you smile more and generally feel more sociable and the jobs you do will seem easier and the mundane tasks will even seem less boring.

When you start to feel the gentle wave of optimism – the general feeling of goodwill that runs through you as you visualize positive things – try to bring this feeling into all your visualizations. Eventually, you can consciously draw on this positive energy as you begin each visualization exercise. This technique strengthens the effects of the visualization you're practising, and over time you start to notice that even when you're not visualizing you still seem to be in higher spirits than before.

Becoming motivated and achieving more goals

Relatively quickly after you start to visualize, you may well discover that you're more motivated than usual. This change can manifest in a desire to do things that you've been putting off, such as redecorating the house, practising a musical instrument, remembering to write your diary, taking up a new hobby, or visiting friends and relations.

Even if before you start visualizing you feel too tired or that not enough time is available to become the person you want to be or to attain your ambitions, after you begin your visualization exercises your desire to succeed strengthens, bringing with it the motivation you need. As you continue to visualize, you start to realise the things that are necessary to attain your goals and so you quite naturally want to do these things more and more.

You may find that you start to get a little fidgety if you watch too much television, that you tend not to sleep in at the weekend, or that difficulties with your current projects (at work or at home) suddenly seem to disappear. This situation occurs even when becoming more motivated (something that I cover in Chapter 9) isn't one of your direct goals. This additional motivation is key to helping you achieve your goals, because you need to be proactive and take conscious steps towards achieving them.

Imagine that you're self-employed (if you aren't already!) and your ambition is to get more customers in order to increase your income. In addition, assume that recently you haven't had much success in this area. In this scenario, when you begin visualizing around your financial goal, ideas start to come to mind about how to contact potential customers. You may find that the increased confidence you begin to exude makes current customers want to give you more business, or recommend you to colleagues. Perhaps you see new opportunities that require a few extra hours work a week. You discover that you now have the necessary motivation to keep working at getting that extra business.

With visualizing, all the things you need to achieve your goal become apparent, as does the drive and motivation to do so. Simply keep on visualizing and the goal you desire works its way into your life, and really doesn't feel like hard work at all.

Developing greater energy

When you're actively pursuing a goal through creative visualization, you may also find that you have an abundance of energy. Usually, this energy is sufficient to keep you going to achieve your desire, but often you notice that you also have extra energy to employ in other areas of your life. You may suddenly have the urge to go on walks or start cycling, or visiting a gym regularly. You may find that listening to other people (whom you previously found tedious) is now a lot less boring and that the things they say are quite interesting. This result is due to the fact that now you have the energy you need really to listen (and not just hear), and in the process discover what you've been missing out on.

Much of the time this energy becomes infectious and you see other people picking up on it: you start motivating them as well. If they comment on your new vigour, thank them (and maybe mention this book, if you're feeling ever so kind!).

When the energy starts to flow, do make sure that you employ it. Use the energy to help achieve your goals, to help other people, and to improve the quality of your life and the lives of your loved ones. If you don't use it, you lose it. But if you draw on the energy, more comes from within you to replace it. And keep on visualizing, because that's the ultimate source of the energy.

Looking at the Unconscious Benefits

When you begin to visualize, many changes take place within you, albeit unconsciously. You may not notice these changes at first, but when you look back at how you were before and compare that situation to how you are now, a great deal of difference becomes apparent.

Three main areas of unconscious benefits are as follows:

✔ You begin to feel less stressful and your anxiety levels fall, even if they're not that high to begin with.

✔ Your mind becomes more settled.

✔ You start to feel more fulfilled.

As you visualize more and more you begin to feel more strongly in control of your life and its direction. Things that normally worry or upset you have less of an adverse effect and you find the motivation and energy to deal with them.

Reducing stress and anxiety

Put simply, stress is unpleasant. Even in very small amounts it can make you psychologically and physically unwell. Yet more often than not you aren't aware that you're under any stress. Or if you are, you may often mistake it for motivation, which it most definitely is not.

Try to avoid stress as much as possible, even when times are hard due to the fact that you can't afford to pay the bills, a relationship is going badly, or you have a boss who puts too much pressure on you. Yes, all these are problems (and quite common ones at that), but you don't need to be stressed by them. In fact, by reducing stress levels you can find that you deal more easily with such problems. Keep reading for some concrete ways to battle stress!

The feeling of being out of control is one of the biggest causes of stress. The exercises in this book related to calmness, anxiety, and stress reduction (check out Chapters 8 and 11) help you to start taking back control of your life.

Here's a simple visualization exercise you can do at any time to reduce your anxiety levels when you feel stressed. Imagine sucking the stress right out of all parts of your body and concentrating it deep in your *solar plexus* (in the centre of your chest, at the lowest part of your rib cage) by breathing in deeply – as deep as you can – and breathing along with the visualization. Now imagine that you're blowing up a meadow-green balloon made of pure energy (green has good healing and relaxation properties).

Puff out as you fill the balloon with the air containing all your worries and problems. When it's full, tie a knot in it and let the balloon float away in the breeze; watch it grow ever more distant and smaller and smaller. Soon it disappears over the horizon where both the stress and balloon simply evaporate away into nothing, taking your problems with them. If you have any more troubles still in you, visualize puffing them into another balloon and let it follow the first one. Do this exercise a few times until you feel better.

Creative visualization can be used as an effective method for reducing the symptoms of stress, as well as the causes. When you know that you can lower your anxiety levels with creative visualization (and have successfully done so a few times), you find that over time your body adopts the stress response less often, until eventually you rarely feel stressed out, if at all.

Obtaining peace of mind

One side benefit of reducing stress and anxiety (as I describe in the preceding section) is that when you look back after having visualized for a few weeks you notice that you've become more peaceful inside. Overcoming stress through creative visualization helps you to maintain a more balanced outlook on life so that niggling little things (such as someone taking a parking spot you were waiting for) no longer bother you so much. As a result, you feel more at peace with the world.

When you have this feeling of peace it frees you from the noise and chatter of your thoughts (both good and bad). It's like the difference between being at a noisy party where you can only hear one or two people close to you, and sitting on a park bench where not only can you easily converse with your friend, you can also see and hear all the sights and sounds around you. Sometimes all we need is a little peace in order to get our thoughts in order.

You're no less energetic or motivated – these things are as strong as ever – but you feel as if a burden is beginning to be lifted from your shoulders, a burden that you didn't even know you were carrying.

Feeling fulfilled

As you reduce stress and feel more peaceful through the use of creative visualization (check out the two previous sections), you may also begin to experience more occasions of personal fulfilment, in which your visualizations help you to realise all the positive things you've achieved and will continue to achieve.

Perhaps you don't even recognise it at the time, but when you feel proud about having completed a project, that sense of achievement may well also be fulfilment.

Fulfilment is the sense that you're in the right place at the right time, and doing the right things. And, of course, that's the case: if you're visualizing your goals, and they're beginning to be realised, you are indeed heading in the direction you want to go.

If you wish to attain this state of being (or any other) more quickly in the future, you may find the technique of anchoring (often taught by Neuro-Linguistic Programming practitioners and hypnotherapists) to be useful. With anchors you can quickly recall desired memories or change mental states using a variety of methods including physical gestures and verbal phrases.

Whenever you feel in a state of mind that you'd like to easily recall at a later date (such as feeling fulfilled), you can perform a unique gesture like tapping the point of your nose twice (or anything you choose) to lock it into your memory. Then, when you perform the same gesture another time, it'll help to quickly recall the same feeling you had when you stored the gesture in your memory.

Instead of a gesture you can also choose a phrase such as 'I feel fulfilled' which you repeat to yourself a few times when you first experience that feeling. Saying this phrase again in the future will help you to recall the feeling. Chapter 11 makes use of anchoring to help overcome fears and phobias by helping you to recall relaxed states of mind when approaching something that scares you.

Tracking your progress

In any personal improvement process it's important to track your progress so you can tell how well and at what rate you're progressing. Seeing your progress also works as an additional motivator (just like seeing you've lost a couple of pounds at a weekly dieting weigh-in) and keeps you going when the progress seems difficult.

To prove to yourself that you're benefiting from your creative visualization practice, I recommend that you fill in the first column of Table 3-1 (or a photocopy if you prefer), marking each of the rows with a number between 0 and 100 for how strongly you feel that particular characteristic right now. Then enter today's date at the top of the column. This entry serves as a baseline summary of who you are now. The additional columns can then be used to detail your progress as you bring visualizing more into your way of life.

Complete other columns in the chart from time to time (at periods at least a week apart) and prove to yourself just how well creative visualization is working for you. The chart contains 12 columns and so you can use it to measure your progress during a 12-week period, or a full year of 12 months. Or simply fill in a column as and when you remember or feel like it.

This chart is a visualization reinforcement that (as the scores slowly go up) serves to increase your belief in how well the system works, and therefore leads to even greater effectiveness.

Table 3-1   Personal Development Progress Chart

	Date	Date	Date	Date	Date	Date	Date	Date	Date	Date	Date	Date
Attention span												
Career/Occupation												
Compassion												
Confidence												
Contentment												
Conviction												
Courage												
Creativity												
Determination												
Drive												
Empathy												
Energy												
Enthusiasm												
Finance												
Fitness												
Focus												
Fulfilment												
Generosity												
Happiness												
Health												
Honesty												
Humility												
Kindness												
Knowledge												

	Date	Date	Date	Date	Date	Date	Date	Date	Date	Date	Date	Date
Love												
Mindfulness												
Morality												
Motivation												
Optimism												
Passion												
Peace of mind												
Positivity												
Reliability												
Relationships												
Resilience												
Respectfulness												
Responsibility												
Security												
Spirituality												
Stamina												
Wellbeing												
Willpower												
Wonder												

Enjoying the Physical Benefits

The physical benefits of creative visualization manifest even when your goals aren't physical. As I describe in Chapter 1, your mind and body are part of an organic whole. Improvements in your mind also have positive effects in your body, and vice versa. For example, shy people tend to keep their eyes averted and often adopt a slightly stooped posture which is bad for the spine and muscles around it. But when you're confident you tend to stand tall with a straight back, which is a much better posture that helps make you less prone to back problems in later life.

Your body and mind are closely intertwined with each other. What you think reflects in what you do. And what you do changes how you feel. For example, simply forcing a smile when you're unhappy shapes your facial muscles in such a way that your brain responds by releasing chemicals that lift your mood, and you become happier. In fact this is an exercise that you can never fail to be impressed with. Simply smile as often and as widely as you can, especially to your friends, and you can't help but have a sunnier outlook on life.

Becoming fitter

When you visualize, you tend to become more physically active (due to increased motivation, energy, and strength). As a result, you automatically start to get fitter because you're exercising your muscles more; you may also lose some excess weight.

Make sure that you harness this increased fitness level as positive feedback by enjoying and using it. When you feel energised and fidgety, get up and do something, even if it's just a bit of extra housework or visiting a work colleague down the hall. Getting up and doing something strengthens your visualizations and enhances the mental and emotional changes you desire. Being inactive physically results in less mental activity due to the mind-body connection, and your creative visualization results will therefore come more slowly than if you keep active

Knowing that these physical improvements may occur when you visualize enables you to prepare for them. If you're ready for the changes, you're more likely to notice the improvements, consciously take them on board and make more of an effort to make them permanent changes.

Helping you to lose weight

Although creative visualization can be used as a dieting aid, I don't recommend attempting to lose weight purely with creative visualization. Once you've selected a dieting strategy or programme that suits your require-ments, you can use visualizations to help keep you motivated and overcome temptation and hunger pangs.

For example by holding an image of a slimmer, fitter you in your imagination you can focus on the benefits of losing weight, to overcome the temporary temptation to 'just eat a few biscuits'. And when you feel hungry use your imagination to remember how it feels when you're full up and not hungry. By holding that feeling in your mind you find it easier to put off snacking until your next meal time.

Consult your GP before embarking on any weight-loss programme.

Increasing your stamina

Not only can you use visualization to help increase your energy and strength, you can use it to develop greater stamina too. As you become more used to obtaining results from your visualization you find you choose to visualize more frequently, resulting in finding more time to visualize and more time for doing whatever it is you're visualizing about. What's more, the target of your visualizations becomes easier as you practise it more and become more focused on it, and you find you can manage it for longer periods too.

Your body needs to get used to all this new strength and stamina, and so take things easy when you start to become more active. That way you can avoid overexerting yourself too much and too quickly.

Reducing your aches and pains

As you become more confident and relaxed through creative visualization, you may become less prone to aches and pains because, due to the mind–body connection, the less stressed and happier you are the higher your pain threshold becomes. Inversely, the more depressed you are, the more you tend to feel minor aches and pains as being greater than they really are.

A lot of minor pains are psychosomatic – put simply, they're 'all in the mind' – and often a symptom of stress; as you reduce your stress, they fade. (Flip to the earlier section 'Reducing stress and anxiety' for more on the benefits of keeping stress in check.) Other aches can occur as a result of under-using your muscles, so that they become weak. But as you become more active (another benefit of practising creative visualization), the muscles grow and the pains diminish.

If you suffer from frequent headaches, you may find that they start to occur less often, are less severe, and last a shorter time. In turn this improvement does wonders for your thinking – which becomes clearer and less distracted by the headaches – and your emotional state, which becomes brighter and more positive.

Again the reason for this is down to the mind–body connection. Stressed and depressed people are not only more susceptible to minor aches and pains, they also tend to catch colds more easily and often suffer from more headaches too.

By using creative visualization to improve how you feel and become more relaxed, your immune system is boosted by this newfound positivity, your pain threshold rises, and you may suffer less from headaches.

Medical conditions such as migraine headaches which are being treated with medication should continue to be treated this way, but you may find that creative visualization helps reduce their intensity or frequency.

You may also notice that if you have a skin condition such as eczema or another condition such as a pollen allergy, it also begins to improve. This is because a person who consistently thinks positively tends to have a stronger and more active immune system than one who doesn't. Many years ago I used to suffer from several colds each year, but now I seem to not catch any more than one every couple of years – even when the children come home from school with streaming colds they've caught there. I put this down to a generally elevated level of positivity in my outlook.

Even if you're young, fit, and healthy and less likely to feel tiredness or to suffer from other physical ailments, you should still notice some positive physical improvements as a result of visualizing. These improvements can include catching fewer colds, faster healing cuts, getting a better night's sleep (waking up relaxed and fresh), and even healthier-looking and feeling hair and skin.

Lowering your blood pressure

Stress sometimes causes high blood pressure (hypertension) and so you may find that this problem begins to improve when you practise creative visualization. If you have a blood pressure monitor, keep a note of the readings in Table 3-1 to verify any improvement. If things get better, it could be that it's the result of reducing anxiety and stress in your life.

Remember that creative visualization isn't an alternative form of medicine to use in place of regular medicine. It's about bringing together all the things that help you, and that includes modern medical techniques, therapies, and drugs. Therefore always consult a physician or other medical professional if you're in any doubt about physical problems that don't settle down after a short period.

Part II
Discovering How to Visualize

The 5th Wave   By Rich Tennant

"Creative visualization can certainly help you, but first you have to want to quit trampling villages."

In this part . . .

You'll learn how to use the various techniques of creative visualization: visualizations, affirmations, mental flash cards, and written goal setting. You'll also begin to prepare yourself for making changes to your life by focusing in on the things that are most important to you. When you're ready you'll then look at choosing the best places for you to practice your visualizations.

Chapter 4

Exploring the Different Types of Visualization

*T*here are a number of different ways in which you can visualize the changes you'd like to make in your life and how they'll affect you once they're achieved. You can use audio or video sources as inspiration or guidance, and there are ones where a friend leads you through your visualization. You can employ mental flash cards which are like a quick, five-second visualization you can call on when you need sudden inspiration, or to quickly summon the energy or motivation to do something.

To accompany these types of visualization you can use affirmations where you repeat positive phrases about a trait you'd like to improve or a goal you'd like to achieve. These affirmations can also be written down and read out loud from time to time to increase their results.

By understanding the different types of visualization techniques and how and when to use them, you can make more efficient use of your time, and the exercises you practise will achieve better results. This chapter discusses all these techniques and explains how they work and how to use them.

Understanding Unguided Visualization

In Chapter 1, I talk about daydreaming as an example of a type of visualization that you probably practise without even realising it. Other types of visualizations that you're likely to be carrying out already in everyday life include dreaming and lucid dreaming, visualizing a vista (a panoramic landscape view) when listening to music, and imagining a story as you read it.

These visualizations are *unguided,* in the sense that you don't consciously direct them. In fact, much of the visualization you already do is probably unguided: you simply follow the flow of your thoughts, wherever they may lead, acting as a detached and passive observer. Perhaps you daydream when you're bored and your thoughts wander about and constantly change as new ideas pop into your head; or when sleeping, you have long and highly intense dreams in which a whole multitude of different weird and wonderful events occur.

Sometimes you can have flashes of inspiration in which a picture comes suddenly into your mind. The 'picture' can be the solution to a problem, or a religious vision or epiphany, or simply one of those 'Aha' moments when something suddenly makes sense, just like a light bulb lighting up over a character's head in a cartoon.

For example, it could be raining and you may be pondering about how to quickly fix a leaky roof when you suddenly remember that you have some garden pond sealant that works under water, and therefore you ought to also be able to apply it to the roof (even in the rain) to make a quick temporary repair.

These types of flashes happen to us all day long, and are so common we probably don't even realise that they're a type of instant visualization.

You probably carry out some form of unguided visualization every day. No surprise, therefore, that creative visualization works so well: it's something that's already part of your unconscious behaviour.

In this section, I describe sleep dreaming and daydreaming and how you can turn both events to your advantage.

Defining daydreaming

Daydreaming is a partner to sleep dreaming. When you daydream you tend to un-focus your sight and gaze into the distance to remove distractions from your view, which serves a similar purpose to closing your eyes when sleeping. Most daydreaming happens when we're tired or bored.

Like me you probably recall being at school and sometimes staring out of the window, daydreaming instead of working on your maths problems. We lapse into daydreaming when there's little outside stimulus, or the stimulus happens to be too brain-consuming (like maths!) and we need a rest from it.

Of course, in your daydreams you have more control over what you think about because you're awake. This means you focus in more closely on things that have importance to you. But then your thoughts hop all around those things, often leading off at wild tangents and then back again.

This type of reflection helps to order your thoughts and perceptions to better understand them and the connections between them, and serves the purpose of rebuilding neural pathways in your brain (the process through which all learning occurs, where neurons create new connections or strengthen existing ones – think of it as a sort of 'reprogramming'). The reason for it is to help you cope better with life by constantly analysing it in your daydreaming downtime, as also happens in real dreaming, but on a far deeper and more abstract level.

Daydreaming is a natural mechanism that has worked well for human beings for thousands of years, although it can also work against you if you allow negative spirals of thoughts to enter your daydreams, which can potentially bring on depression. But if you augment your daydreaming with creative visualization, you can avoid or reduce the occurrence of these negative spirals and, more than that, you can create positive feedback to change your emotions and many other aspects of your psyche and physique.

Positive feedback is the opposite of a negative spiral. In the latter, the worse you feel, the more depressed you get. But in the former, when you're more positive, you begin to feel happier, and that makes you even more positive. I describe positive feedback in more detail in Chapter 1.

Dreaming lucidly

You can achieve all sorts of life changes while you're awake by practising creative visualization. But what about when you're asleep? Well, a phenomenon exists called *lucid dreaming*, which occurs when your conscious mind 'wakes up' in the middle of a dream and starts to take control.

Like daydreams, sleep dreams serve a purpose, which is to rebuild neural pathways in your brain (the physical process behind all learning and other mental and psychological change) so you're better adapted to the world in which you live. Unlike daydreams, however, your unconscious mind guides sleep dreams, and the unconscious has its own agenda and puts you in scenarios you'd never deliberately visit in a daydream.

That's why you sometimes have nightmares, for example. when the images you see frighten you.

So you don't consciously choose to have your dreams (good or bad), but your unconscious thinks that you do and it sometimes appears to use your dreams to send you messages. For example, falling dreams may serve to remind you to be careful when in a position in which you may fall (physically or metaphorically). The same goes for dreams in which you're sinking in water or being chased by someone or something. These sleep dreams arise due to your fears and help to guide the things you do in the same way that when you first touch something really hot, you very quickly learn not to do so again. Of course, like everyone, you have worries and concerns of which you're unaware, and if you have frequent bad dreams this may well indicate that an issue in your life needs addressing.

The important use of dreaming is to help make sense of your day and to lay down those memories that are important. This is done in an abstract way, which isn't yet fully understood, but is what subsequently results in your dreams. I sometimes think people can over-analyse their dreams, (although strong Freudians will disagree with me), and that simply experiencing them is all we need to do.

It's up to you how you interpret your dreams. Studies have shown that about three quarters of dream content or emotions are negative, and because of this, dreams (other than lucid ones) are not a helpful means of creative visualization.

When you dream normally, and unlike in daydreams, you feel more like an active participant than merely an observer. But have you ever tried to change a sleep dream as it unfolds? Most people find this next to impossible, which is because dreams are controlled by your unconscious, not your conscious mind. For example, no matter how hard or how often you flick a light switch, the light refuses to turn on; or if you mislay an item, such as your wallet, you often can't find it. And if you're having the very common naked dream, you normally can't find your clothes anywhere!

When you lucid dream, however, you feel as if you've woken up, but you know that you're still dreaming. You can turn around and look closely at objects. For example, if you're near a tree you can walk up to it and examine a leaf and see its structure down to the finest detail and subtlest colours.

A lucid dream generally occurs when something so totally absurd (even for a dream) occurs to you, or an outside sound or commotion raises your consciousness enough to know that you're dreaming, but not so much that you wake up. The common metaphor people use is pinching themselves to see whether they're awake. If you find yourself in a position to pinch yourself in a dream and it doesn't hurt, you may be experiencing a lucid dream.

If you choose, you can float up into the air and effortlessly fly around. When you do so, you can see how all the objects around you appear realistically in three dimensions and that you and they move absolutely correctly with respect to each other, as they would in real life.

Once in a lucid dream, I floated into space and sped up time and was able to watch the planets rotating around the sun, each in its own orbit, with the earth's and other planets' moons whizzing around them. At the time the dream seemed like a hugely expensive digital animation.

If you've never experienced a lucid dream, explaining them can be difficult and you may find this section quite hard to believe. On the other hand, if you've had any lucid dreams you may well think that I hardly scratch the surface!

Taking advantage of a lucid dream while it occurs

When you think that you're in the middle of a lucid dream, I recommend that you spend a little time verifying it for yourself. If you can think 'I'm in a dream', you've probably woken up your conscious mind sufficiently, and your dream is going to be lucid. If you can't produce this verification, you may still be able to transform a normal dream into a lucid one (check out the following section 'Turning a dream into a lucid dream').

Try exploring the world you find yourself in. Touch and feel things. Breathe in and smell the air. If you're like me, most of your lucid dreams have a natural or nature-like essence, often taking place in rich and vibrant countryside. So try flying over the landscape and feel the breeze rushing past you. Perform magic. Make rabbits appear out of thin air, or build a castle with a wave of your hand.

I find that about five or ten minutes is the standard length of a lucid dream (or at least in dream time it feels like five or ten minutes), after which your unconscious takes over again, just as it does when you fall asleep. So after a minute or two of enjoying the lucid dream, you can really live your visualizations by incorporating them into your dream. Take a look at the following examples for ideas of how to use your lucid dreams to your advantage:

- ✔ If you want to become fit, make yourself totally healthy and strong as an ox. Practise running a mile in five seconds, leaping over tall buildings and mountains, or bouncing up to the moon.

- ✔ If you want to become more self-confident, imagine yourself as the most confident person on the planet, standing 100 feet tall.

- ✔ If you want to pass exams, imagine yourself reading every book on the subject and all the information flowing quickly into your brain; feel it all clicking into place like pieces in a jigsaw puzzle.

- ✔ If you want to improve your finances, see yourself as already wealthy; imagine that you're completely financially secure and can produce a wheelbarrow full of cash any time you need it. In fact, visualize paying a wheelbarrow of cash into your bank while you're at it.

Whatever your goals, simply act them out as if they're real, but use the super-powers you have in your lucid dream to exaggerate them to the fullest. By doing this you'll have the most vivid and strongest visualizations possible, because what you imagine will seem almost real. Therefore the results of visualizations within lucid dreams are among the most effective you can have.

Many people have difficulty getting into a lucid state while dreaming. So if you can't lucid dream after following the advice later in this section, don't worry about it as it's not an essential element of creative visualization. However, if you do find that you can go lucid while dreaming then it is a tool you can use to augment your creative visualization.

Turning a dream into a lucid dream

Lucid dreaming is most likely to occur after any long period without sleep. Also, if you're so lucky as to be able to take a nap for just a few hours after a main sleep, that sleep tends to be much lighter and your conscious mind is far better equipped to take over and produce a lucid dream. In fact, middle-of-the-day naps tend to be excellent for successful lucid dreaming. Be aware that lucid dreaming is a possibility in these cases, so that you recognise it when it happens and can take full advantage.

You can also use creative visualization to help bring on lucid dreaming. Simply visualize yourself asleep and then 'waking up' into a lucid dream, and imagine the things you'd do in that state. After a while, your unconscious realises that you want a lucid dream, and it may choose to relinquish control to your conscious mind in some dreams.

To bring on lucid dreaming and to continue experiencing it, keep the concept at the forefront of your thoughts. Google 'lucid dreaming' from time to time (loads of useful information is available online) and read books about it. You'll be glad you did because your first lucid dream is a sensational experience.

Visualizing on the spur of the moment

You don't always have to set aside time, get yourself relaxed, and find the right mood to visualize – or indeed fall asleep. In this section, I describe a couple of powerful visualization techniques that you can practise in a second or two.

Experiencing Reinforcing visualizations

Reinforcing visualizations are ones in which you practise building on an existing situation or skill. For example, athletes who visualize may reinforce their feelings of strength and endurance, or people giving up an entrenched habit, such as smoking, carry out reinforcement visualizations that help to maintain their willpower. Both negative and positive reinforcement visualizations exist, but the positive ones always seem to work far better, and therefore I don't include negative reinforcements in this book.

As an example, when trying to quit smoking, you can focus on not having all the nasty tar and pollutants coating your lungs. But this is a highly negative image that's not as effective as imagining the exact opposite; clean, healthy energetic lungs, and being able to walk up hills, breathing easily and without getting out of breath or coughing.

Whatever you visualize, your unconscious mind will focus on it. So if you visualize a negative thing, even if only because you want it to stop, you actually tend to reinforce it unwittingly.

Using Interrupt Visualizations

Interrupt visualizations are those in which you follow through a course of action that normally leads to an undesired ending, but then you interrupt it just before that ending, and make something else happen instead. For example, if you're on a diet and (almost without thinking) you tend to reach for a chocolate chip cookie when it's left on a plate, you can use an interrupt visualization to follow through the process of reaching out your hand to the plate. At the last minute, however, imagine moving your hand away to a glass of water, which is then picked up and drunk in place of the cookie. Performed enough times, an interrupt visualization helps to replace old unwanted patterns with new desired ones, and the old habit fades away.

As you get more accustomed to visualizing throughout the day, ample opportunities present themselves for you to do a quick visualization. Try to take advantage of as many of them as possible, because each one helps to reinforce the others and is another step towards achieving your goals.

As part of my goal to make this book as interesting and useful to as many people as possible, whenever I take a break from writing I imagine briefly different types of readers ⊘ teenagers, athletes, retired people, entrepreneurs, and so on – reading the book and discovering something beneficial. This way I hope to ensure that I include as wide a range of examples and exercises as I can for use in a variety of typical situations.

Getting to Grips with Guided Visualization

Guided visualization is where you consciously take control of your visualization and guide it on a course from start to end.

When you're trying to use visualization constructively – for example recalling a map to help you remember how to drive somewhere new – you actively guide your visualization by imagining the map (or whatever you're doing) in your mind's eye.

When people using their imagination in this way are placed inside an MRI (Magnetic Resonance Imaging) scanner, the visual cortex of the brain (which normally processes information coming into your eyes) usually 'lights up'. This response indicates that when visualizing you use the same part of your brain as you do when viewing an object with open eyes, as if you're in fact seeing the thing you're imagining.

As you know, when you see things, you're more likely to remember them (or at least the main points of interest about them, although how much we remember varies from person to person). You find out about the object from its setting and its function – if it has one – and the more information you take on board about the object, the better you remember it.

In the same way, visualizing something in a structured manner helps you to discover or develop a new skill or ability. For example, if you've never played golf before but would like to learn, it'll help you to watch some golf on the television and then imagine yourself as one of the players. Visualize yourself taking the swings and imagine how all your muscles feel as you do so.

When you observe particular actions of others, *mirror neurons* in your brain are triggered so that you too feel as if you've carried out that action. When someone smiles, for example, you feel the smile too. Likewise if a child falls and bangs its head you feel that bump too. In the same way, by watching something happening and then imagining doing that thing yourself, you can already start to build the neural connections needed to learn a new skill.

While unguided visualization can help you to make sense of your current life, this section introduces you to ways of using guided visualizations to shape your future.

Following a visualization plan

The most important thing about guided visualization is that you follow a plan. This plan can be a ready-made exercise (such as the ones in this book) or one that you design yourself (once you've become accomplished at practising these ones) in order to achieve the maximum benefits. Following a plan ensures that each visualization is a complete exercise in its own right – with a beginning, middle, and end – and that while visualizing you don't lapse back into daydreaming or unguided visualization.

Using audio or video assistance

Many CDs and websites are available that contain narrated, guided visualizations for you to use. These guides typically focus on specific goals, such as relaxation, quitting smoking, or losing weight.

If you have difficulty using your imagination, why not get a DVD or Internet video to help you. A simple Google search for 'creative visualization audio and video' is a good place to start.

These types of guided visualizations are really best suited for helping you to get started with visualization. The sooner you're able to do your own visualizing without these aids the more proficient you become.

Being guided by a friend or relative

If you know someone who understands creative visualization, ask her to describe exercises to you so you imagine them in your mind's eye. Even if you don't know anyone suitable, you can still ask a friend to read exercises from this book to you.

Try recording yourself reading the visualizations onto a computer or smartphone and then visualize as you play back the recordings. This approach means that the reading doesn't distract you while you visualize and allows you to commit exercises fully to memory.

Memorise one or two exercises as soon as you can so you can simply recall them as and when you need to do them. In this way, you get started with your visualizations sooner rather than later.

Using mental flash cards

I often use what I refer to as 'mental flash cards' when I visualize. These mental 'cards' are very short distillations of a bigger visualization that I imagine at the same time as the main visualization. Usually they're based on a quick summary of a longer visualization. Then I can do my regular visualizations in my quiet times, and run a one- or two-second flash card when there isn't enough time to practise a longer exercise.

Although I've used visualizations successfully in many areas of my life, I'm still working on reducing my weight. I've had some success, but I need a lot more (as do many people), and so I have a few different mental flash cards to aid with this goal.

One of my mental flash card visualizations is to turn a picture of a biscuit (or other snack food) quickly into half an hour of brisk walking on a treadmill. I force myself to consider two options: whether to refuse the biscuit and save having to exercise; or eat the biscuit and exercise the calories off (or worse still put on some weight). Most of the time I'm reminded that not eating a biscuit takes only a couple of seconds, compared to the 30 minutes of exercise I'd have to spend otherwise!

Throughout Parts III and IV of this book, I provide loads of examples of mental flash cards that you can use to accompany your own visualizing.

Writing Down Your Visualizations

To enhance your visualizations, or if you find using your imagination difficult when you first begin visualizing, try writing them down. The benefit of putting your goals down on paper is that they're easy to return to later. And, because when your goals are in writing they never change (unless you rub them out and change them yourself), this method can be used to help precisely reinforce an objective.

Written visualizations can be pinned to the wall or somewhere that you frequently see them. They can then act as a constant reminder, spurring you on to visualize your goals more frequently.

Setting yourself goals is the main type of written visualization. Simply take a blank piece of paper and a pen and write down half a dozen or so of your most important goals for the following couple of years. Figure 4-1 shows an example. Flip back to Chapter 2 for tips on setting yourself achievable goals.

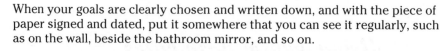

When your goals are clearly chosen and written down, and with the piece of paper signed and dated, put it somewhere that you can see it regularly, such as on the wall, beside the bathroom mirror, and so on.

To keep those goals focused in your mind, read them out loud to yourself at least twice a day.

I find that planning goals over a two-year period is useful, as is updating them each year. I keep the old sheets of paper (which I laminate) and stick the new ones over them. If you do this, each new two-year plan can overlap the previous one by a year, and so you can modify existing goals and continue on from or replace completed ones. Chapter 2 contains other ways of re-affirming your goals.

WRITTEN GOALS FOR 2011/12

* I will pay off all my personal loans and credit cards by the end of 2012.

* I will obtain a promotion at work or a better job with higher pay elsewhere by the end of 2012.

* I will lose 15 pounds weight by the end of 2011, and a further 25 pounds by the end of 2012.

* I will learn to play the clarinet in 2011.

* I will find the time to spend 2 hours extra each week actively playing with the children.

_1/1/11_

Figure 4-1: A typical set of written goals for the next two years.

If you also have life-long ambitions – goals that may take many years (or even decades) to achieve – you may also want to write these down on another sheet of paper. Long-term goals may be becoming company director of a major firm, obtaining a doctorate, bringing up a large family, becoming a head teacher, or anything that takes much of your lifetime to complete. By writing these long-term goals down, you're actively increasing the chances of achieving them.

The importance of written goal setting

In Chapter 1, I write about Napoleon Hill and his book *Think and Grow Rich*. As a young man Hill met the steel magnate Andrew Carnegie who instilled in him several principles that Carnegie used to build his financial empire; the fundamental lesson was the importance of writing down your goals. As Carnegie told Hill, 'It may interest you to know that approximately ninety-eight out of every hundred people are totally without a major goal, and it is significant that approximately the same percentage of people are regarded as failures.'

And Carnegie was very close to the mark with that 98 per cent figure, because in *What They Still Don't Teach You at Harvard Business School*, Mark McCormack cites a Harvard study conducted between 1979 and 1987. In 1979, Harvard MBA graduates were asked 'Have you set clear, written goals for your future and made plans to accomplish them?'

Three per cent of the graduates had written goals, 13 per cent had goals but hadn't written them down, and 84 per cent had no specific goals.

In 1987, Harvard followed up these students and found that the 13 per cent with unwritten goals were earning twice as much money as the 84 per cent with no goals, and that the three per cent with written goals were making ten times as much money as the other 97 per cent combined.

Chapter 5

Preparing Yourself for Change

● ●

In This Chapter

▶ Yearning for positive change

▶ Adapting to new routines

▶ Taking ownership of changes

● ●

*T*he one thing about life that never changes is the fact that it always changes, and particularly so when you set out actively to achieve specific goals. As the playwright George Bernard Shaw said: 'Progress is impossible without change, and those who can't change their minds can't change anything.'

The ultimate aim of any personal improvement programme is to become a changed person – to bring out those latent qualities in you that you desire and quell your less desirable qualities – and using creative visualization is no different. This chapter addresses preparing yourself for a programme of change, and why it's important to want and anticipate change in your life before you visualize. It also discusses the need for making room in your life for the change so that it fits in snugly, and how to prepare yourself for changes that in some cases may mean getting used to a different way of life, and even letting go of some cherished behaviours and assumptions. The good news is that you've already started: Reading this book marks the beginning of your personal journey that's going to lead to plenty of improvements.

Wanting to Change

Before you can bring about any improvements in your life, you need first to really want to change. Vaguely feeling that something isn't quite right and perhaps needs changing (as long as you don't actually have to do anything!) isn't sufficient. If the issue doesn't really bother you, and you're happy to struggle on through if change never happens, you're going to have difficulty maintaining your change programme.

From this desire springs motivation, and from that comes decision, which leads to energy and finally action. But the change starts with a little seed: a burning hunger or longing for something new and different in your life.

Knowing that you must truly want something to change

Like many people, you may intuitively feel that you want different things from your life, and you may even understand and accept that you have to change in order to achieve those things. But this feeling is more of a detached reali-sation without any depth of conviction, and certainly the desire for change may not be very strong. But if you can imagine having already achieved your goals, how does that emotionally feel? What scenes do you imagine as a result of this achievement? By visualizing having achieved your goal you begin to invoke sensory images which in turn induce unconscious behav-ioural and cognitive leaps.

To help you with this, Figure 5-1 uses the metaphor of life as a car journey that requires you to change a wheel when you want to change yourself. Wheel A represents the general pattern of going through life without thinking about change.

Often people drive through their lives with wheel type A attached because they've tried new things before and failed. Perhaps you've attempted to quit smoking a few times and then given up on giving up, or maybe you know your clothes size is creeping up each year but you've stopped letting yourself worry about it.

But the time comes when these things begin to bother you much more and you want to make some changes. Then, generally, you decide to swap your old wheel for wheel B, in which the typical change cycle is as follows:

Figure 5-1: Three wheels represent- ing different approaches to change.

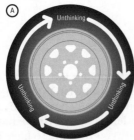

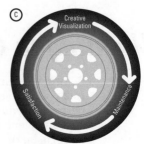

1. **Unthinking:** Living with your initial frame of mind.
2. **Contemplation:** Becoming aware of a need for change.
3. **Decision:** Deciding which change to make.
4. **Preparation:** Getting ready for the change (psyching yourself up).
5. **Changing:** Making the change in practice.
6. **Maintenance:** Continuing the change.
7. **Willpower:** Using willpower to stay focused.
8. **Relapse:** Relapsing when willpower fails.

This cycle explains the reason why people so often fail at making changes: willpower ebbs and they tend to relapse into old ways.

Sadly, you often start to address problems in earnest only when they get in the way of what you want to do. And so when you finally decide to do something, you find out that a bigger task is far harder than if you'd made the change earlier. By then, for example, your health is worse, you've put on more weight, or other problems are more pronounced, and all this makes sticking with the change even harder.

But fortunately, creative visualization offers a means to break the change/ relapse cycle, as shown in wheel C in which you achieve full maintenance of the change by continually visualizing. You need to try to move your change to this wheel as soon as you reach the maintenance part of the wheel B cycle.

When you use wheel C, you maintain your change through creative visualization and feel satisfied as a result; therefore, you want to continue visualizing to maintain the pleasure. In wheel C, creative visualization takes the place of willpower in wheel B by removing the opportunity to relapse if your resolve weakens. Instead, you maintain a positive reinforcing cycle that doesn't require immense internal strength to keep up.

Making the change one of your main desires

To achieve and maintain important and real improvements, you have to want them to happen, and so you may need to work on how much you desire a change before you set out on making it.

I recommend spending time to reflect on aspects of your life that bother you and you want to modify; in particular things that may normally be below your mental radar so that you don't think about them that often. Then decide whether you ought to work on any of these aspects. If so, you can begin to visualize wanting the thing to change so your desire for this change grows.

And wherever you can, make sure you visualize successful achievement of the desired goal and the impressions you feel about this achievement. This helps to bypass any mental roadblocks you have in place that have been preventing you from trying to achieve a goal.

Anticipating the change eagerly

Instead of just making the desire to change one of your main goals, motivate yourself as fully as you can so you become excited about and eager for the change. You can accomplish this aim by using visualization to realise and concentrate on how much happiness, health, joy, wealth, and so on the change is going to bring.

Maybe you've added up all the hours that you spend watching TV, calculated that the number is too high for your comfort, and want to cut back. In this type of change, which releases time back to you, you need to find other things to do with this time, and so you can concentrate on these new time fillers. For example:

✔ If you can play a musical instrument (or want to learn), think of all the enjoyment doing so is going to bring you. You may even write some songs or tunes, or join a band, local choir, or other musical group. Imagine all the great music and new friends you'll make.

✔ If you love reading and want to do more of that instead of watching the TV, think of all the great books you've never found time to read before, but now you can. Visit an online bookseller and browse through your favourite categories, maybe even add some to your wish list – such browsing doesn't cost a penny but helps you further build up your anticipation.

✔ If you love cooking, visualize the feeling, smells, and flavours as you spend the evening baking instead of slumped in front of the TV. Picture the admiration from friends enjoying your cakes and then asking for the recipe. Maybe you decide that you can make some money by selling the cakes to a local coffee shop; if so, imagine how you'd spend those earnings.

If you're looking to make a change for the sake of your health, such as quitting smoking or starting to exercise or diet, visualize the benefits. Imagine feeling far healthier, having more energy throughout the day, experiencing the sense of achievement, and all the other positive aspects of the new, fitter, healthier you. Get excited about the benefits and bring them into your life so you simply can't wait to get started!

Making Room for Change

Developing a desire for change in your life (as I discuss in the preceding section 'Wanting to Change') is one thing, but having it happen in reality is quite another – particularly when the change comes unexpectedly or too quickly to digest easily. This section covers some of the changes that may occur and helps you plan for them.

Ever since national lotteries were invented a large percentage of winners have ended up unhappier than before, many even stating that they wish they'd never won in the first place. But why does the dream of owning huge amounts of money turn into a nightmare for so many? Well, apart from all the 'friends' and relatives who suddenly appear out of the blue, as well as litigants who believe they can legally win some of the money pot, the biggest reason is that many people don't adjust well to the massive changes the lottery win creates in their lives. Many lottery winners are quickly thrust into the limelight and their previously private world is swiftly replaced with a whirlwind of people and huge changes taking place, almost daily. As well as all this unsettling new activity, winners also generally have no prior understanding of the complexities of managing a great deal of wealth, and some go on to lose every penny. The huge win is simply too much, too quickly for some people.

Similar problems can arise with musicians and actors who become suddenly famous. Because the change is too fast, they feel overwhelmed – in many cases leading to a downward spiral of alcohol and drug abuse.

In contrast, people who have a goal, who work hard towards it, and visualize and plan for it, manage their success quite naturally. The difference is because part of the planning and visualization process involves consideration of what things are going to be like when they reach their goal (which is, after all, why they have the goal in the first place), and so success doesn't come as such a shock as sudden good fortune.

Modifying your regular routines

The first things to do when planning any life change are to modify your regular routines and create time and space in which you can progress your change effectively, as I describe in the following two sections.

Changing your patterns

You can find that your daily routine is impeding your attempts to change and needs altering.

If you're quitting smoking you really need to (at least initially) avoid those situations in which you're most likely to smoke, such as directly after a meal, with a drink, when taking a work break, and so on. To help do so, after a meal at home you may decide to do the washing up immediately. If you used to smoke when consuming a particular drink, replace it with a different one or on work breaks don't go near the back door where the smokers hang out, but instead go somewhere else or take a quick walk.

Making time for the change

You may find that creating the necessary time to visualize and pursue your goal is difficult, particularly when your desire is something time-consuming such as completing a degree via a correspondence course. In these cases, effective planning is essential.

Whatever your goal, determine how much time you need to set aside and allocate at least that much as soon as you can, even before you start out. Given how people are usually very optimistic in these types of estimates, I'd go as far as recommending that you allocate twice as much time as you think you're going to need and make sure that you use it all performing the necessary tasks.

It's sometimes difficult finding the time needed to introduce changes into your life, which is one of the biggest reasons you put things off. But you actually have plenty of time available, and you just don't realise how much of it you spend watching television or doing nothing in particular.

To find the time for something that may take, say, 30 minutes a day, all you need to do is spend a minute or two each day, for a few days, imagining that you've already found the time you need. See yourself with a free, 30-minute slot doing the thing you need to do, and fast forward through the full half-hour noticing how nothing and nobody interrupts you.

A person can have so many goals that listing them all is impossible. But whatever your ambitions, you need to create new routines to facilitate them as soon as you can. Humans are creatures of habit and the sooner you instil a new (more positive) habit in place of the previously undesired one, the quicker it becomes ingrained – and the faster any stress caused by the change dissipates.

Accepting that your assumptions may change

Often when you make changes in life you don't realise that the way you think is going to change as well as your behaviour. People who successfully quit smoking often become very anti-smoking, whereas they simply disliked it before stopping. The same goes for people who stop other habits such as excessive drinking. Try to remain aware of this change in attitude before-hand, because people who give up bad habits can often come across to other people as quite irritating in their new-found zeal.

Of course, you want to talk about your success to everyone because you've learned the lesson yourself and are reaping the benefits. Being open about your change also helps to further reinforce it, and that's fine. But try to temper your enthusiasm a little.

After you've worked through a tight spot, such as a very tough financial situation, and things are looking up, you can often forget just how hard things were for you before and begin to look on other people in the same situation a little less sympathetically. This unfortunate reaction is human nature: people tend to relate mainly to their current situations and so, psychologically, the better things are going for them, the less time they seem to have for others who are worse off. They forget how they struggled through difficult patches themselves.

Your assumptions also change in positive ways. For example, as your desired changes begin to manifest, you expect them to do so more frequently, as you become accustomed to the fact that creative visualization works. Therefore, you spend less time thinking generally 'what if?' and more time thinking positively 'when?'.

Knowing that your life is going to be different

When you use creative visualization to bring changes into your life, that's exactly what happens: mostly good but also occasionally problematic changes. Your life is going to be different. After all, that's what you desire. But even so, seeing exactly what differences occur can still come as a surprise.

After stopping smoking, you have much more disposable income, you feel much fitter, you don't have a hacking cough, and you can run up the stairs without getting out of breath. In addition, food tastes much better, and you may find that you start preparing and consuming food more, perhaps with dinner parties or dining out more frequently. An unexpected side effect of the latter change, however, is that your weight may come under pressure.

Whatever your desired change, things are going to be different and being aware of the possibilities can help you cope with them:

- ✔ If your goal is simply to be happier, you can find yourself spending more time socialising with friends and others, but there may be negatives, such as having less time to spend on your hobbies.

- ✔ If your aim is a promotion, your work life may change, bringing you into different circles of colleagues and new responsibilities, but be aware that you may have less time for family and friends.

- ✔ If improved finances are your desire, you'll worry less about bills and have more disposable income to spend, but you may gain a tendency to overspend in the new excitement.

- ✔ If you want to get to a good college or university, just about everything in your life may change, which includes the positives of being far more in control of your own life than ever before – but then again, there are no parents to kick you out of bed in the morning, and you may miss your friends and be homesick.

- ✔ If you want to find a partner, your romantic life may blossom, but the amount of time you get to spend with your existing friends will also be correspondingly reduced.

For hints on handling the negative changes, check out the later section 'Seeking ways to accommodate the good and shun the bad'.

If you practise any of the techniques in this book to bring changes into your life, you can be certain that when they happen, things are definitely going to be different – mostly in positive and pleasurable ways.

Welcoming the Changes

Your creative visualization improvement programme is going to bring changes with it, and you need to be ready to welcome them and strive to integrate everything new into your life as seamlessly as possible. As a regular user of creative visualization, try to get into the mindset of always giving positive changes a good home, whatever they are and however they manifest.

Unforeseen negative changes and reactions can also arise, however, often as side effects. Fortunately, these negative aspects tend to be minimal (generally just annoyances really) and you can easily handle them. Read on to find out how.

Understanding that all changes are part of the overall plan

As you accomplish your goals, things around you change and continue to do so as long as you set new goals and visualize attaining them. After a while you may have some goals fully achieved, some partially realised, and others on which you're just starting to work. Therefore, your life is a constant supply of new events, new people to meet, new activities to get involved in, and so on.

The life of a creative visualizer is one of constant changes, all of which are part of your overall life plan. Even though you may not know it, all your different goals are part of an overriding strategy you've chosen, which is to better yourself and those around you.

Seeking ways to accommodate the good and shun the bad

As well as all the good that arises from positive thinking and creative visualization, other people may sometimes get jealous of your achievements and you may find that gossiping or even backstabbing can occur, particularly at work. Why? Because the status quo is changing, with you as a rising star. As Woodrow Wilson (28th President of the United States) said: 'If you want to make enemies, try to change something.'

As part of your response to any such negativity, understand why it exists and where it comes from. Be thankful that you're doing so well as to cause others to have these reactions. Of course, other people being negative towards you is unpleasant, so try to visualize positively for them to lessen their impact on your life (as the following visualization describes).

Spend some time thinking about how all people are individuals just like you, made up of trillions of atoms all connected in complicated and amazing ways to form a living, walking, and talking human being. In other words they are amazing too. They have friends and family, and mothers and fathers who love them. Wish them well, and even imagine them equally surrounded in the loving energy you sometimes imagine for yourself in various visualizations in this book.

But choose in your mind not to be negatively affected by them. Their life is theirs, and yours is yours. You'll be kind, civil and, yes, friendly towards them. But you actively choose not to be bothered by any of their negativity. Once you've tried this technique for dealing with people that hurt you, you'll find it far more effective and positive, and far less blood boiling than getting angry about them!

Incorporating the changes into your way of life

All the changes that arise as a result of your change programme amount to a new way of life, one that itself keeps changing and continues to improve as you work on your goals.

The people around you, the objects you possess, the places you go, and the events that take place are all now your way of life. They may be different from before but they're your life. Acknowledge them as such and take ownership of it all, knowing that your desire for positive change is shaping this way of life, benefiting you and those around you.

Chapter 6

Choosing the Best Times and Locations for Effective Visualization

. . . .

In This Chapter

▶ Ensuring that you're free to concentrate

▶ Increasing the power of your visualizations in the unconscious

▶ Using music and video while visualizing

. . . .

*W*hen setting out on a path of personal development through creative visualization, ensure that you do everything possible to get great results as early as possible; doing so helps to reinforce your belief in the techniques and encourages you to use them more.

Not that you must have faith for creative visualization to work – the techniques are tried-and-tested psychological means of connecting with your unconscious mind. You need only to practise them and, even if you're sceptical, they work. As long as you're objective in your analysis of the results by noting actual goals achieved rather than vague feelings of being different, you're going to notice changes taking place in your personality, body, and life in general.

The more fully you visualize, however, and the more convinced you are that the practice is going to work, the faster results come and the quicker you benefit from a happier, more fulfilled life.

Every little advantage can help to achieve this aim. In this chapter, I describe how to select the best times and places to carry out your visualization sessions and provide a few tips on enhancing the process. I also help you to understand the vitally important role of the unconscious mind in effective visualization.

Being Able to Concentrate

With the exception of those who meditate or practise relaxation techniques, many people tend to have busier minds than is good for them. Although to a certain extent a busy mind can help you achieve more things by multitasking, over a certain level the speed of ever-changing thoughts become a burden as they run into (and often conflict with) each other. For people with extremely busy minds, concentrating on any single task can be very difficult.

Therefore, a mind that's too busy is overloaded and needs slowing down somewhat, which happens with repeated visualization. Calming your mind and relaxing goes a long way towards helping you to concentrate, but the benefits are negated if distractions are preventing you from keeping focused.

The most important thing you need to be able to do when you visualize is concentrate. If you lose concentration and let your mind wander from what you're imagining, your visualizations tend to revert to simple daydreams, with none of the added benefits of guided imagery.

The following sections help you to find spaces, times, and privacy for your visualizing.

Choosing your visualizing space

The first and most obvious thing to do when you start to visualize regularly is to find somewhere quiet with little likelihood of distraction.

A good place to visualize is in bed, at the start or the end of the day (or both), unless you're too tired, because then you risk your visualizations quickly turning into dreams. That doesn't sound too bad, but most guided visualizations have a beginning, middle, and end, and often the end part is crucial to the whole exercise; visualizing the first two thirds without the final part, because you've nodded off, can have the opposite effect to the one you desire. If you've only visualized as far as the before part of an exercise (the thing you want to change from) and omitted the after part (the goal you want to achieve), the wrong part of the visualization is emphasised.

If you do choose to visualize in bed at night, only run quick imagery through your mind, such as mental flash cards. If you're sufficiently awake in the morning, though, that's a good time to perform longer visualization exercises.

Another environment that's conducive to successful positive visualization is somewhere in the home where you can't hear other people or perhaps in the garden as long as distracting traffic isn't going on.

You can often also visualize during parts of your commute if you're a passenger and your mind is free to concentrate properly on the exercises. While travelling to work on buses and trains most people are quiet and read a book or newspaper or use their laptops; but gazing out of the window and visualizing is just as easy.

At the risk of stating the obvious, don't try any type of visualization while driving a car, because you need to keep your full concentration on the road at all times. If your vehicle is stationary, however (for example, at traffic lights), you can sneak in a quick five-second mental flash card.

Some people also seek out good places to visualize that are away from their usual routines. For instance, if you live or work near a park you may enjoy going there specifically to visualize. And if you have a dog that needs walking, you have a wonderful opportunity for visualizing.

Weigh up a few places you can easily access and where you're most able to visualize properly, and try them out. If some appear more promising than others, concentrate on those places to start with, but other locations may well turn out to work better than you think.

But if you can't find somewhere quiet it's more important that you visualize than not, so instead try to find places where you can snatch brief moments of maybe 10–60 seconds. In these circumstances restrict your visualizations mainly to seeing your goals accomplished and contemplating the positive effects on your life of having done so.

By doing this you find that you strengthen your ability to concentrate and block out unwanted noise, so that over time you find yourself able to practise longer visualizations in a very noisy environment. The key is to discover how to get into the visualizing, trance-like state so that you can ever more easily get back into it when you need to, even under difficult conditions.

Preventing interruptions

When you begin to visualize, you may believe that your partner, friends, relations, and so on consider that what you're doing is a little crazy (unless they also visualize, in which case they're bound to be totally supportive). They probably don't think you're crazy yourself, but if the thought of that bothers you, simply don't tell people.

If someone interrupts you during a visualization to ask why you're being quiet, or offers a penny for your thoughts, quickly think about something like a recent holiday you enjoyed (or plan to enjoy) and then (truthfully) say 'I'm just thinking about the trip to Cancun' (or wherever the holiday destination is).

Over time you're going to feel less silly about visualizing, especially as you see the results, and perhaps even want to tell others about it. But don't feel that you need to until or unless it feels right, although you may need to tell certain people if they're not used to frequent moments of quiet contemplation from you. If you live a hectic life with children rushing around all the time, or have flat- or room-mates who always party, let them know that you sometimes need your 'thinking time'. In such situations you may need to specify certain times of day during which you ask not to be disturbed. You need only five or ten minutes a day away from the noise and distraction to begin to see results, and so you're being quite reasonable with such a request.

Of course, if you really want to bring change into your life and have some major goals in mind, spending an hour or more each day working on your visualizations is going to benefit you. This time is a total figure, though, and so it can be six blocks of ten minutes, twelve of five minutes, or any combination. If you visualize for this long each day, however, you're going to have to find ways around all the potential distractions.

I have a home office that looks out across the street to a busy Greek restaurant. Customers are continually coming and going. When I'm visualizing I like to stare into the distance and unfocus, but the scene over the road is sometimes too distracting for me. I tried putting a blind up in the window, so I could simply twist the slats to close them when visualizing, but then the room became darker and with only the blind to stare at in front of me it just didn't feel right.

In the end I moved the office around and placed my desk under a side window, which simply looks onto the side of the house next door and a few trees. Now any time I look up is perfect for a quick visualization.

In the 1990s, my British software company set up a branch in the US, and I had to rent an apartment in Pasadena that had extremely noisy neighbours both above and below. Most of the time I dealt with this noise by turning up the music or the TV or opening the window to let in the noisy street sounds (and the heat).

In the end, the solution I found was a pair of noise-cancelling headphones I picked up at the airport. They worked great on the plane and were just as good in the apartment. Of course I didn't wear them all the time, but when I had some research to undertake or wanted to visualize they were perfect. Give it a try!

Finding your best times of day

The times at which you visualize most effectively are going to be quite different from other people and depend on your lifestyle; whether you work or are a student, if you have children, if you're retired, and so on.

I recommend that you draw a line between your work and your personal visualizations so you don't run the two together. Of course your work and home life are closely connected, but separating the two is good for your mental health and is only fair to your employer. And being fair and honest is one of those things you need to be if your visualizations are going to be fully successful.

Use full visualization exercises at work only if they're somehow work-related. In fact, many successful business people use creative visualization as a work productivity tool. For example, if you're suddenly handed a difficult project to bring in within a low budget and in a very short period of time, spending some time visualizing the entire project is quite acceptable because that's part of your planning process.

In the earlier section 'Choosing your visualizing space' I discuss making use of your commute to work for visualization time, but why not also consider the morning and evening hours as well, before you leave and after you arrive home.

Some people enjoy visualizing while munching away at their toast or breakfast cereal. You can start off by imagining a positive and productive day (to set the day up in your mind), and then move on to your goals and life changes.

After work or other quiet times are also suitable for contemplation and visualization, such as while watering the plants, cooking meals or washing up, doing the ironing or vacuuming, and participating in a hobby.

I don't advise that you practise longer or more complicated visualizations while watching TV. Television has a way of grabbing you almost hypnotically, so the words you hear and things you see just flow into your brain without the usual level of conscious scrutiny you'd normally bring to bear (which is why advertisers love TV so much). If you try to visualize with the television on, some of the events on the screen break into your imagery and distract you. Others creep past and into your unconscious, so it receives both your visualization and (perhaps) an advertisement for soap powder at the same time (check out the later section 'Understanding the Role of the Unconscious' for more details on the relationship between the unconscious and conscious minds).

If you need to visualize when the TV is on or other distractions are in the room, give yourself a few minutes without that distraction. The bathroom – which everyone visits alone a few times each day – is always a good place for a quick visualization.

Clearing your schedule

If you're so busy that you need to keep a schedule of appointments, activities, projects, and so forth, the only way you're easily going to make time for creative visualization is to clear your schedule, leaving suitable times of the day just for this activity.

All you need to do is set aside a few minutes between appointments. What's more, when you use these times to visualize they also act as a powerful energy-restoring exercise, preparing and refreshing you for your next appointment.

If you can't set aside the same times each day to visualize (and so get into a routine), you're going to need to pre-book some reserved slots into your busy schedule.

Even if you're not hyper-busy, when you start visualizing you may find that setting notifications on your phone or other scheduling device is helpful to avoid you forgetting to practise your visualizations.

Understanding the Role of the Unconscious

The more effort and focus you invest while visualizing, the more effectively it works, because these things impress upon your unconscious mind, which then listens more closely to your conscious mind. Therefore, effective creative visualization requires an understanding of the unconscious and its relation to the conscious mind, something I provide in this section.

Your *unconscious mind* handles dozens of essential jobs at any single moment, including: managing your breathing, heart rate, temperature, and digestive system; monitoring your organs; controlling thousands of individual muscles; and much, much more. It encompasses your belief system, memories, skills, everything you've been through and seen, and all you've ever learned.

Tricking your conscious mind . . . up to a point!

Your conscious mind can love and cry, and perform arithmetic or create music. It understands the surrounding world and can tell the difference between good and bad, even in complex situations such as serving on a jury.

It also acts as the doorkeeper to your unconscious mind, letting through only those things that it deems relevant or worthy, something that hypnotism takes advantage of by silencing the conscious mind and/or sneaking commands past it through misdirection techniques.

But the unconscious mind isn't stupid; it carries out checks and balances and refuses to act on any commands it believes are dangerous or immoral – you're unlikely to comply with requests to hurl someone off a bridge or jump off yourself when hypnotised. But if a hypnotist tells your unconscious to pretend to be Elvis Presley for a few minutes it probably doesn't object; in fact, usually it participates by freeing up your conscious inhibitions so that you can really plunge yourself into the role, generally resulting in quite a good impression!

owever, at the risk of offending practising therapists, I should point out that stage hypnotism is a far cry from the clinical and professional practice of trained hypnotherapists, who can help with a wide range of emotional and other problems using tried and tested psychological and hypnotic techniques.

One useful analogy is to think of your unconscious as your autopilot: you program it and then sit back as it moves into cruise control, taking you through life in ways that it feels are most beneficial to your wellbeing. Therefore, your conscious mind is left free to do the thinking and making complicated decisions. Whereas your unconscious performs loads of duties simultaneously, your conscious mind can manage only a few functions at a time, although it does them very well.

While you're performing creative visualization exercises using your conscious mind, your unconscious mind is listening and taking it all in. The more sincere you are, the more emphasis it puts on what you tell it. And at the same time it senses how you feel too, because that's vital information to help decide how to process the data it's receiving. The unconscious records whether you're sad, happy, or excited, and makes a note of any pain (or pleasure) you feel and anything else coming in through your senses, such as tastes and smells.

All these different aspects crunch together in the supercomputer of your unconscious, with the result that it acts for your best interests to make the goals you visualize come true. The wonderful thing about your unconscious is that it's a major part of the organic whole that's you; it's the down-to-earth, childlike, ever-pleasing, inner you. It loves the whole you (not just your conscious mind), and so you need to love it back. Just think how tirelessly it works on your behalf, 24 hours a day (even when you're sleeping).

The job of your unconscious is to keep you well and get you through life in the way it thinks you want to go, as healthily and comfortably as possible. Be positive and it's positive. Be negative and it's negative. Whether during visualization or in life in general, treat your unconscious like your best friend (which it is), be good to it, and provide it with plenty of positive encouragement and direction. If you do, it responds in its fullest capacity.

Whatever your unconscious sets out to do, it always tries to do its very best and has powerful ways of getting things done. The more it knows that you deeply desire something, the harder your unconscious tries to bring that desire to fruition; which is why you must always be as positive as you can, whenever you can.

The ability and determination of your unconscious mind to attain goals is the power that lies behind creative visualization, and one of the main reasons why guided imagery works so effectively.

Enhancing Your Visualizations

The more energy, emotion, and feeling you put into creative visualization, the better and faster it works. This section takes you through a few ways to give a little back to the unconscious mind that works so hard for you (as I describe in the preceding section), and helps you to connect with this part of your mind as you visualize.

Going somewhere you love

To maximise your visualization sessions, give as much as you can to your unconscious mind in the form of encouragement and information, but not in a logical or factual manner. Your unconscious mind thrives on abstractions and emotions as well as physical sensations, so if you have any favourite places you like to visit, make sure that you visualize as fully as you can whenever you're there. Feel all the emotions you can summon and speak to your unconscious with them.

Whether the place is a particular park, a playground, the seaside, a mountain view, or whatever, if you feel strong and inspired and simply love to be there, breathe it all in and visualize. First, experience the 'now' and how much you're enjoying yourself at the moment. Second, move on to visualizing your goals; use the positive feeling you have to feel the same way about your ambitions as you imagine achieving them and how your life is going to be when they're achieved. All the time, feel the power and inspiration that your special place brings you.

Playing your favourite music

Music has a special place in most people's lives, maybe because it's built from vibrations and harmonies – something the brain fully understands since it vibrates at various frequencies (known as brain waves) according to your mental state. But whatever the reason, almost everyone has a few pieces of music that they simply adore and that light up their souls.

When you listen to a piece of music that you feel strongly about, instead of simply enjoying it, drop in some occasional visualizations of your most important ambitions. Tie the music and your goals together and float them into your unconscious, which appreciates how important they are to you and works all the harder at obtaining them for you.

Your unconscious is a creature of feeling and emotion, and so responds very positively to the feelings the music brings you, and also to the music itself. If you like it that much, you can be sure that your unconscious does too – after all, you're one and the same person!

A web search for 'meditation music' turns up thousands of websites containing music (some of it free) that's been especially written to help with meditation and visualization. Much of this music isn't as bland as you may imagine, and you can sample most of the paid music before you buy anyway, just to be sure that it's right for you.

You can also use any other music that you find uplifting and relaxing to help get you into the right state of mind for successful and positive visualization, as well as help reinforce your imagery.

You can also light some scented candles, or take your MP3 player and headphones with you on a country walk or into your garden. The more senses you can bring to a visualization party, the more you enjoy it and the quicker the results come and the greater they are, which, in turn, makes you look forward to your next visualization session.

When visualizing, avoid music with lyrics that distract you from your visualizing. Of course, if the words apply directly to the theme of your imagery, that's fine, but otherwise restrict yourself to instrumental music.

Watching specially created videos

Generally, when visualizing I advise against watching anything more than what you can see by gazing idly into the distance (or closing your eyes), and that particularly means no TV or films. However, many videos have been produced as aids to relaxation and visualization, and if you have difficulty getting started you may find that they help.

To find some free videos, search for 'relaxation' or 'visualization' at YouTube (`www.youtube.com`) on the Internet. Many DVDs containing relaxation and visualization imagery are available from online stores, such as Amazon (`www.amazon.co.uk`).

Although these aids are helpful, try to move on to visualizing only in your mind as soon as you feel ready, so the imagery comes entirely from within you. The more you can build up and practise your own visualization exercises, the more quickly they become a part of you and are absorbed into and acted on by your unconscious.

Part III
Visualization Exercises for a Happier, Healthier Life

The 5th Wave   By Rich Tennant

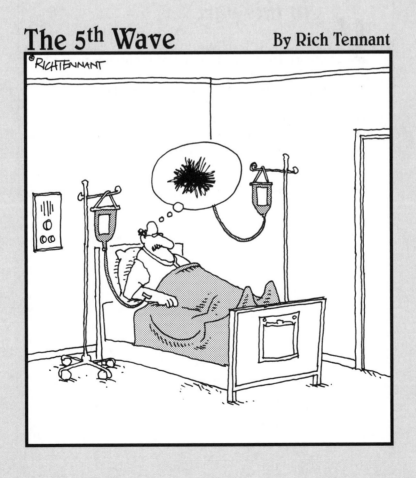

In this part . . .

You get down to the nitty-gritty of actually visualizing, starting off with simple exercises for becoming happier and more fulfilled. If you have issues with anger or stress you'll be provided with positive exercises you can practice to alleviate anxiety, and you'll discover how to motivate yourself and gain greater mental energy. This part of the book also focuses on improving your physical and mental health, overcoming phobias, and improving your relationships with other people.

Chapter 7

Being Happier and More Fulfilled

. . . .

In This Chapter

▶ Maintaining a calm mindset

▶ Adopting a positive point of view

▶ Reflecting on your previous successes

▶ Loving life to the full

▶ Becoming a source of good

. . . .

*W*hen setting out on improving your overall level of happiness, and to help become more fulfilled with your life, you need to focus on the following five aspects that together form the acronym STARS (what positive thinkers want to be!):

✔ **S**tay calm

✔ **T**hink positive

✔ **A**ccept success

✔ **R**elish life

✔ **S**upport others

In this chapter, I examine steps you can take and visualizations you can practise to lift your outlook on life, which are broken down into five main areas comprising the five points of the STARS model.

This convenient acronym is handy when you're not feeling your best and want to do something about it. At such times work through the five elements of the STARS model and see if one or more of its five components can be visualized on to raise your spirits.

Starting with a Simple Visualization

The simple visualization exercise in this section allows you to experience just a little of the power of creative visualization for yourself. This exercise is just a bit of fun with no other psychological benefit, but by doing it you create new neural pathways in your brain (a subject I discuss in Chapter 4), and it takes only a couple of minutes:

1. **Make yourself comfortable and relaxed.**

2. **Visualize a shiny green apple floating in the air in front of you.**

3. **See how ripe it looks.**

4. **Take a bite, noticing how juicy and delicious it tastes.**

5. **Imagine the apple slowly growing until it's more than twice your height.**

6. **Visualize a shovel in your hand and start using it to cut out a doorway into the apple, pitching the removed fruit in a big pile behind you.**

7. **Keep on digging into the apple until you've completely hollowed it out, and then cut out two or three windows for good measure.**

8. **Look out of one of the windows and see all the other apple houses around you; some are small and some are huge skyscraper apples, in varying colours of shiny green and red.**

9. **Walk around inside your apple, feel the squidgy floor ooze into your barefoot toes and look out at the view from the other windows, all the time noticing the sweet smell and taste of the apple.**

10. **Realise that in fact you're in the Big Apple: New York.**

11. **Go outside and pop into the corner convenience store (also an apple), which smells different, a bit like a cooking apple perhaps, and visit a few other apple buildings too.**

When you've had enough, stop the visualization. For the next few weeks and months, whenever somebody mentions the Big Apple, you're going to remember your apple house in the apple city. If you do this visualization a few times a day for a week or two, it may never leave you (although I don't recommend it, unless you're a real apple lover!).

With this visualization as an illustration behind you, think how easily you can use the same techniques to create the positive changes you desire by visualizing about them. Read on to get started.

Staying Calm

The first and most important point in the STARS model is to stay calm and try not to worry. (Chapter 8 contains much more on keeping calm as well as several useful calming visualization exercises.) Saying 'try not to worry', however, is a bit like saying 'don't think of a pink elephant' – it ends up achieving the opposite and making you think about it!

The point is that most of us do worry a lot of the time and we need to acknowledge this fact (and that it can lead to stress) and move on by choosing to become calmer. So sit back, relax, and allow the creative visualizations in this chapter to sink into your unconscious mind and bypass any stress or worry you may be feeling. (For more on the power of the unconscious in visualization, check out Chapter 6.)

When you're generally tense, worried, or simply not very relaxed, try to ensure that you're calm whenever you visualize, otherwise your mind is full of distractions and you have trouble concentrating. Being relaxed also lets your unconscious mind pay attention to your visualizations and not to whatever may be bothering you. Turn to Chapter 1 for details of a relaxation exercise.

Looking on the Bright Side

The second point in the STARS acronym is 'Think positive'. As I explain in the following section, thinking about one thing leaves little room to also consider (that is, worry about) other things at the same time. So be positive, and don't give room to negative thoughts.

When you want to make a change in your life, such as improving your level of happiness, remembering that you *can* change is crucial (check out the later section 'Realising you do have power' for more). After all, life is made up of constant change. So when you feel like you're stuck in a rut and every day seems the same, remind yourself that you have the power to change things. The first step towards changing your life is wanting to change, and the second is knowing that you can change, which in turn helps you to decide what to change.

Armed with these thoughts and decisions, you can then set out on making the changes themselves, something that creative visualization helps you do effectively and quickly. Flick to Chapter 5 for more on preparing for and making changes.

Understanding why positive thinking works

Typically, you can fully concentrate on only one thing at any one time. When you want to turn your attention to something new, in order to experience it properly you have to take your mind off whatever you're currently focusing on.

For this reason, many countries ban the use of mobile phones and texting while driving; the attention the phone requires takes away from that available to keep an eye on ever-changing road conditions. And yet, due to a mental block, many people think that they are able to text and drive safely. The truth is, however, that when your conscious mind switches from one task to another, it completely forgets the previous one, so while texting a message you don't see the car in front of you coming to a sudden stop, or realise that you aren't paying attention to something much more important (the road), until it's too late.

You can see a powerful illustration of this mental block on the Internet at `www.visionlab.harvard.edu/silencing`. In this short video clip, several dots forming a circle continuously change colours, but then the circle begins to rotate and suddenly the dots appear to stop the colour cycle. But if you watch the clip again and this time follow the dots as they move you see that, in fact, they never stop changing colour. This optical illusion demonstrates how you use a single part of the brain for both colour awareness and movement, and therefore it can only easily manage one or the other job at a time. On the same website, three other similar videos show how motion also silences the perception of changing brightness, size, and even shapes.

To be as efficient as possible, the human brain evolved over a very long period not to waste programming power. If a part can perform more than one task (although not at the same time) then all the better, and this is the case – very few parts of the brain seem to perform only one function. For example, thanks to Magnetic Resonance Imaging (MRI), scientists now know that professional musicians use parts of the visual cortex when playing an instrument, which may explain why so many close their eyes when performing. Interestingly, non-musicians or beginners don't use the visual cortex in this way.

Bearing this fact in mind helps you understand one of the reasons that positive thinking works. When you replace negative thoughts with positive ones, the brain has less space to process the unwanted thoughts because it's busy handling positive ones.

By focusing on and visualizing the good things in your life, you edge out the bad. The *synapses* (junctions that connect neurons to each other) that previously connected up in a vicious circle of negative thinking stop being reinforced, and your brain forms new positive connections. Over time, these new connections become greater in number than the old ones and replace the previous ways of thinking. So it really does pay to look on the bright side.

Being optimistic

Removing negative thinking (which I describe in the preceding section) isn't the only reason for being positive; it's just the start. By adjusting your attitude to something – whether a task to complete or someone you know – you begin to look at the task or person in a new light. Where you may previously have noticed only the things you dislike, by being positive you start to see things you approve of and even admire.

You also begin to see how you and the thing or person can better relate to each other. For example, a difficult work project that you don't want to undertake becomes far easier when you discover things about it that you like and that interest you. The same goes for an acquaintance who normally annoys you – when you pay attention you often find that this person does have some interesting things to say, or even shares an interest in the same hobby as you.

The benefits of thinking positively about any situation, person, or thing massively outweigh the benefits (if any) of thinking negatively. Where your options before seem extremely limited, when you adopt an optimistic outlook they open up and reveal many new possibilities that you never previously noticed. Negativity is limiting and destructive, but positivity is empowering and brings abundance and happiness.

Realising you do have power

One of the first steps towards making any personal development change is to understand that you can do something about your current situation; that you're in control of your own destiny and aren't caught up in something over which you have no power. Even locked up and deprived of social contact, you can still improve yourself because you have control over your mind.

Nelson Mandela spent 27 years in prison, 18 of which were on Robben Island (South Africa's equivalent to Alcatraz island in San Francisco). While in prison Mandela completed a law degree and steadfastly kept his resolve, refusing opportunities for freedom in return for renouncing the struggle of his fellow black citizens. When Mandela was eventually released, was he bitter?

Far from it. As soon as the world saw him, it knew he had developed an air of grace and statesmanship far different from his earlier years as leader of the African National Congress's armed wing. He was mildly spoken but determined and led his party through difficult negotiations towards free and open elections, in which he was voted president. Crucially, he ensured that the country avoided the violence that many more negatively minded commentators had predicted.

Fortunately most people in the West have political freedom, and yet they so often build psychological prisons around themselves. They limit what they allow themselves to do by thinking 'I can't do this' or 'I'll never be able to have that' and so on. Keep in mind the words of American car pioneer Henry Ford, who said, 'Whether you think you can, or think you can't, you're quite right,' and Richard Bach, author of the magnificently uplifting book *Jonathan Livingston Seagull*, who wrote, 'Argue for your limitations, and sure enough they're yours.' Don't let your thinking limit you in life.

Even something as simple as putting a brave smile on your face can help improve a situation that's bothering you. And believe it or not, a brave smile pretty soon turns into a real one. So realise that you can do something about your situation and move towards achieving happiness, even if you don't yet know precisely what to do. As you become more optimistic you discover more and more ways in which you can positively act, feel, and respond, even within what may seem to be very limiting circumstances.

Every situation is unique, but you can always try this simple visualization exercise to increase your awareness of the control you have over your situation and personality. Its purpose is to inform your unconscious that you want actively to do something and to prompt it to start considering its options and coming up with new ideas to help you:

1. **Sit back in your chair, close your eyes, relax, and imagine your spirit gently separating from your body.**

   You're that spirit now. You have the same shape and size as your body but are composed of a semi-transparent, smoke-like substance. Slowly drift backwards so you can see your body in its chair, resting silently and calmly a few feet from you.

2. **Start to shrink your spirit form down, compressing and pulling it together until you're only about an inch tall.**

   Notice that although you're small all your muscles and limbs work as normal and, although a little more solid, you're still able to float in and out of things and through walls.

3. **Head gently back towards your body and imagine that behind your body's eyes is an amazing cockpit, like the inside of a million dollar super car, with the eyes as windscreens.**

   Float into this space and seat yourself in the pilot's chair, fasten your seat belt, and start the ignition. All the controls you need to drive your body are within easy reach. At your feet are the accelerator and brake pedals, and the steering wheel in your hands directs your body anywhere you want it to go. In the dashboard, you can see the controls for your emotions, with knobs and switches to make your body feel excited, sad, happy, or any other emotion. Next to these is a microphone, so your body repeats whatever you speak, and next to that is a flight mode lever.

4. **See yourself seated comfortably and your body revving to go; imagine pressing the buttons and turning the steering wheel to make it stand up and walk around the room.**

   Practise having your body say things such as, 'It's such a nice day', and then walk it outside, press the flight mode lever, and zoom up into the sky.

5. **Fly somewhere you've never been but always wanted to go, somewhere special to you.**

   After landing, disengage flight mode and resume walking and explore the place. Actively control the wheel to move your body to the left or right and to climb steps, and use the grab button to pick things up, bringing them up to your body's eyes so that you can see them just outside of the 'windscreens'. Press different buttons to let your body experience any emotions you like.

6. **Notice that after a while you can't keep the spirit you reduced down to your one inch size and so you start to grow.**

   Your arms fill into your body's, your legs into its legs, and so on until you and your body are one again.

7. **Spend some more time exploring the special place, now using completely natural movements – with no buttons to press or levers to pull.**

   Simply walk your body where you want to go and do all the things you want to do.

8. **Get swiftly and easily back into your real place and time in your chair when you finish exploring.**

   Simply sit down in the visualization and close your eyes. Then fade your imaginary place to black over a few seconds – just like in a film – and over a few more seconds fade from black to the last view you saw from your chair. Then open your eyes.

This exercise is quite a long visualization that may last up to 15 minutes or so. If you perform it every now and then, when you feel like circumstances are out of your control, it provides tremendous relief. Visualizations like this awaken your unconscious mind's imagination, spurring it to help find more opportunities than you realised were available, and opening your mind to the things you can control rather than those you can't.

Seeing light at the end of the tunnel

Being unable to see the light at the end of the tunnel can hold you back from happiness. When you eventually get to the other side you can forget how life was before, and you almost think, 'What tunnel?'. Therefore it helps to give yourself a little something to go on; some encouragement or glimmer of hope that you're progressing. This helps you keep up your resolve and stay committed to achieving your goals.

Often you can make the mistake of thinking of happiness as the condition you hope to feel as a result of the changes you plan to make. Perhaps money is really tight right now, and you're sure that you're going to be happier when things sort themselves out. And perhaps you do, for a while. Then other things start to bother you and you think to yourself that after they're sorted out you're going to be happy.

If you continue at this rate, you end up postponing your happiness forever. If your goal is to be happy in the future, remember that now is the future of your past, and that back then you thought you'd be happier by now. You need to start being happy right here, and right now. Stop focusing on how you're going to feel at some future date, and start to feel some of that now. Remember some events in your past and remind yourself that you've come through many tough times, and that the current situation is just one more that you're going to overcome.

1. **Open up a tunnel in your mind's eye through which you can see the resolution of your current difficulty.**

   Imagine that right at the end of the tunnel the solution to your problem or completion of your goal is waiting,

2. **Let the light from there shine brightly through the tunnel.**

   Although you may not see clearly what's at the end of the tunnel you can make out odd shapes and see that there's definitely some light.

3. **Let some of the light reach you now and lift your spirits.**

   Feel the light entering your eyes. It shines from a resolved future at the tunnel end. Know that the answer and solution is there and that you'll reach it soon.

4. **Allow yourself to enjoy some of the happiness you've been saving for your future.**

   Unlike a birthday present that's accidentally revealed to you early, there's no disappointment in taking some of the enjoyment from your future by experiencing it now, because when you get to your future you can enjoy some happiness from its future too, and so it goes on.

Recognising that the sun will rise tomorrow

Life changes. Good times always follow bad ones. The lesson is to enjoy good times and keep your chin up during difficult ones. Even if the weather is cloudy today and the sun out of sight, it's going to rise in a clear sky tomorrow (or one day soon). It will be a new day packed with new opportunities – to enjoy life, achieve things, make plans, begin or continue changes in your life. As the old saying goes, 'It's not the end of the world'.

You can use visualizations or affirmations to make today and tomorrow a good day. Get into the habit of repeating some or all of the following positive affirmations out loud a few times each day:

✔ Tomorrow is going to be a very good day.

✔ Every day is better than the last.

✔ I'm really looking forward to tomorrow.

✔ I'm thankful for the time each new day brings.

Try as hard as you can to mean what you say, even if you only feel it somewhat. By repeating these affirmations regularly you come to believe them more and more, and so look forward to each new day.

Mental flash cards for becoming happier

Here are a few mental flash cards you can use when you have a few spare moments, or when you think you need to raise your spirits and feel better and happier.

✔ **Loving your home:** Imagine your home – your favourite rooms, your family, your pets, a warm fireside, a comfy bed, partying at birthdays and special occasions, and anything else you love about your home. Flash the images through your mind like photographs, feeling warm and good about each one.

✔ **Loving yourself:** Feel the love within your heart, and imagine arms around you as if being cuddled by another. Love your unconscious mind that helps you so much, and love your body that keeps you alive and lets you do the things you love. Love the fact that you can love.

✔ **Loving others:** Think of people you love; your partner, family, and friends. Imagine love flowing from your heart into theirs. Realise the joy of having them in the world with you.

✔ **Loving living:** Imagine a sunrise or sunset, or sunny weather, rain, snow, blizzards, or balmy calm days. Feel the pulse of your heart, the joy of each new day, and of resting after living that day to the fullest. Breathe in the freshest air ever and breathe out endless loving life.

✔ **Loving giving:** Feel the joy and gratitude as someone you love opens a gift you give him. Grin as you write out a donation cheque or give directions to a lost driver. Smile as you imagine spending time listening to someone who's lonely.

Being Proud of Your Successes

The third point in the STARS acronym is 'Accept success'. If you want to achieve change but think that doing so is impossible or at least very difficult, remember those things that you've already accomplished. You see, when you find yourself trying to achieve something, you can easily forget all the other times you've been in this situation before.

Recognising your successes

You've accomplished so many things already in your life and yet you probably don't often think about them. For example, you learned to read and write and you know how to do arithmetic. You can also probably ride a bicycle and drive, and maybe you can use a skateboard or even a unicycle.

Perhaps you can juggle or are good at cooking, or maybe you have a way with plants or are good at playing a musical instrument. You've certainly completed many projects, both at school and possibly at college or university, or in a work environment.

Many people have diplomas, degrees, or other qualifications. Most people overcome their fear of public speaking to give successful talks or presentations, and nowadays nearly everyone is proficient with technology, such as computers and mobile phones.

You may like to try and surprise yourself by taking a pen and paper or opening up a new document on your computer and spending the next ten minutes listing all the successes you've had. And as more of your successes occur to you over the following few hours and days, be sure to add these to your list as well. This simple exercise makes an excellent starting point for visualizing – particularly for improving self-esteem and overcoming obstacles blocking your goals.

Your life is packed full of successes, both small and large, and so from time to time consider them and give yourself a little pat on the back in acknowledgement. Doing so reminds you that you can and do achieve things, and that you can continue to do so.

When you go to the effort of summarising your successes in life, also recognise that *you* achieved them (not anyone else). No doubt you had assistance from parents, friends, teachers, and associates, but in the end your achievements are down to the effort you put in.

To be successful (or more successful) you need to build and maintain the mindset of success in your life. And success doesn't mean becoming a business mogul or earning millions; it simply means achieving something that you want to, which can be anything you choose.

The more you feel like you've been successful in the past, the more you're going to be successful now and in the future.

Remembering how you succeeded

One vital key to continued success is to repeat a formula that worked for you. Einstein said that the definition of insanity is 'doing the same thing over and over again and expecting different results'. If something you try doesn't work, maybe you need to change an aspect of that attempt before you try again (but you must try again). But if something worked for you before, repeat the process as long as it continues to do so.

Think about the process of acquiring a new skill. For example, say you successfully taught yourself a new language (a foreign or computer programming one), how to play a new musical instrument, or how to plaster a wall. Ask yourself the following questions:

✔ **How good were you at this skill when you first started?** Possibly not very good.

✔ **What did you do to improve?** Probably practise.

✔ **How much did you practise?** Most likely for many, many hours.

✔ **Did you repeat things over and over again until you were satisfied with them?** Almost certainly.

✔ **Did you visualize the process as you went along?** If so, you know that it helped.

✔ **What time of day was it and where were you when you were learning most effectively?** For example, some people take in information better in the morning and others later in the day.

These types of questions help you analyse how you accomplished mastering a new skill.

The same logic applies if you successfully quit smoking or lost some weight. Think about how it felt, the motivators you used to keep up your willpower, and the distractions you used to take your mind off cravings.

Spend time thinking about your successes to get in the frame of mind and the right mood to embark on your current projects or personal development goals.

Realising what your successes bring to your life

The previous two sections help you to bring many of your successes to mind and how you set about achieving them. In this section, you think about the benefits your achievements have brought to your life. Doing so reminds you and your unconscious mind why making the effort to accomplish things is important – the fact that many benefits ensue.

If you earned qualifications, consider what they helped you to do. Probably they assisted you in getting a job in your field of interest and may also have had an effect on the salary you take home. If you learned a foreign language, perhaps you travelled or got a job abroad; or maybe playing a musical instrument helped you meet more people and join a local band or musical group. Or achievements such as quitting smoking, losing weight, or overcoming depression led to a healthier and happier life.

Only you know what you've achieved and how it affected your life positively, and so only you can recognise the positive benefits you've seen from your achievements.

And here's a benefit of your successes you may not have realised: When you contemplate the positive effects your accomplishments have had on your life, you build up the motivation you need to make more changes. By accepting success, you motivate yourself in your goal to have more successes.

 Whenever you feel a little detached from one of your life goals, perhaps because you lack energy or enthusiasm, run again through the exercises in this whole section to re-invigorate yourself and get your motivation back on track. See Chapter 9 for further information on becoming more motivated.

Focusing on Good Things

Part four of the STARS acronym is 'Relish life'. I can't emphasise enough that when you focus on the good things in life and strive to enjoy them, you leave less room to dwell on the bad things.

I bet that the people whose company you enjoy the most tend to have a positive approach to life, and that one of the things you like about them is that their attitudes rub off on you. Becoming the same sort of person isn't hard. All you need to do is enjoy those things that you like anyway – just try to think about and appreciate them a little more.

Enjoying friends and family

You may read this heading and wonder what I mean. After all, of course you enjoy your friends and family (well, those that you get on with, anyway). But because these people are usually very close to you, you can get used to them and almost take them for granted. So, from time to time, focus on consciously enjoying the time you spend with people who come into your life. Say to yourself, 'I'm enjoying this person's company', and smile.

 Avoid gossiping about other people, because despite what you may think, doing so serves only to raise your own negativity level. If someone else starts to gossip negatively, just say something like, 'Yes, but did you know that. . .', and mention something good about the person. Go ahead, try it, and be amazed how the other person changes tack and the whole conversation develops a more positive tone. In addition, other people like and respect you more when you're positive in this way.

Appreciating nature and wildlife

If you have a pet, next time you stroke or pat it just think about the enjoyment that owning this pet brings to you. If the birds outside your window wake you up in the morning, spend a minute appreciating the dawn chorus brought to you directly from nature to herald a new day.

If you have a garden, spend some time in it just pottering about or sitting and enjoying it. In the summer months it can be the most relaxing part of your home, but even in winter have an occasional wander round in the snow or rain and appreciate the nature around your house.

Of course, when you visit a park or go to the countryside or beach you're thoroughly surrounded by nature, and so breathe it in, listen hard, and look long. Feel at one with everything around you, at peace with the world. Flip to Chapter 6 for more on using a special place in this way.

Savouring food and drink

Eating and drinking are two of life's greatest pleasures and they use all of the classic five senses: for example, smell and taste (of course), but also the look of food (such as a luscious chocolate cake) and the feel of it on your fingers and in your mouth. And you even hear the cake as it's cut and when the knife touches the plate, and (believe it or not) you hear the sound of chewing as you eat. But so often people are in a rush and make do with a quick hamburger or sandwich on the go, hardly noticing the experience.

When you sit down to a proper meal, ensure that you enjoy everything about it. Taste the flavours by chewing slowly, sense the smells, and savour tastes and aromas. If you're eating out, soak in the atmosphere too. If at home, enjoy being with your family and any guests. After all, if you want your life to be happy, meal times have to be one of the best parts, and so discover how to enjoy them to the fullest.

Because you eat three times (or so) each day, you can use meal times for regular visualizations. I tend to allow a couple of mental flash cards to run through my brain at the start of a meal (different ones according to how I feel), just to tie them into the eating experience. Doing so takes only a few seconds, nobody notices, and it makes the rest of the meal time somehow more enjoyable.

Indulging in hobbies and activities

Nobody should be too busy to spend time on hobbies or activities. But sadly, as people move on from their teens into their 20s, get jobs, and/or start families, hobbies seem to drift by the wayside because so many different parts of life begin to infringe on time.

Even so, people still find the time to watch several hours of television each week, often justifying it by telling themselves that they're tired and that TV helps them to rest. This may be true – to an extent – but after an hour of television you often find that your willpower to do anything else has been sapped. The box in the corner has an amazing power to suck you in and slow down your brainwaves into a lazy and compliant state. So if you know that you have couch potato habits, maybe you need to consider finding something else to spend a little time on each week; something that you can really get stuck into and enjoy.

Start with something simple, such as jigsaw puzzles and constructing models, things that you can do on the kitchen table. If you need a reason or incentive, do the hobby with one of your kids. Or if your body is a little out of shape, go swimming, running, or even just take an hour-long walk once a week. Doing so helps keep you fit, gives you thinking and visualizing time, and helps to energise you.

If you have a garden, try tending some flowers or planting a few fruit trees. Maybe buy a cheap plastic greenhouse, seed the lawn to bring it back to health, dig a fish pond, or build and put up bird feeders.

Most people love music and, believe it or not, researchers have found that people of any age can learn to play musical instruments. Electronic keyboards are very cheap these days, and you can even download free and very inexpensive apps for smart phones and tablet computers – you can always use a pair of headphones if your practising irritates others.

Try buying a beginner's book for your instrument and see how you get on. If you don't know what instrument you want, visit a local music store; they're almost always happy to let you try them out – as long as you don't play 'Stairway to Heaven' or 'Smoke on the Water'!

Whatever hobby or activity you come up with (and regularly changing them is a good idea) enriches your life and enjoyment of it, and helps towards the other goal of this chapter which is to be more fulfilled. By participating in activities or working on projects, your sense of fulfilment really starts to take wings and fly.

Loving being alive

Always make an effort to love life itself; after all, it's the most incredible gift you've ever been given, and the more you invest in it the more it keeps on giving. Life is energy and emotion, movement and love, and isn't hard to find because it's simply everywhere!

Try to imagine that you're that spark of life; infinitely small, yet so full of potential – you have the ability to create life itself, in all its wonder and variety.

1. Close your eyes and imagine your consciousness leaving your body and shrinking down to a tiny spark the size of an atom.

   Although you don't have eyes and ears you can sense everything around you just as if you're seeing and hearing.

2. Hover close to a small stone on the ground and then lightly touch it with your flame of life.

   See how the stone slowly awakens and begins forming itself into a living, breathing frog, which then croaks and hops away.

3. Now try giving life to a larger stone.

   Touch it with your flame and watch it slowly change until you see the gaping and yawning mouth of a lion, which then saunters off in search of prey.

4. Repeat this with a few more stones and pebbles.

   Animate them into real or imaginary beings of your choice.

5. When you're ready, return your consciousness to your body.

   Imagine floating back to a point somewhere between your eyes, then blink a couple of times to return to normality.

This exercise helps you and your unconscious mind to contemplate the amazing force behind life, and creates a metaphor for injecting life into everything you do, people you know, and so on. Practised a few times this exercise will help you become more interested in life itself and enjoy being alive, which naturally will lead to elevating your general outlook on life.

By reading this book you've shown that one of your desires is to effect one or more changes in your life. And this goal exists because deep down you enjoy living and want to get more out of it (and put more into it). So try your best to appreciate life to its fullest. You can never spend enough time simply loving being alive.

Seeing Yourself as a Source of Good

The final point of the STARS acronym is 'Support others'. If you want to feel more fulfilled, supporting others is vital, because you're highly unlikely to find anything more fulfilling than helping another person to achieve or come through something difficult.

Think about which you prefer or enjoy the most: giving or receiving a gift. Most adults enjoy the former far more. And each person has tremendous power to do good in other people's lives through simple acts of giving, helping, and listening. These acts generally cost little time or effort and the rewards you receive in turn are many times greater in terms of real value – that is, things that matter to you.

Having compassion for others

To become a source for good in the world you need to have compassion for others. For sure most people have compassion and give to charities for needy children or starving third-world families. But if you want others to care even more about you, you must care more about them, not just through charitable giving to people you don't know, but to everyone you have contact with or make a difference to.

Humans are cultural beings who create family units that come together into communities. People like to work and play together and they value each other's support and encouragement. The more you participate in society, the more you get back out of it. Everyone has problems and simply existing can sometimes be quite hard. So developing a strong sense of compassion for the circumstances and emotional states of those around you benefits everyone, yourself included.

Radiating love

When you have compassion for others (see the preceding section), you want the love you feel to radiate out.

One of my first forays into visualization in the early 1980s was when I discovered the Steve Hillage album *Motivation Radio,* a concept album that starts with the track 'Hello Dawn' and continues through others including 'Motivation', 'Light in the Sky', and 'Searching for the Spark'. The album's a very psychedelic, almost trippy, album in which Hillage encourages you to find your motivation and then use it to bring 'light and love and laughter' to the world. One of the songs, 'Radio', is about tuning into a radio frequency of love being beamed from the cosmos. I like this idea, and so I devised a visualization reversing this in which you become the radio transmitter.

Here's a great visualization that really gets you psyched up and keen to help other people:

1. **Picture yourself standing with your arms outstretched in the middle of a huge grassy field.**

   Towns and cities are all around you.

2. **Imagine that you're slowly growing until you're hundreds of feet tall, the size of a large communications tower.**

   Feel how strong and powerful you are.

3. **Begin transmissions – the programme you're broadcasting is nothing but pure love.**

   Feel the power shoot out from your heart and up and down your spine, tingling throughout your body before it then pulses out from you in waves of love enveloping everywhere in all directions for dozens of miles. Feel the power move up from your heart to between your shoulder blades, where it creates shivers (as if you're getting a shoulder massage), before it shoots to the back of your head and vibrates away behind you. Now see the golden orange energy beaming in waves from your wide spread finger tips, writhing and wriggling over the horizon, and the beams themselves shooting more energy beams down to the land below, like a sort of lightning.

4. **Look around you slowly with eyes that beam pure love and joy to wherever they gaze.**

   Know that your energy is being received by everyone within a radius of many miles. As you transmit the power of love, feel more welling up from your heart, which contains a reservoir of more than you can ever need, with more being created all the time.

5. **Hold this vision for a few minutes.**

   Project nothing but love, peace, goodwill, and boundless energy to everyone around you. If you're religious now is also a great time to offer up prayers for all these people. Ask your higher power to look after them and for their lives to be enriched.

6. **Turn the beams of energy slowly off.**

   Gently power down, shrink back to your normal size, and return to your place in reality.

This visualization allows you to increase your capacity to love and the power of your unconscious mind, and you also get in some practice, so feeling love comes much more easily to you in future.

Remembering to listen

Sometimes you spend so much time thinking, doing, and telling that you forget to listen – whereas listening is, in fact, one of the most powerful things you can do.

Do you ever find yourself engaged in conversations that are getting boring and into which you try to inject some life without success? Whenever that happens to me (and if I catch myself doing it), I stop and try to just listen to what the other person is saying. Often this action results in the conversation getting back on track and becoming interesting again.

If you simply hear what people say and don't pay full attention, you can find that the other person often reciprocates and you both end up talking pointless small talk, and not for long. If you're work colleagues, after a while you probably just end up nodding at each other as you go past.

But when you really take the effort to try and understand what people are saying to you (and take the time to read between the lines), you can discover important new information, such as the other person is upset. Listening helps your relationship with the person to change and develop in positive directions (as I outline in Chapter 12). The other person also listens more intently to you, and so you find out more about each other.

Paradoxically, sometimes your closest friends are the ones you listen to least, because you feel as if you've heard everything before and you automatically pay less attention. If that happens with any of your friends, or your partner (or any family members or close friends), next time you see the person, make sure to do less taking, more listening, and ask questions.

Praying for other people

If you're religious you already know about praying for other people; it's a common practice that takes place in all the major religions and in this context involves asking God to help someone out in a time of need. By praying you not only let God know that you care for the person and want that person to be protected or to be happy, but you also tell your unconscious mind and, if you pray out loud, other people too.

Prayer is a central part of any religious person's life and I encourage such people to integrate prayer into their creative visualizing.

Of course, agnostics and atheists can also express their compassion and desire to help other people. You can do so internally or out loud, whether or not you believe that God intervenes. Why not pray to and for the world, Mother Nature, or the cosmos. Or simply wish for someone to be well or happy (which is strong hope coupled with the intention to act) and try to help the person if you can do anything.

Whether you pray or wish, and especially if you do so with other people, I believe that the recipient usually benefits. This statement is a strong one which operates at the point where scientific, biologically and psychologically based creative visualization blurs with mysticism, religion, and parapsychology. No one can prove that praying doesn't work, and scientists make astonishing new discoveries every day. What everyone does know, for sure, however, is that praying can't hurt.

Therefore, if prayer helps you to visualize better (and vice versa), please do combine the two. The results of your visualizations are enhanced as a result.

Being a healer

Many things can heal. Bandages and antiseptic can heal cuts and wounds, medicines can cure illnesses, and time can heal mental pains such as grief.

But people can also help to heal other people. Those with illnesses respond better, and are more easily cured, by thinking positively (check out the earlier section 'Looking on the Bright Side' for more on positive thinking), something that you as a friend can help with. The only caveat is that you and the ill person must have high expectations as well. Having low expectations for an outcome that you visualize about returns limited results, if any.

Research proves that positive visualization accompanied by positive expectation hastens the cure of many illnesses. For example, people suffering from cancer have been able to recover more quickly using visualization techniques.

Here is a visualization that you can use yourself to help speed the recovery of wounds or as an aid to medical procedures or medicines.

1. **Imagine that you have X-ray vision and can see inside your body.**

   Use this power to look at your veins and then use your super microscopic ability (that you also have) to zoom in and study your white blood cells. (These are the ones employed by your immune system to seek out and destroy foreign cells.)

2. **There are five different types of white blood cell and they are all created in your bone marrow. Imagine each of these types of white blood cell as different knights in different colours of armour.**

   You have white knights with shining swords, black knights with menacing lances, red knights with huge iron balls on the end of a chain, green knights with giant clubs, and blue knights with sharp axes.

3. **See all these little tiny knights galloping through your veins on mighty horses directly towards the source (or sources) of your infection or wound.**

   Imagine them fighting away with all the foreign invaders, quickly killing them, so they die and float away in the blood to be expelled from your body. They are your personal army at your control, and are a mighty force to be reckoned with.

Because of the mind-body connection, your unconscious mind will respond to these visualizations by doing everything it can to ensure a plentiful supply of white blood cells. This positive thinking has been shown in many studies to significantly boost the immune system in many people. (Chapter 10 includes more information on visualizations to become healthier.)

Having and demonstrating a positive attitude towards yourself can also help inspire someone else who's ill. By simply sharing your time, belief, and optimism with someone in need, you can help the person recover his health that much sooner. If you have strong expectations of early recovery, so does the other person and that helps with the healing.

Encouraging success

Several studies have looked at the effectiveness of visualization in many areas. One in particular included people who were in the process of various things such as job seeking, searching for a partner, and preparing for exams. What it was that they were aiming for wasn't important for the study; only whether or not and how quickly they achieved it.

These people were then split into groups where some visualized and some didn't, while others were positively encouraged by the observers (to give them greater expectations of results), and some were not. This provided four groups:

Group 1 No visualization and no encouragement

Group 2 Encouragement but no visualization.

Group 3 Visualization but no encouragement.

Group 4 Both visualization and encouragement.

The results these groups attained increased in order: Group 1 achieved the least, Group 2 did a little better, Group 3 did exceptionally well, and Group 4 performed even better than that.

This demonstrates that positively believing and expecting success actually nets results (as creative visualizers already know), but it also shows the importance of other people in helping us to achieve our goals more quickly and with even better results than simply visualizing on our own.

Take an interest in other people, listen to them, have compassion, and encourage them, and you may well help the healing process and many other aspects of their life. At the very least you're providing precious support.

Chapter 8

Overcoming Uncontrolled Anger and Stress

*N*ot all anger is bad. For example anger can lead to civil rights protests and movements in which collective anger is channelled to change society for the better, and in psychotherapy and counselling sessions, anger can be used to channel the strength needed to deal with depression or other negative emotions. We have the emotion of anger for a reason; because it is useful to us.

But that said, many people feel they have too much anger in their lives, and this can easily happen because expressing a little anger does have a tendency to lead to more. For example, after telling off one of my children recently for being very naughty, I caught myself still being harsh to my wife when I spoke to her immediately afterwards (and had to apologise), because the anger behind the telling off I gave was still in my system. Uncaught this could have led to me being cross for much longer than necessary.

This chapter deals with managing and diminishing the extremes of uncontrolled stress and anger, and isn't intended for minimising levels of controlled anger or stress, which are generally thought to be beneficial and at times quite useful.

Understanding Why You Have Strong Emotional Responses

Anger is a powerful emotion and one of the most fundamental responses formulated in response to threats by a region in your brain called the amygdala. Each of us has two of these *amygdalae*, which are small tonsil-like objects that manage your basic emotions, including anger, fear, and hatred, as well as your sex drive. Deep within the temporal lobes, the job of the amygdala is to handle your responses to certain conditions as quickly as possible.

When stimulated by an appropriate trigger, the amygdala informs the rest of the brain. If it senses potential attack, the amygdala sends appropriate messages to the parts of the brain that can release a range of chemicals such as adrenaline to pump energy quickly into the muscles and increase the heart rate and breathing to get more oxygen to where it's needed. Or if a partner shows interest in you, your body prepares in slightly different ways. For example, your pupils will dilate and your breathing and heart rate will increase.

By adopting a basic emotion, a person quickly summons all the things needed to deal with a situation. Which emotion (or combination) emerges is down to the possible risks and rewards as determined by logic centres in the brain, which pass their evaluation back to the amygdala so that it can create a suitable response: anger if you need to fight, fear if flight is the best option, and so on.

Feelings such as anger and fear are primitive reactions that date back to humans' cave-dweller ancestors. For example, you get angry to put down a challenge from someone else trying to surpass you in the tribe's hierarchy; or you get the primitive urge to provide a speedy punishment such as a slap to an insolent or unruly child. Fear, on the other hand, serves to help keep you out of harm's way.

But humans have come a very long way in the last few thousand years and societies are now advanced and complex. People now have non-violent means (such as the law and courts of justice) to deal with disputes, and much healthier ways to discipline children than hitting them (such as positive and negative reinforcement). Nevertheless, the emotional responses remain in humans as strong as ever.

What's important is that you understand these responses rather than beating yourself up about them. You can't (nor should you even try to) eliminate these emotions, because they're an important part of who you are. But you can discover how to live with and experience stress and anger with altered and more positive responses. Read on to find out how.

Controlling Your Temper

You've no doubt lost your temper many times; everyone has (well, except for saints, but they're pretty rare). If you have children you've witnessed temper tantrums dozens of times. But as you grow up you (usually) discover that better ways exist to get what you want, such as being nice to your parents rather than screaming and stamping your feet. But the fact that young children lose their temper so easily shows what a basic human response it is.

For some people, however, controlling their temper can be quite hard. Perhaps your parents let you tantrum rather than deal with the problem, and so you never developed the self-control required. Or maybe you're so stressed by other situations in your life that you're easy to anger. But whatever the cause, you can't deny that being too angry, too often isn't good for you.

When you're angry your pulse rate rises, you breathe harder, your voice rises, adrenaline pumps through your body tensing your muscles, and the amygdala (which I describe in the earlier section 'Understanding Why You Have Strong Emotional Responses') wrests control from your logic centres, so that you have difficulty thinking straight. Instead of considering suitable rational responses to whatever angers you, you want to hit out (verbally if not physically), you want the other person (or people) to shut up and listen, and you seek recompense if you feel wronged (or even lust for revenge).

All these primitive responses aren't good for your body because the anger uses up your energy supply, and getting angry frequently can cause higher blood pressure, frequent headaches, and other symptoms. Also, chronically angry people who have reduced levels of *acetylcholine* (a hormone that tempers the effects of adrenaline) and therefore have difficulty controlling their emotions, can also sustain kidney and liver damage, as well as incurring sustained high cholesterol levels. And that's not even considering the negative effects that anger has on other people.

The bottom line is that anything you can do to control your temper is going to be good for you and those around you.

Isolating and managing known triggers

One of the first things you can do when deciding to control anger is to become aware of possible triggers so that you can be prepared for them. Two of the most common triggers of anger are violation of expectation and blocking of goals. Just a few possible examples of your expectations being violated include:

✔ Terrible service in a restaurant.

✔ Somebody lying to you, letting you down, or standing you up.

✔ A lazy child who refuses to clean her room.

✔ Somebody getting angry with you.

✔ A product that fails when you need it.

Examples of goal blocking include:

✔ Someone blocking your way while driving.

✔ Someone disagreeing with you or denying a request.

✔ Someone getting in your way or making you wait.

✔ Someone demanding your attention when you're busy.

✔ Someone in an official position thwarting your efforts, such as a referee disallowing your team's goal.

Use the examples above as memory jogs, and then follow these steps:

1. **Create a 'Controlling My Anger Triggers' list.**

   Put down as complete a list as you can of the things that have made you angry in the last few months.

2. **Write an affirmation list underneath.**

   For example:

   I'm aware that the above things can trigger my anger and I choose to prepare myself so that when they happen again I won't leap into my previous behaviour.

   Because I'll be ready I'll recognise the potential for anger but choose not to give it any power.

   Instead I'll breathe in deeply and slowly and then count to ten as I breathe out, before considering any further action.

3. **Sign your name at the bottom and put the paper somewhere where you can frequently read it.**

   Stick it to a wall or fold it up and put it in your wallet or purse; or leave it anywhere you readily access.

4. **Make a routine of reading the entire page to yourself at least once a day.**

   And believe every word you've written. After all, you've signed it so it's a contract with yourself.

If you're able to read your list a few times before the next anger incident, your fury still wells up but so does the memory of your affirmations, strongly enough that you acknowledge the anger but choose not to let it overwhelm you. This pause gives you time to consider alternative and more appropriate responses in place of the usual knee-jerk reactions of the past.

Turning anger into humour

If you consider all the symptoms of anger and put them into a caricature of a person, for example Homer Simpson when he gets mad, you have to admit that being angry is sort of funny, at least afterwards when the adrenaline's stopped flowing and you're looking back. And have you ever laughed at any of the clips on the Internet of people who flip out and start throwing things about? Actually, this type of laughter is often nervous rather than a belly laugh.

Have you noticed that when people meet each other for the first time and are nervous, you hear lots of nervous laughs? You laugh at things you say and do, and what other people do, but not in a bad way. This type of laughter isn't normally about anything funny; it's simply a natural reaction that tells the other person that you're nervous too, but you're friendly.

Here's a visualization you can try to head anger off at the pass next time you hear it coming:

1. **Imagine one of your triggers has happened and you're fuming.**

2. **Focus on how cross you are (you may even notice your pulse rate increasing as you do so), and how it makes you feel.**

3. **Switch suddenly to seeing yourself laughing out loud at a funny joke or situation (maybe recalling something funny you've seen or a joke you've been told).**

4. **Try laughing out loud and feel the laughter bubbling out of you (if nobody's near you to think you're crazy, of course!).**

Carry out this exercise regularly and the interruption you've introduced into your mind (from anger to laughter) kicks in the next time you're angered. Use the humour to shrug off the anger in your mind and say to it, 'I refuse to give you the power to make me feel bad – I prefer to laugh'. Become aloof from whatever triggered the anger, and smile. You can. Doing so is easy – as you see if you practise the exercise.

Explaining why you're unhappy

If someone frequently triggers anger in you, such as a child persistently leaving a completely messy bedroom, choose a time when you aren't angry to sit down with the person and explain why these actions upset you. Discussing reasons for your anger with someone who causes it, when you're both calm and collected, allows you to offer reasons and explanations and perhaps come to agreements or compromises. You simply can't do this in the midst of an argument or when you're furious.

If you've already tried talking with the person who's annoying you and don't think you've been very successful, or if you're nervous about how well such a discussion may go, I suggest that you visualize the whole discussion first in a positive manner.

Visualize both of you relaxed, communicating, and sharing your viewpoints, and without creating a particular outcome imagine that you end up with a positive agreement of some sort. The result may well be a compromise that you have to negotiate, and so include negotiations in your visualization. Just generally feel good about the discussion and its outcome.

After visualizing along these lines at least once, leave it for a day or two and maybe do the exercise once or twice more. Then select a suitable time for this discussion and most likely it'll go as well as you envisioned.

Developing your ability to forgive

Sometimes people let themselves get angry because they have little forgiveness in them, and so they let even small things trigger their temper. But you can become less bothered by these triggers if you practise forgiving people in your visualizations.

Say that your partner has a habit of assuming that when you're discussing some work that needs doing around the house, you're actually telling your partner to do the work (and probably right now), and he or she then jumps down your throat as soon as the words are out!

Visualize this situation happening, and realise that your partner has simply misunderstood, and that perhaps you didn't phrase the comment in the best way. Then forgive your partner for jumping to conclusions, and forgive yourself for not communicating better.

The more you practise, the more you automatically start to phrase things differently so that your partner doesn't misunderstand; and your partner stops triggering you by getting cross at something that you didn't mean.

Even if you're pretty sure that something isn't your fault, well, you have to live together. So discuss the problem with your partner and visualize forgiveness so that the behaviour stops bothering you. You may well find that your partner becomes less inclined to trigger you in that way because you no longer supply any response.

Forgiveness works wonders for your blood pressure and diffuses the tension in most difficult situations. And remember that you may be partly to blame, so forgive yourself too and vow to do better next time.

Letting off steam in your head

Sometimes you need to relieve the intensity of your anger without lashing out.

You can practise this visualization when you're calm and bring it into play when you feel infuriated. This exercise helps to reduce the level of anger and its symptoms:

1. **Visualize your head as if it's a kettle full of boiling water.**

   Sometimes that's what feeling angry is like, anyway.

2. **Take a deep breath and imagine that the intense pressure of steam blows the small lid right off the top of your head.**

   See the lid fly away.

3. **Let the steam slowly escape from the hole in the top of your head.**

   As you let the steam out, make the noise through your pursed lips of escaping steam.

When your breath is fully gone, so is all the steam and the pressure is completely relieved. If you like, you can make the sound effect out loud – it's better than swearing!

This visualization is an alternative to the well-known 'breathe in and count to ten' exercise, and you may find it more effective because you really feel what you're imagining – especially if you practise the visualization a few times in advance so that it comes to you naturally.

Keeping Yourself Calm

This section provides exercises you can use to help with your general levels of calmness. They serve to reduce your anger and also lower any anxiety you feel. Whenever you have difficulty relaxing, feel uneasy or nervous, or your emotions are overwhelming you, flip to this section and try one or more of the exercises.

Also try to memorise one or two of the following visualizations (pick the ones that you feel work best for you), so that you can recall and practise them on demand.

To help control your temper and stay calm, use the mnemonic QUIET, details of which follow and are in the next five sections:

- ✔ **Quietness:** Go to a quiet place.
- ✔ **Unspoken:** Speak quietly, or not at all.
- ✔ **Interval:** Wait before taking any action.
- ✔ **Existence:** Focus on the fact that you exist.
- ✔ **Thinking:** Stop thinking – just be.

Going to a quiet and safe place

To start calming yourself, visit a quiet place. This location is somewhere with few distractions and little noise, where you can feel more relaxed and completely safe. If you can't do so, because (say) you're in the middle of something important or at work, try to visit a mental quiet place. The following visualization helps you to create such a destination for when you need it.

The object of this visualization is to create an imaginary place that's calm, joyful, free of all distractions, and where you feel safe. So imagine an idyllic, undiscovered tropical island as follows:

1. **Visualize yourself lying on a golden sandy beach on a warm day.**

   A cool breeze gently wafts over you. You can see birds swooping and soaring in the deep blue sky, while the smell of the fresh salty sea tingles your nose, and the white noise of its rhythmic lapping onto the beach lulls you deeper into your relaxed mood each time you hear it. The sun is warm (but not too hot), energising your body.

2. **Stand up and take a walk on your imaginary beach.**

   While you amble along, feel the dry and cool sand pushing up between your bare toes, while every now and then a shallow wave of water washes it away. Inland, the palm trees sway slowly in the breeze, and behind them a tree-covered hill rises up towards its pinnacle at the island's centre. This island is yours. Nobody else knows of its existence and you're never disturbed here. You can get to it whenever you like and leave when you're ready. On the island you need nothing. You're never hungry or thirsty and no man-made items are here unless you bring them. You can walk all the way around the island in less than an hour, and when you're tired of the beach you can explore the woods, grassy clearings, and wildlife farther inland. Sometimes you climb the hill, which has winding pathways where harmless rabbits and wild sheep roam. From the windy summit you have a full view of the ocean. All around is nothing but deep blue sea. And yet you're never lonely. This island is your quiet place and you can come and go as you please.

3. **Come back and explore whenever you like.**

   The first time you perform this visualization simply go with the major themes: the sun, sea, sand, and nature. But remember that you're creating your personal quiet place, so explore it each time you visit. Discover all the pathways and get acquainted with landmarks such as particular trees or oddly shaped rocks. Surprise yourself when you find little babbling brooks or waterfalls, and go swimming in the crystal clear water. This world is yours and you can do what you like with it. Perhaps you want to take a few tools with you and build yourself a hut; or bring a ready-made one with you. You can transform the island into your own perfect sanctuary, and even give it a name if you like.

You can safely lose yourself in this visualization just before going to sleep because it has no structure, no beginning, middle, or end: it simply is. And you can stay in the visualization for as long or short a time as you wish, it's up to you.

Lowering your voice

When you're stressed or angry you may have less control over your voice. You shout or have difficulty finding the right words, and your mouth may be dry. Therefore, if you can, say nothing – unless you have to speak to others, in which case try to keep your voice down so that you retain more control over it. The following visualization helps by concentrating on bringing your voice more fully under control:

1. **Imagine that you're standing in the centre of a town square with buildings all around.**

   In your hand you have a large box with a single knob on it, just like the chicken-head knobs on old-fashioned wireless radios. Around the knob is a dial with settings marked from 0 to 10, and a final setting, 11 , as shown in Figure 8-1.

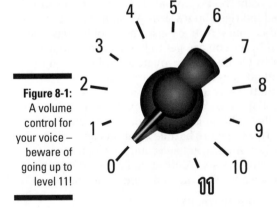

Figure 8-1:
A volume
control for
your voice –
beware of
going up to
level 11!

2. **Visualize turning the knob to setting 3 (and feel it click as it passes each setting), as you start to sing a long and constant 'laaaaaa'.**

   Or sing any tune you're comfortable with. Hear how your singing is coming out at just a conversational level.

3. **Now turn the knob to level 6.**

   Listen to your voice booming across the square

4. **Turn the knob all the way down to 1.**

   Hear how your voice is now a very quiet sound, like singing a lullaby to a baby.

5. **Try a few different levels in your mind to get the hang of them, and then turn the knob up to setting 9.**

   Hear how your voice carries into every alley and side street, and comes echoing back.

6. **Nudge the knob up to level 10.**

   Listen to how deafening your voice has become, as the windows all around rattle and shake and your eardrums hurt. If you were to turn the knob up just one more notch those windows would start to break and come shattering down to the ground. But you don't want to do that.

7. **Slowly turn down the dial.**

   Hear your voice get quieter and quieter until you get to level 0 and, although you're still singing, the town square is totally silent – nothing is coming out of your mouth.

Next time you notice your voice is raised, imagine the volume control and note the level. If it's greater than about 3 or 4, maybe you need to visualize turning it down to a lower level. When you do so, your own voice level follows because the visualization serves to make you aware of the sound of your voice in terms of volume, whereas previously you may not have even been aware that your voice was raised.

Practised now and then, this exercise gives you tremendous control over the volume of your voice and, much like a trained actor, you find you can easily select a level fitting to the current situation and environment. Even when your hackles are raised, you're able to keep your voice low and controlled.

Taking time out

Taking a break is great for re-invigorating yourself. Simply waiting before taking any actions and letting yourself cool off allows you to avoid making bad decisions (or saying something you may later regret) and gives your inner store of energy time to replenish.

You need up to 20 minutes for all the chemicals that anger releases to leave the bloodstream, and for the ability to process information properly to return – even if you quell your initial response quickly, you still need up to ten minutes. Until then, you're unable to comprehend explanations completely, come up with solutions, or undertake problem solving. You're simply not thinking straight. So taking time out is a very important part of calming down after getting angry.

This fact is also worth bearing in mind when dealing with angry people. Until they calm down, they can't understand or even consider any argument you try to make (however logical). Generally, any such communication attempts simply provoke their fury further, so give people space and time before you approach.

One way to take time out is to go for a walk around the block, office, or garden, or wherever you are. The changing scenery and reasonably fast pace helps to clear your mind. But if you can't leave your current situation, even for a few minutes, the following exercise gives you mental time out at a fairground (remember to evoke the carnival atmosphere, the happy mood, and the smell of candy floss and hot dogs):

1. **Visualize a fairground ride, say, a rollercoaster or merry-go-round.**

2. **Picture yourself getting seated and preparing for a short ride.**

3. **Imagine your ride starting slowly and then speeding up.**

4. **Feel the vibrations coming through the seat and the wind whipping past your face as you immerse yourself in the next few minutes of fun.**

5. **Dismount when the ride is over, take a deep breath in, breathe out, feel refreshed, and take a step back into reality, ready to get on with what you were previously doing.**

Focusing on existence

Whenever anything is weighing heavily on your mind or you're concerned or worried about something, taking yourself out of your current situation and considering the big picture can help. By remembering how huge the universe is, how small you are in comparison, and the amazing fact that you exist at all, the negative effects of your troubles can be severely diminished because they're placed in a different context. The following visualization takes you on a short journey to help achieve this viewpoint change:

1. **Imagine that you're a spirit-like being unaffected by the laws of space and time.**

   You're outside the universe looking in at the hundred billion galaxies.

2. **Fly into the universe and through all these galaxies until you see the Milky Way with its hundred billion stars.**

   Follow one of the long arms of stars that radiate out from the centre of the galaxy until you're about halfway to the centre, where you find an interesting star called Sol, surrounded by several planets and plenty of large asteroids. Fly on past the strange planet with a ring around it called Saturn, as you head closer to the Sun, past the giant Jupiter and the dead, red Mars until you see a beautiful blue, green, and white pearl float into view – the planet Earth.

3. **Keep flying in towards the planet Earth until you can see your continent and then your country, and then start descending to your present location.**

   Float through any obstructions such as roofs and walls until you see yourself.

4. **Drift down and merge with your body.**

   Feel it and you breathing together until you're one. Sense the life flooding through your veins. Feel the warmth of your body and the thoughts in your head. Consider how amazing it is that in the whole, vast universe you're alive and able to experience it. Is this an amazing coincidence? Is it through God's creation? Either way the fact of existence is huge, and you've received the incredible gift of life. Compared to the grand view obtained from your lightning tour of the universe, your current troubles and cares are insignificantly small. Rise above them.

Stopping thinking

Whatever else you do when upset, stressed out, or angry, one of the easiest and most powerful exercises to bring you back to a state of calmness is simply to stop thinking. If you have no thoughts, nothing exists to feed the feedback cycle and your negative mood dissipates.

Sometimes I suggest replacing negative thoughts with positive ones (as I describe in Chapter 7), but that requires work and concentration, and can be hard to do when adrenaline and other chemicals are coursing through your veins as a result of being angry. So at times like these, try to think of nothing.

In the following visualization, you practise an exercise that snips each thought in the bud as it happens, until you stop having any thoughts at all:

1. **Imagine your thoughts as weeds.**

   The definition of a weed is a flower in a place where you don't want it. Think of your thoughts as weeds: they may be valid but right now they're unwanted.

2. **Visualize each thought that arises in your mind as a weed starting to grow out of the ground in front of you, and simply pluck it out and toss it away.**

   At every new thought, pluck and toss. As you continue doing this action you notice that you have fewer thoughts. Weed out that thought too – it's unimportant. Concentrate only on weeding your mind garden until no more thoughts take root.

3. **Simply be.**

   Expert meditators aim to experience a rare state of complete calmness in which they're thinking of nothing at all, but you don't want to strive to attain anything at this time. Enjoy simply being and not thinking. If you like, look around and just experience. And if a thought occurs, just pluck it out and throw it away.

When you first try this exercise, you may have limited success because you're so used to thinking constantly. If you can, therefore, try adopting the classic meditation pose with your legs gently crossed and hands resting, palms up, on your knees. Or you can do the exercise lying on a soft carpet or yoga mat; don't use a bed or couch though, because that's too comfortable and you may simply fall asleep. These postures have become commonly used because they've been found to be the least intrusive on your meditation, and yet not so comfortable that you fall asleep.

> ## Mental flash cards for relieving anger and stress
>
> Use the following mental flash cards when you have a few spare moments (or when you think you need to use them); they help reduce the risk of becoming angered and relieve any stress:
>
> ✔ **Zooming out into space:** In this visualization you can quickly take yourself away from any situation by zooming out into space. Maybe you can orbit the Earth, visit the dark side of the moon, or zoom out past the planets and on towards other galaxies. It's quick, easy, and very effective.
>
> ✔ **Dressing as a juggling clown:** Humour works wonders, so why not imagine yourself as a silly clown with a painted face, hugely baggy pants, and shoes that are way too large. Now try juggling some balls and dropping them everywhere, throwing custard pies, and falling over. (Not one to try if you have a fear of clowns, though!)
>
> ✔ **Sunbathing on a sandy beach:** If you regularly practise the exercise in the earlier section 'Going to a quiet and safe place', you have a suitable beach of your very own already, so go and sunbathe on it from time to time.
>
> ✔ **Receiving a back and shoulder massage:** Physically, apart from exercising, massaging comes a close second in helping you to relax. Curiously, you can also get some of the calming effect of a massage by imagining being given one. Move your shoulders and neck about as you visualize a massage and you may even send a shiver up your spine.
>
> ✔ **Feeling a fan or breeze blowing peace:** Visualize the feel of a gentle, cool breeze blowing in your face. Perhaps it also has a slight scent of lilac or lavender. Feel it bringing peace, calm, and coolness into your mind.

Reducing Stress

As I discuss in Chapter 3, stress is not only an inconvenience, but also causes unhealthy effects on your body and mind and can make you ill. At the very least you become less efficient and less able to function in a normal manner, and therefore anything you can do to reduce your stress levels is beneficial.

Exercising regularly

Believe it or not, one of the most effective stress relievers is exercise. Keeping active increases your sense of wellbeing and positivity, partly due to you becoming fitter, but also because your body releases a reward chemical when you exercise called *dopamine*, which naturally elevates mood and counters depression.

Dopamine is central to the reward systems your body uses to incentivise you; your body releases this chemical when you eat, during sex, and in positive social interactions. In fact, dopamine is often abused: many drugs, such as opiates, cocaine, alcohol, and amphetamines, actively interact with dopamine and change its levels, which is why so many people find drugs addictive.

But instead of taking artificial drugs (with all their dangerous side effects), through the simple action of exercising you can release large amounts of dopamine and enjoy a free and legal 'high', as well as getting fit. It's a win-win situation.

However, most people live busy lives and finding time to exercise isn't always easy, particularly when you feel stressed out. Fortunately, at these times you can turn to creative visualization. Flick to Chapter 5 for techniques to help you find the time you need for a new activity such as exercising.

Comparing yourself with people worse off

One of the best stress-relieving visualizations is more of a realisation really, which is to acknowledge just how well off you really are by comparing your situation with those of other people around the world.

When you feel stressed, just remember that you're probably in the top few percentage of people in the world in terms of standard of living, health, and most other indicators. Others would be happy to have the worries that are causing you stress, such as needing to find the money for a child's piano lessons, or having to replace a broken mobile phone. Try to put your problems into context and gain some perspective; and realise that in the scale of all things, you actually aren't really as badly off as you may sometimes think.

Imagining yourself in two years' time

When you're stressed, facing the future and seeing an end to your problems can be difficult. To counter this feeling, try evaluating your goals, confirming their practicality and the feasibility of achieving them, and then looking at the end results. For example, right now you may be stressed and even depressed, but as long as you're working on it through creative visualization and other means, the stress and depression is going to go away.

To help keep your spirits up and stay motivated to make the changes you want, the following visualization lets you experience yourself at the other side of the tunnel:

1. **Imagine yourself as a spirit being.**

   The laws of space and time don't apply to you.

2. **Whizz quickly forwards through time to today's date in two years' time.**

   Watch yourself as you do so. Try to go at a speed of about a month every couple of seconds, so that you reach your destination of two years ahead in about a minute. As you travel through time see how, month by month, you become more relaxed and active. You look healthier and seem a lot happier as each few seconds goes by.

3. **Feel good about the future.**

   You can't look accurately into the future, so your precise location and what you're doing may not be clear, but you can tell that the future you is a much brighter and more fulfilled person who's leading a more active and stress-free life. Feel how good, fresh, and natural that is.

4. **Let your future you simply fade away like a puff of steam.**

   Don't fly back through time. Just allow the current world to fade back in.

This exercise helps you to feel less anxious and causes your stress levels to drop – and that's what the future is going to be like, only better.

Using imaginary balloons to float away bad thoughts

In the earlier section 'Stopping thinking', I provide an exercise in which you suppress all thoughts – good or bad – in order to achieve a level of calmness. When you have less time available, however, you can use the following exercise to deal with your negative thoughts.

When bad thoughts keep coming and are getting in the way (and depressing you), take a few moments to sit or position yourself comfortably. As each thought arises, blow it out into an imaginary, self-sealing balloon and let it float away high up into the sky. Being light and insubstantial, the balloons easily pass through the ceiling or any other obstructions and keep on rising until they're out of sight – and out of mind. Keep visualizing balloons in your mind until the level of bad thoughts slows down enough for you to be able to get on with whatever you're doing.

Visualizing meditation

As I discuss in 'Stopping thinking' earlier in this chapter, meditation has a powerful calming effect and is one of the best things you can do to relax. But when adopting the appropriate posture is impractical – for example, because you're sitting at a desk or on a train – you can use visualization to put you in the right 'position'. That's right, creative visualization is powerful enough that you can visualize meditating and it has a similar positive effect. You can then visualize wherever you are and whatever you're doing, as long as you have a couple of minutes to spare.

Try this exercise for visualizing meditation:

1. **Visualize yourself lying on a comfortable and supportive yoga mat with your eyes closed and arms down beside you.**

   Picture yourself somewhere relaxing, such as your quiet place (from the earlier section 'Going to a quiet and safe place'), or anywhere calm. Feel yourself as you sink gently into the mat.

2. **Concentrate on your breathing.**

   Your breathing comes slowly and steadily. Become aware of the sensation as your breath enters and leaves through your nostrils. Notice your chest rising and falling in time with your breath. Whenever thoughts occur to you, ignore them, nip them in the bud, or float them away in balloons (as in the earlier sections 'Stopping thinking' and 'Using imaginary balloons to float away bad thoughts'). Whatever you do, dispel them quickly and get back to concentrating on your breathing. Count each breath from one through to ten and then start again. Go round a few times until your breathing is all that you sense and then you can stop counting.

3. **Stay in the zone and simply experience it.**

   You're now thought-free and still, and around you is silence. No thoughts, no worries, no judgments. All that remains is you. Stay that way for as long as you like (or have time for).

4. **Count down from ten to one when you're ready to finish.**

   Become more alert at each step until you're completely back to reality.

With practice you can even do this visualization with your eyes open and nobody else noticing, and you still come away with a feeling of overwhelming calmness and a sense of harmony with the world.

Focusing on a single positive outcome

The following stress reduction technique concentrates on one single positive outcome, and one only. Doing so focuses you clearly on a single goal, therefore helping you to unclutter your mind and concentrate more easily:

1. **Choose a single benefit of reducing stress in your life.**

   Don't select a negative reinforcement, such as having less of something (like fewer headaches). Instead, visualize something you want more of, such as increased enjoyment of life – in which case the positive outcome is joy, so concentrate on that concept.

2. **Feel joy well up within you as your stress goes down.**

   Notice how you want to smile – so do so. Maybe you feel like laughing, and if you want to, go right ahead.

3. **Revel as fully as you can in the feelings of joy.**

   Let them run up and down your back, along your arms and legs, and throughout your body. Tell your unconscious that this feeling is the real you, not the stressed-out worrier. Demonstrate to your unconscious mind what the feeling is like.

Of course, you don't feel intense joy like this all the time when your stress is reduced. But the idea of this visualization exercise is to communicate your desires strongly to your unconscious mind, which does its best to help you attain them (check out Chapter 6 for more on the nature of your unconscious). So enjoy the joy that you visualize, because it's, well, enjoyable.

Chapter 9

Finding More Motivation and Energy

· ·

In This Chapter

▶ Drawing on your inner energy

▶ Accessing external power sources

▶ Using rewards as incentives

▶ Diminishing apathy and overcoming procrastination

· ·

*E*veryone wants to do certain things in life or achieve certain goals, but often, for one reason or another, they never quite get around to doing so. People's lives are less rich as a result. Of course, the phrase 'for one reason or another' is vague; the truth is that motivation and energy are lacking. If you can bring these two powerful attributes together you can accomplish almost anything you set your mind to.

In order to become more motivated and energetic, you need to visualize wanting something as much as possible. Building an increased desire for certain outcomes causes the mental barriers preventing you from taking action to drop away, and your determination, willpower, and energy increase sufficiently for you to attain the goal.

In this chapter, you acquire techniques you can use to increase your levels of motivation and stamina, making it easier for you to get started on a project you're having difficulty setting out on. It also helps you feel the inner energy to draw on when you're tired, and the commitment to stick with goals through to completion.

Incentivising Yourself

Everyone loves incentives – probably because brain chemistry is based on an incentive and reward system. And the more positive an incentive, the better it seems to work, whereas negative incentives (anti-rewards, or punishments) are usually less effective. That's why the brain has many chemicals designed to create a state of pleasure.

To make incentives even more effective, break them down into parts so that you reward yourself incrementally for each portion of a goal achieved. But keep the incentives reasonably small, to avoid replacing the overall reward of finally attaining the goal.

Turning desire into motivation

Understanding the difference between wanting to do something and being strongly motivated to do so is crucial.

When you *want* something, you'd like to have it but your desire isn't overwhelming. For example, you may want to stop smoking but feel that too much effort is required, so you don't bother. The same goes for wanting a fitter body; because it takes exercise and time to achieve, you put the goal off. Or perhaps you've always thought that getting into an art form such as oil painting may be interesting, but you know it requires purchasing all the materials, setting up a space in the house to use, and plenty of practice before you become good enough to really enjoy it.

The problem with these scenarios is that you have insufficient motivation to take the wanting any further, and this lack has the knock-on effect of ensuring that you don't have the energy to undertake the task anyway. It's a negative double whammy!

In contrast, when you really desire something, obtaining it becomes much easier because the motivation built up by the desire expresses itself in sufficient energy to achieve the goal.

If you meet someone you really like and with whom you want to be in a relationship, you do everything in your power to make this happen. You change work schedules to have the same time off, you arrange to go to the same places so that you can get to know each other better, and you probably buy new clothes, get a haircut, and so on. All these things require time or energy or cost you money (which you earn through using your time and energy), but you see that the potential reward is worthwhile.

Reward is the key to motivation.

Humans are highly reward-led creatures whose neurochemical makeup provides rewards in the form of serotonin, dopamine, endorphins, and epinephrine. These chemicals are called *neurotransmitters* and they send signals to reward centres in your brain that provide feelings of pleasure. Attaining this chemical reward is one of the biggest reasons people do things, and without this incentive system in place humans would be very lazy beings indeed.

People discover from a very early age that they feel good when they do certain things or achieve goals. They also instinctively know that some actions lead to them feeling a little better and others make them feel extremely good; the difference is generally the amount of 'happy' chemicals released into the brain. Therefore, the greater the effect you can visualize a reward having, the more motivation you have to attain the special feeling from success.

So that's how motivation works chemically. Practically, though, in order to become more motivated you must visualize wanting something as much as possible. By building increased desire for a certain outcome, mental barriers preventing you from taking action are dropped and your determination, willpower, and energy increase sufficiently to attain the goal.

Focusing on the rewards

You set every goal in life for a reason, and that's because you want something. Perhaps you want to be slimmer or better off, or maybe you want to quit smoking or learn to play the saxophone. In these examples the basic rewards are a slimmer, sleeker body that looks and feels better; an improved standard of living from more money; health and money-saving benefits by stopping smoking; and the enjoyment of playing a musical instrument.

When aiming for a goal, constantly visualize the rewards that success is going to bring you. Like a young child expecting a birthday, live in eager anticipation of the reward. Keep it uppermost in your mind so that it drives much of what you do.

So don't think 'I want to be slimmer'; instead think 'When I'm slimmer I'm going to buy these clothes'. Focus on what you're going to do and how you'll feel as a result of achieving the goal.

Imagining a difficult project has been completed

Suppose that you set yourself the task of fully decorating your house, because you want to freshen it up or sell it. Even for a smallish property, that involves a lot of painting and decorating. As a do-it-yourselfer with only a few hours available per week, you may need seven days to properly complete each room, so the whole project could take several weeks, and require real dedication to keep up the necessary work.

Using the following exercise regularly as a project such as this progresses helps you stay on track and complete the job in time:

1. **Picture the rooms in your house and choose one to start with.**

   Think what needs doing with that room.

2. **Visualize the things you're going to do to improve the room.**

   For example, removing and/or replacing wallpaper, fixing woodwork and window frames, plastering and painting, laying carpets, and hanging curtains.

3. **Imagine the room completely finished, shiny and brand new.**

   In your imagination walk around and look at the clean paintwork, feel the wallpaper or curtains, smell the newness, and enjoy the way everything turned out perfectly.

4. **Visit the next room and carry out steps 1 to 3 again.**

   Continue through each room until you've finished visually redecorating. If you plan to do any work outside, visualize that as well.

5. **Take a full and extended tour.**

   Appreciate how much nicer your home is and (even if you're not going to sell it) how much extra value you added to it.

When you do this exercise, you may well find that you spot things you hadn't planned to do but now want to. Therefore, allow your visualizations to change as your work progresses and they can also help with your planning.

You can use exactly the same approach for any objective or ambition. Create a good picture in your mind of how long the goal's going to take and what's required to attain it, and then visualize the satisfaction you can expect from finally completing it.

If you want to write a book, imagine reading the first copy off the press and showing it to your friends and family; or if you want to set up a large website, visualize thousands of people visiting and making use of it. If your desire is to learn to drive, visualize the freedom gained from getting your licence. Whatever the project is, visualize that you've successfully completed it and are already reaping the rewards.

As with all visualization exercises, keep your goals realistic and attainable and maintain a high expectation of success. A goal without expectation, or expectation without a goal, results in nothing. You must have both. Always be reasonable and positive in your approach to creative visualization, but don't be afraid of exaggerating what you imagine so as to help build the neural pathways in your brain more quickly.

Receiving payment for a job well done

Some tasks are thankless and, frankly, not fun at all, and sometimes you get little reward for finishing a project other than the payment you receive (in terms of money or gratitude). For example, clearing a blocked toilet by replacing broken pipes and drains is a physically strenuous and smelly task that not many people would class as fun. But this job is a plumber's bread and butter (so to speak).

 If you can't think of a reward for a project that you have to do but aren't necessarily going to enjoy completing (other than by having finished it and not having to work on it any more), try to focus on the payment you get in cash or gratitude. Both of these factors are strong motivators.

Looking forward to recognition for your work

Another reward for a job well done is to earn someone's respect. For example, obtaining a university degree often brings with it the respect of your peers and recognition from your tutors. Completing a multi-year course and earning a degree is a major task, and so keep yourself guided and enthused by imagining the respect you get when you finally finish and receive your certificate.

Likewise, designing the artwork for an advertising campaign, organising an important conference, and getting an article published in a magazine are examples of projects that earn respect, which you can use as a motivator.

 Whenever you complete a non-trivial task, other people recognise this fact and respect you for it, especially if you consistently come up with the goods. So when you need a quick incentive to get back on track and do some more of a large project, spend a few moments visualizing the kudos it brings.

Making tedious tasks important

Always remember that even the most tedious of tasks is important if it leads towards attaining your desired goal. Therefore, give every job the value it's worth in your mind so that you don't devalue it and find that performing the task is harder than necessary.

Suppose that you're starting a new hairdressing business and you need to mail hundreds of households nearby. Creating a flyer or letter may be quite good fun, but addressing the envelopes and affixing stamps is nowhere near as enjoyable. Nevertheless, if you focus on drumming up business for the new venture, the task adopts an air of much greater importance and becomes far less tedious and boring.

When faced with any mundane task that you must perform, use visualization to elevate its importance in your mind by focusing on the positive benefits it brings. Then the task becomes a lot less wearying and can even become quite fun if you set little milestone markers, and think (for example) that for every hundred letters sent, you may get one or two enquiries that turn into valuable long-term customers.

Turning Around Apathy and Procrastination

I was going to write about procrastination here but I can't really seem to get around to it, so I've left it until later, when I may feel more like doing it. . .

Seriously, though, procrastination is the bane of most people's lives and I'm sure that everyone's suffered from it at one time or another – simply type the word into Google and you get back over four million web pages on the subject. One of the reasons for this huge number, I suspect, is that when procrastination rears its ugly head many bloggers turn to writing about it in an attempt to beat the block.

But what exactly is procrastination and is it the same as apathy? Well, I believe that they're quite different. *Apathy* indicates a general laziness and lack of interest, while *procrastination* can arise in even the most motivated people.

As far as I can tell, I tend to procrastinate with my writing when I'm not entirely sure about the subject matter, and therefore my unconscious holds me back until I do something else such as read a book or do some research, after which I generally have the facts and assurance I need. Other times, procrastination creeps up on me when I'm in a really productive flow, often caused by tiredness beginning to set in and my not wanting to start writing nonsense (well, not too much of it anyway).

Whatever the reason, procrastination can sometimes be tremendously difficult to overcome. To help, the following sections present tips and visualizations you can use to deal with the problem.

Doing something because you want to

The first key to overcoming procrastination or apathy is to really want to do something. The more you can increase your desire for a goal, the more you find the willpower to get started.

Use the following visualization to reinforce your goal setting by maximising how much you want to achieve something:

1. **Think about your goal.**

   Don't worry about the precise nature or details of your goal, just focus on it and start thinking about how important it is to you and how you really want to achieve it more than almost anything else.

2. **Imagine that you feel really good inside.**

   Your body feels vibrant and energised and you feel super-excited. Increase the intensity of this feeling so that it's as strong as, for example, anticipating meeting your partner after you haven't seen him for a month, revealing the winning picture in a group on a lottery scratch card, or preparing for your first child to be born.

3. **Return to visualizing your goal while the good feeling from Step 2 stays with you.**

   If the good feeling fades a little, return to thinking about the thing that gets you excited again until the feeling's sufficiently strong for you to return to contemplating your goal.

What you're doing here is creating a strong connection between your goal and the intense feelings so that the two become associated with each other – by you, your unconscious mind, and also through new and reinforced neural pathways in your brain.

By repeating this exercise for a goal that isn't as highly motivating as other goals, you increase your desire for it and find any apathy greatly diminishes.

Breaking big tasks into smaller parts

Some projects are so large that they can become overly daunting and the crushing weight of the huge amount of work required can stop you right in your tracks.

You can always break big projects down into smaller parts, each of which you then tackle independently, making the whole job much easier to complete. In this way, you also get regular boosts of encouraging satisfaction as each small task is completed.

Mental flash cards for overcoming procrastination

Here are a few mental flash cards for when you need to overcome apathy and prevent yourself from procrastinating:

- **Freeze-framing yourself:** In your mind freeze yourself and stop the world, and then step outside your body. Visualize what things you can easily accomplish towards your task and then look at yourself sitting there doing nothing about it. Understand how you can simply get up and with very little effort do just one thing that moves you nearer your goal.

- **Boosting procrastination to the moon:** Take a good look at your procrastination and see it as a heavy weight pressing down on you and preventing you from acting. Now summon all your strength, pick the procrastination up, and heave it towards the moon where, after a couple of orbits, it lands on the far side. You're now free and unencumbered, so get on with what you know you ought to be doing.

- **Reviewing a previous, similar project:** Think about any project you may have previously completed that's in any way similar to the current one. View it as a completed whole that you managed to finish and of which you're proud. Now turn to the project in hand and know that this one is exactly the same. You're going to complete it and you'll be proud of it.

- **Imagining a ten-year-old completing the task:** Imagine a child doing the thing you can't get around to doing yourself. See how easily the child manages, and feel almost ashamed at how you as an adult can't bring yourself to work on the task. If a child can do it, so can you.

- **Laughing at how easy the task is, when you thought it was hard:** Laughter is the best medicine (I seem to have read somewhere). Laugh in the face of hard work and it really becomes less daunting. So even if a project looks impossibly difficult, just visualize yourself laughing at how absolutely simple it is, and it becomes so.

Whether you're undertaking a building or renovation project or a major marketing push at work, or emigrating to another country or something huge like that, consider only the elements that comprise the whole. You can break building projects down by room and the type of work such as painting, wallpapering, bricklaying, and so on. You can divide and conquer marketing by working on a series of small promotions or on a customer by customer basis. And relocating abroad involves the subtasks of finding a new job, locating a new house, choosing good schools, and so on.

Whatever you're working on, you can always rely on the *two-minute rule*, which states that if something can be achieved in under that time no apathy or procrastination barrier applies and you can easily do that job. Thirty different two-minute items in a day result in an hour of work in which you've completed thirty things, most of which you may not otherwise have attended to.

The two-minute rule is great for all those little tasks such as tidying your desk, filing paperwork, paying a bill, making a phone call, and so on. In this way, you can clear away a huge amount of the tedium from your day, leaving more of the fun tasks that you enjoy.

Using mind movies to view the whole project

Mind movies are a perfect technique for better comprehending and approaching large projects.

The idea is to visualize the entire project from start to finish as if you're filming a movie. This approach makes you pay attention to detail and film all the parts. It also stores the movie in your memory so that you can then rewind and fast-forward through it to any point and then play back the scene. The best way to use a mind movie is to film it and then view it straightaway, either in your mind's eye, or imagining viewing it externally on a movie screen, which can provide an element of separation from the mind movie, enabling you to be more objective. Remember you can also run the movie backwards so that you create all the back scene links as well as the forward ones.

You can then call on the mind movie whenever you like to strengthen your motivation for certain parts of a project. It also helps to reveal aspects you didn't plan for, and is therefore a great productivity tool too.

Seeing yourself doing a better job each day

Regular improvement is a great motivator – just ask anyone who's success-fully dieted about the wonderful feeling of seeing the pounds fall off at regular weigh-ins. So when you're actively working on a project and starting to lose some of your initial spurt of energy, try the following generic visualization, which you can tailor to your specific circumstances to keep yourself focused and engaged:

1. **Think about something that you recently accomplished towards achieving your goal.**

   Consider how much it contributed towards achieving your final aim.

2. **Visualize yourself doing the same again but just 1 per cent faster and 1 per cent better.**

   Increasing any level of productivity by a single percentage point is easy; you hardly notice it. But 1 per cent is still more than last time and it feels good to improve.

3. **Imagine that the next time you work on the task you beat that performance by another 1 per cent, in both the speed and the quality of your work.**

   See how good you feel knowing that you're continuously improving.

Think about that fact each time you improve your efficiency even a little: you may finish the project sooner or improve its implementation – or maybe both.

This drive for constant improvement and the regularity of visualizing in this way really help to override any procrastination that starts to set in, especially when you're even further into the project; when you look back you can see how much your ability improved and how the effort you put in increased.

Listening to your motivational theme tune

If you're like most people, many songs probably pop into your head according to different activities you perform. Some of them are soulful and reflective, some happy, some funny, and so on. So have a think about what speaks to you musically when you're really engrossed in something.

Think of a song or tune that you find yourself humming or whistling when you're being productive, almost without realising it. That's your motivational theme tune, and recognising it as such is important. See it as being the MP3 player of your unconscious. Then, when you find apathy rearing its ugly head, recall the tune to change your mood and get yourself motivated.

The tune can (and probably will) change from time to time, which is fine and quite normal. Just like you, your unconscious updates the things it enjoys over time.

Harnessing the Power Within

You can't get the energy or motivation you need to accomplish a goal from outside yourself, and neither can someone else give it to you – not the type of energy you need to make big changes or achieve life goals, anyway. No, the energy you need must come from inside you, and when you don't have much of it (or think you don't) you may feel unable ever to muster enough.

You most certainly can find all the energy you need, but you have to be fired up or motivated about something first. So, while reading this section, bear in mind something in your life that you're passionate about and participate in actively (not as a spectator).

You can choose any sport; a hobby such as playing a musical instrument, painting, or photography; visiting museums and places of architectural or cultural interest; cooking speciality cakes or your own chilli recipe; walking or cycling in the country; climbing or hiking up mountains; swimming; or, well, the list is endless. Whatever you choose, find an activity that motivates you and keep in mind how it makes you feel.

Recognising the energy within you

I hope that you've come up with an activity from the preceding section that drives you, because you're now going to examine how it makes you feel. As this activity is a passion for you, sense the excitement that looking forward to it brings you right now, and feel the associated energy – the energy that comes from inside that you use to perform the task.

Perhaps you like to jog and the endorphin high is one of the things that keeps you going; if so, imagine that experience now, and feel the energy that wells up in you, enabling you to keep running (check out the 'Incentivising Yourself' chapter earlier in this chapter for more on rewards).

When you work on something you enjoy (or in order to achieve something that you desire) the energy you need to do it is always available. It is deep down within you, waiting to be drawn on in abundance.

Here's an exercise you can perform to become more fully aware of all this latent energy and bring it out more easily:

1. **Visualize yourself with your arms and legs outstretched, each capable of touching the edge of a large hoop.**

   Recall the world-renowned painting by Leonardo da Vinci 'The Vitruvian Man' to help you with this visualization.

2. **Imagine that right in the centre of your body (at your solar plexus) a sun is squashed down to the size of a golf ball.**

   This sun radiates power – it's a fireball of energy.

3. **Sense the energy fireball just below your sternum radiating heat, light, and energy throughout your body.**

   Feel it tingling along your limbs, up and down your spine, and in your head. See the sparks flying out from the tips of your fingers and toes.

4. **Imagine that whenever you touch anything you transfer some of your limitless energy to it.**

   Imagine the battery in your car is flat and refuses to start. Lift the bonnet, point one hand in the battery's direction, and fully charge it with a single jolt of power. Now imagine a global power outage has taken place due to a magnetic storm in the sun, but you easily emanate waves of energy into the wiring of your house to keep all your lights and appliances running. Visualize the neighbours asking you to power their houses too, which you accomplish by upping your power output.

5. **Take the visualization a step further by giving more power.**

   Increase your power level. Decide to help out your country and transmit enough energy back into the grid for everyone. Imagine opening your power output to maximum and beam your energy to all the electricity grids of all countries in the world. Keep this up for a minute or two, until you see that the magnetic storm is over and the power stations come back online.

6. **Power back down again.**

   Your energy fireball is now simply pulsing away quietly, waiting to be drawn on again when needed.

Unleashing your inner life force

The visualization exercise in the preceding section makes use of an invented fireball of energy to create the feeling of energy, and it's quite powerful (forgive the pun). After you've practised that exercise a few times, move on to recognising the inner life force within your own body with the following exercise:

1. **Visualize yourself with your arms and legs outstretched, and this time focus on the physical energy you have in your body.**

2. **Think of your left leg and feel the strength in its muscles, starting with your toes and up to your hips.**

3. **Think of your right leg, and then do the same with your left and right arms.**

4. **Feel the muscles in your torso, your shoulders, and neck, and then try to sense all your muscles simultaneously – each and every one is ready to perform your bidding whenever required.**

5. **Feel your heart pumping powerfully and regularly, pulsing life into your body once every second or so.**

6. **Sense the blood in your veins as it's being pumped around your body, bringing energy and nutrition where needed and removing dead cells and toxins.**

7. **Notice how warm you are as your body creates and radiates heat, and concentrate on the life force within you.**

Practising this exercise helps your unconscious mind to recognise the physical strength and power of life within your body, so that you can draw on it as and when required.

Building your inner feeling of strength

Sometimes you don't feel like doing something because you're too tired and don't have the energy; it seems to you that physically you're simply not strong enough. Usually this is simply an illusion brought on by inactivity, which can be remedied by substantially increasing your inner impression of your own physical strength with a simple visualization.

In this section you work on building up your inner feelings of fitness, strength, and stamina. This won't make you stronger physically but should make you feel as if you are and it may help towards motivating you to become more physically active. (For exercises to help improve your physical strength and sporting ability, please refer to Chapter 15.)

In this exercise your aim is to build up a mental picture of your own physical strength, imagining it to be far greater than it really is:

1. **Imagine that you're standing inside the famous prehistoric monument Stonehenge, in south-west England.**

   Stonehenge is a huge circle made from roughly rectangular upright boulders, with others placed above them as lintels. Over the centuries some of the lintels have fallen down and many of the uprights have toppled over too.

   Around you, on the ground, are several smaller boulders and stones, with some as small as your fist.

2. **Pick up a small stone.**

   Note its texture and weight.

3. **Look around for another stone about twice the size and pick that up.**

   Feel how this stone is somewhat heavier and you have to use more strength, but lifting it is quite manageable.

4. **Pick up more stones, increasing in size each time until they get large enough that you need two hands to lift them.**

   See how, although it takes some strength, picking up large stones is easy.

5. **Work your way through the other fallen rocks, again increasing the size of each that you lift up until they begin to get as large as you.**

   At this point they probably weigh a ton each, but you have no problem heaving them up above your head and dropping them back down again.

6. **Rebuild Stonehenge.**

   Make the stone monument look just how it did thousands of years ago. Lift and heave all the upright stones back into place. Bed them back into the ground by twisting them so they don't fall down again. Grab hold of all the fallen lintels, lift them onto your shoulder, and heave them up onto the uprights. Pretty soon you see that you've restored several hundred tons of stones back into a full circle and you hardly even feel tired.

Of course, like many of the visualizations in this book, what you've imagined is impossible. But that's why the technique is called *creative* visualization. By seeing things in a new and out-of-the-ordinary way, you help to build new neural pathways in your brain, including those involved in muscle control, and this exercise serves to prepare your body for becoming mentally stronger – and also physically too, since this type of positivity often results in more interest in being active and exercising in general.

Drawing on your willpower

When you have a difficult goal to attain, especially one that involves changing a deeply ingrained habit such as quitting smoking, you're going to need as much self-control as you can muster. To help, use the following interrupt visualization exercise to increase your willpower and practise the act of ignoring temptation:

1. **Imagine something that you want to do a lot but would rather not.**

   For example, drink a glass of beer or cola, eat a cake or pastry, or smoke a cigarette or cigar.

2. **Select something healthy that you'd rather do.**

   For example, you'd rather drink a glass of water or fruit juice, eat a carrot or celery stick, or do something with your hands such as juggling.

3. **Perform the first action, but at the last minute interrupt this activity and perform the new one.**

   For example, if your action is to drink a glass of cola and the alternative is to have a glass of water, visualize reaching out for the cola, getting ready to pick the glass up, and then turning at the last minute to a glass of water instead, which you then drink. If you chose a cake and a carrot do the same thing: reach for the cake but at the last minute pick up a carrot and bite off a chunk. The same goes for smoking: just before picking up the cigarette, grab a set of juggling balls and start juggling.

Understanding why creative visualizations are so strange

You may be asking yourself why some of the visualizations in this book are so impossibly weird and wonderful, and whether more down-to-earth exercises would work better. The answer is absolutely not, because the brain has learned over many years to pay less attention to normal things and really notice anything unusual.

People who can perform incredible memory feats know this fact and use mnemonics to recall huge amounts of data, such as thousands of decimal places of pi. For each number they associate a wacky image and link it to the next one with another equally weird image. The brain takes note of these strange inputs and quickly makes neural pathways from them that can later be recalled in perfect order.

If you simply try to force yourself to memorise long sequences of numbers (or anything), you're going to get stuck after less than ten items, because your brain has no new neural pathways in place due to it finding a list of numbers mundane and unremarkable. For this reason, always try to be extra creative with your visualizations, so that your unconscious mind sits up, listens, and takes note.

You can practise these interrupt visualizations or ones of your own devising, but try to make the latter realistic. Each time you do so, you change the neural pathways in your brain such that the previous automatic pattern of consuming the thing you're trying to avoid is replaced with a new automatic pattern. Practised frequently, your unconscious starts to help you, and your willpower is strengthened so that making these substitutions becomes ever easier.

Using pattern interrupt visualizations in this way is far easier and much more effective than simply trying to draw on inner willpower alone, with the result that you achieve your goals much sooner and with less effort.

If you rely purely on willpower to make a change you run the risk of giving in before you've accomplished what you set out to achieve, because willpower seems to only have a limited duration (or shelf-life) before it fades. Therefore, increasing your willpower is an important aid and should be part of your overall strategy, but not the only tool in your kit. Make sure you use the other techniques in this chapter too so that you stay on course and motivated.

Passing on your energy to others

As always, when looking for a more fulfilled life, you get the best results by being prepared to share your own abundance with others. You also get the most rewards and greatest fulfilment.

When you have excess energy, put it to use helping other people. Maybe someone you know is disabled and has difficulty getting out and about. If so, offer to help with the shopping or other things. Perhaps a neighbour has a high hedge that's hard to reach that you can trim, or a local kids' sports team needs a coach. A multitude of things exist that you can help with in your family and local community, and the more you do, the more energy you find you have.

Even if you're initially sceptical about having more energy, please bear in mind the possibility. And when you see the results of practising the visualizations in this book, and find yourself with excess energy and at a loose end, think about the positive use you can put this energy to.

Absorbing Power from Outside

You take energy into your body in three main ways:

- ✔ You consume calories in the form of food and drink, which you can then burn chemically to produce energy.

- ✔ You breathe oxygen (which comprises about a fifth of the atmosphere) into your lungs, from where it's transported in the blood all around your body and exchanged with carbon dioxide, which you then breathe out.

- ✔ You receive energy from the environment in the form of warmth from the air and direct sunlight.

These processes all supply physical energy, and as long as you're healthy, eat well, and exercise regularly, they give you all the energy you need.

But other kinds of energy exist too, such as spiritual and motivational energy. Although not scientific forces, they feel very powerful, so you can easily confuse lack of motivational energy with lack of physical energy, and vice versa.

The visualization exercises in this section help you to keep all types of energy topped up and ready to be drawn on by maintaining them uppermost in your mind, reminding you and your unconscious that you *do* have all the energy you require for your goals.

Refreshing yourself with spiritual energy

If you believe in God, you already have a tremendous source of inspiration and motivation on your side. Whether you're a Christian, Muslim, Hindu, Buddhist, Jew, or a member of any other (organised or not) religion, all you have to do is pray for the energy that you need to accomplish the goals that you set – ask for the motivation and willpower to maintain the work required to finish.

Even non-religious people may be able to benefit from the feeling of spiritual energy through the power of visualization. By imagining an all-powerful being or presence from whom you can request assistance, you may be surprised at how often this help manifests itself. Don't discount the effect simply because you don't believe in where it comes from, because your unconscious is always looking and listening when you visualize, and that alone is sufficient reason to visualize a higher power helping you.

However, if you have difficulty with this kind of imagery you can instead focus on the human 'spirit'; the wonderful and only partially understood quality within us that lets us love, laugh, sing, paint, and enjoy doing all these and so many other things. Try to use this spirit as a source of inspiration from which to draw your motivation.

Research shows that positive expectation is important for achieving major goals, and by requesting assistance from a higher power (or visualizing doing so), you may find that you can draw on this spiritual energy.

Sunbathing mentally in light, heat, and other energy

I avoid including a visualization exercise based on consuming food or drink as a means of obtaining energy, because most people have enough trouble keeping their calorie intake down anyway. But concentrating on energy that you absorb through your body has no potential negative side issues. In fact, the following exercise not only helps to re-invigorate you, but also serves to bring calmness and deep relaxation:

1. **Imagine yourself lying alone on a beach.**

   In Chapter 8, I discuss visualizing going to your own private location. You can use that place for this exercise or see yourself lying on your back on any bright and warm beach with the waves whooshing and lapping, a gentle cool breeze, and a very warm (but not burning) sun beaming down onto your outstretched body.

2. **Feel the warmth from the sun as it soaks into every pore in your body, bringing warmth and energy.**

   Breathe slowly as you do so and feel the moist air refreshing your lungs. Try to think of nothing but the warm glow and your quiet breathing. After a while, turn over, place your head face down with your arms under your forehead, and let the sun's rays play on your back for a minute or two.

3. **Imagine that the Earth is also sending its heat to you.**

   You can feel it gently pulsing from the molten iron core at its centre.

4. **Feel the heat from the galaxy.**

   Billions of celestial bodies exist in the Milky Way galaxy. Although the other suns are light years away, feel the combined heat from all the tiny pinpricks of energy all around, behind, and in front, to your sides, and above and below you. Together they combine to add an exquisite extra energy vibration to the warmth you already feel.

5. **Feel the heat from other galaxies.**

   Trillions of stars are out there, all sending energy through the cosmos. Step up your imagination and picture yourself receiving just a little from each.

6. **Feel tiny particles all around.**

   Scientists believe that stars emit tiny particles called *neutrinos*, which pass through matter undetected due to having no mass. These neutrinos are flying around the universe with billions of them occupying every cubic centimetre of space (including the Earth and your body). Imagine that they lightly tickle and gently heat your body as they pass through, leaving you feeling energised and powered up.

   As well as heat, light, and neutrinos, the Sun (like any star) gives off many other forms of energy, including radio waves, gamma rays, and X-rays. Some of these are harmful, but the Earth's atmosphere filters the bad ones out. So imagine all the output that gets through to you from the Sun and other stars as a wide range of healthy, healing, and life-giving rays of energy soaking into your body and recharging your inner battery – a bit like taking multi-vitamins, but in energy form.

7. **Finish the exercise any time you feel ready.**

   When you're ready, just like finishing regular sunbathing, you can imagine picking up your towel and returning to normal life.

This visualization is a great one to practise in bed at night, because along with the energy it gives you an overwhelming sense of calmness and leads you into a pleasant and restful night's sleep.

Breathing in the life-giving power of oxygen

Much life on this planet requires oxygen to keep alive, including human beings. So, it's no surprise that oxygen is key to feeling healthy. If you don't get enough, for example because you have a problem with your lungs, you quickly get out of breath and must rest after even the smallest physical exercise.

Also, up to 30 per cent of people suffer from reduced oxygen intake at night as a result of *sleep apnoea* (relaxed muscles along the air intake system reduce the airway and sometimes close it). The sufferer wakes up in order to take a breath when the blood oxygen level gets too low, which can happen dozens of times a night, and lead to excessive daytime tiredness. Often, sleeping medication, excess weight, or alcohol exacerbates the problem.

Visualizing breathing in oxygen serves as an energy metaphor for your unconscious mind. It also helps to reinforce the importance of oxygen, which can encourage people who lack energy due to not breathing in enough of it to take appropriate measures, such as giving up sleeping tablets, losing weight, or drinking less (you can find out more on getting to sleep naturally through visualization in Chapter 10.)

Don't forget to consult your doctor about reducing any prescribed medications you take, and do so only in the manner advised (often medication reduction must be undertaken slowly and carefully).

Here's an exercise that strengthens your awareness of the importance of oxygen and helps reinforce your overall feelings of strength and energy:

1. **Breathe in slowly and then out again.**

   Think only about your breathing.

2. **On each inhalation, think 'energy is entering'.**

   Understand that life-giving oxygen is being sucked deep into your lungs from where it passes into your bloodstream to be pumped around your body.

3. **On each exhalation, think 'tiredness is leaving'.**

   All the unwanted carbon dioxide in your body is being swept up by your blood and returned to your lungs, from where you're now expelling it.

4. **Maintain the exercise until you feel energised.**

   When your inner battery has been recharged take one final breath in of oxygen to ensure it is fully topped up, and breathe out once more to end the exercise.

When you breathe in you take in life-giving oxygen, and when you breathe out you return life-giving carbon dioxide into the atmosphere for plants and algae to breathe – part of the circle of life. So don't imagine you're breathing out a poison or something useless when you practise your visualizations; instead, think of yourself as giving back to the planet the carbon dioxide it badly needs.

Now, of course, in the current industrial age due to burning fossil fuels, humans create an awful lot more carbon dioxide than the planet wants. But this situation has only occurred in the last couple of hundred years, whereas animals and plant life have co-existed for a vastly longer period.

Think positively. One day when the fossil fuels are spent and/or technology is in place to 'remove' all emissions, the planet will again return to the natural gas cycle; plant to animal to plant and so on. So concentrate on this cycle as it was and will be.

Chapter 10

Being Healthy and Banishing Bad Habits

*B*ad habits start off innocently enough. Perhaps you over-indulge in the holiday season and then never quite get back to your previous level of eating; or maybe you make some new friends who like to drink socially and so you end up drinking more alcohol when you spend time with them. And when you're young, peer pressure to adopt bad habits is almost irresistible: you try that first cigarette to look cool or avoid being the only one not smoking, which leads to another, and so on. The same process can happen with illegal drugs and alcohol.

Other people fall into different unhealthy traps. For example, after a difficult situation or event you decide to go shopping to cheer up, and pretty soon you find that you're only happy when shopping and consequently spend far too much money (perhaps more than you earn) just trying to keep your spirits up. Gambling can also start off quite innocuously. You have some loose change and play a slot machine while on a visit to Las Vegas, and six hours later you've reached the daily withdrawal limit on your debit card.

In this chapter, I concentrate on the big three bad habits that many people want to break: smoking, drinking, and over-eating. Of course, many others also exist, such as gambling, swearing, over-shopping, hoarding, bad hygiene, impulsiveness, and so on, but you can easily tailor the techniques I use for the three main examples to any other habit you want to get rid of.

Having a Healthy Body and Mind

In order to have a happy and healthy mind it's important to maintain a happy and healthy body. However, in the modern age of easy access to rich foods, cheap and fast transportation, and the migration of jobs from physical labor to more sedentary occupations such as office work, this is easier said than done.

I've spent the best part of 25 years sitting at a desk, and have gone from a highly active and healthy lifestyle in my first job, caring for physically disabled people in residential homes, to a few years ago bordering on the clinically obese and having a body mass index (BMI) of over 30.

Fortunately, with the help of creative visualization, I've been able to take stock of my situation, and make necessary cutbacks such as reducing my drinking and eating to healthier levels, and quitting smoking.

So, if like me you find yourself with a body that you may have let slide, then the visualization exercises in this section will help you to begin returning your body to a better shape and level of fitness.

Using positive thinking in healing

One of the best guards against ill health is to have a healthy mind. The mind and body are intricately connected, and so being depressed or suffering from other psychological problems often causes your body to become unwell – you may put on weight, suffer from aches, pains, and headaches, and catch more than your fair share of colds. Likewise, it stands to reason that the knock-on effect of being unwell physically is mental fatigue and other issues.

Luckily, positive thinking in the form of creative visualization can have remarkable healing effects; simply by imagining being well you can improve your health. In many studies of ill people, researchers found that concentrating on combating an illness mentally can reduce the severity of symptoms and improve a person's quality and length of life.

Although creative visualization is a powerful tool for helping to deal with many problems and ailments, remember that it works best alongside tried and tested procedures and medicines, not in place of them. Please always ensure that you get the best professional care and advice you can to help manage medical problems as promptly and effectively as possible. Then use the power of creative visualization to try and hasten your recovery and increase its effectiveness in conjunction with professional assistance.

Cancer patients are often asked to spend as much time as they can visualizing their white cells bustling around their body (and especially at the sites of any cancer), destroying and removing all cancerous cells they find and allowing normal cell growth to resume. How this technique works exactly isn't known, but indications suggest that the unconscious mind works with the autonomic nervous system and the immune system in response to the visualized suggestions, and this association helps them to target the causes of the illness.

Of course modern medicine provides a range of treatments for many diseases, including cancers, and so always maintain any treatment agreed with medical professionals. But by visualizing at the same time, you increase your weapons substantially for battling illness.

You form a partnership between you, your physicians, and your body. The doctor determines what's wrong with you and begins whatever medical treatment is available. You then also take the information gained on where the problem is and pass that onto your body through visualization so that it can work on the problem from its side.

Visualization can help with combating serious illnesses and beating minor ones. Have you ever discussed the topic of colds with a person who never seems to catch them? The person often says to you that she's 'not a cold person' or that she 'chooses not to have them'. In other words, she adopts a positive outlook on her health, which keeps her immune system in tip-top condition. In contrast, when you discuss colds with long-term sufferers, the picture you get is quite different.

Flick to Chapter 7 for more on positive thinking and how you can use it to help other people who are unwell.

Building strong core muscles

As you age, if you don't keep active but allow your muscles to weaken, your joints can calcify, leading to osteoarthritis. If you're young and active you may not want to think about this problem, but when you reach middle age you start to notice your first joint aches and pains. Therefore, you need to start doing what you can to keep your muscles in good condition; and now is as good a time as any.

Obviously, you can't build muscle simply by thinking about it. Visualization can, however, help you build your muscles more quickly and easily (and achieve the motivation to keep looking after them, as I describe in Chapter 9). Remember that your mind and body are a team; they're each part of an interconnected and organic whole.

So, like it or not, you need to get physical if you want to be healthy, and particularly develop your core muscles that run through the central section of your body: that is, the spine, pelvic girdle, and hip joints. The main muscles that you may have heard of in this area are the six in the abdominal muscle group (the abs), but some 30 different core muscles reside in this region (mostly with long Latin names).

By toughening your core muscles you achieve the following:

✔ Improved posture and reduction of lower-back pain.

✔ Toned muscles, averting potential back injury.

✔ Improved physical performance.

✔ Minimised muscle aches.

✔ Lengthened leg muscles, which helps you maintain better balance as you age.

Here's a combined physical and visualization exercise that emphasises to your body and your unconscious the importance of keeping these core muscles fit and strong, and also helps your desire to continue the necessary exercise. Physiotherapists and Pilates trainers view this technique as central to developing core stability, in which the abdominal wall, pelvis, lower back and the diaphragm all help stabilise the body during movement.

1. **Sit up in an alert position and (while you maintain a steady breathing rhythm) try to pull your navel inwards and back to touch your spine.**

   Don't just imagine this action, carry it out if you can. The technique is called *abdominal bracing*.

2. **Feel the muscles that are being employed as you hold your navel in.**

   Visualize yourself pouring energy into the muscles from within your core.

3. **Hold this position for up to five minutes if you can.**

   As a beginner, hold for at least 30 seconds. Remember to keep breathing evenly all the time and don't hold your breath.

Although this technique does give you a little muscle toning, no substitute exists for proper exercising. Each time you do this exercise try to apply feelings of power, vibrant health, and motivation to give yourself the get-up-and-go to match your visualizations with physical workouts.

If you have any existing health issues, consult your doctor or relevant health professional before starting a physical exercise programme.

Looking after your heart

Ensuring that your heart is as healthy as possible allows you to obtain a wide range of benefits due to increased blood flow and oxygen distribution around your body, including the following:

- ✔ Increased energy levels and endurance.
- ✔ Lower blood pressure.
- ✔ Reduced body fat and a healthier weight.
- ✔ Reduced stress, tension, anxiety, and depression.
- ✔ Improved sleep.

The general consensus is that aerobic exercise is the best way to look after your heart. _Aerobic_ means 'with oxygen' and refers to exercise that causes you to breathe deeply and bring up a slight sweat for at least 20 minutes. Aerobic activities include fast walking, biking, jogging, swimming, and cross-country skiing.

As a guide, you should be able to carry on simple conversations during aerobic exercise, but if you become short of breath you're exercising too hard.

The only way to become and stay fit is to exercise, and so the following visualization is targeted at motivating you and increasing your desire to exercise aerobically as frequently as possible, or if you've never jogged before, to go out and try it:

1. **Get ready to go out for a 20-minute jog in your mind's eye.**

   Mentally make sure that you're wearing suitable clothes that are loose fitting and airy, such as shorts or jogging bottoms and a T-shirt, and that you have on a good pair of running shoes.

2. **Imagine yourself in the suburbs or on a country lane and start jogging.**

   Feel how your shoes fit just right and your feet feel like they're bouncing with each step. Your legs feel strong and powerful. Notice your arms going back and forth in counter-rhythm to your legs; they feel strong too, but are relaxed and simply swaying to keep you balanced.

3. **Realise as you jog that, far from being tired, you feel energised and can quite happily keep this pace up for the full 20 minutes.**

   Notice a slight sweat building up on your brow; mop it away with the soft armband on your sleeve. Also note how your body feels more supple and is moving more easily.

4. **Imagine passing trees, houses, and side streets as you continue.**

   Nod or wave to people you know. Enjoy that they're seeing you exercising because they know that you're being serious about your health. Experience breathing in cool and exhaling warm air. Feel how the oxygen is refreshing your lungs and energising your body.

5. **Continue until you feel you've finished jogging.**

   See yourself slow down and return to normal walking pace and note how you feel fit and healthy. Remember that after this type of exercise your body maintains its increased level of activity for many hours, burning more calories (even when you're seated) than it otherwise would.

While this visualization is fresh in your mind, start planning for going out and jogging for real. Perhaps pop out to the shops and get yourself some cheap jogging gear and do a 20-minute jog today – no time like the present.

After completing your first jog, you realise how easy it is and how little time it takes out of your day. The current health advice is that you need to do this jog only three times a week to maintain a healthy heart. But, of course, if you choose to do more, all the better.

If you're unfit or have current health issues, take advice from a medical practitioner before embarking on any exercise regime such as jogging; and always stop if any exercise becomes painful or you become short of breath.

Building stamina

You need *stamina* to persevere with changing bad habits and becoming healthier – stamina that keeps you going through thick and thin, giving you the energy to work on things over the long term. Physically, stamina is the kind of energy that you draw on to run a marathon, and mentally it's the ability to stick with something until its completion, no matter how long that takes.

The next exercise is a breathing one, because such exercises increase your stamina and endurance for many activities, including running, swimming, martial arts, and even singing. The technique used is called *Chi breathing* and the goal is to remove the emphasis from the shoulders and chest, and instead breathe from deep within your abdomen:

1. **Sit upright and hold your hands over your lower stomach.**

2. **Breathe in as far as you can until you can't draw in any more air, and then let it all out again, until the very last gasp has been exhaled.**

3. **Repeat this action a couple of times.**

4. **Imagine that as you breathe in, your hands are somehow sucking the air all the way down your torso and into them.**

5. **Visualize that as you exhale, your hands are pushing the air back through your stomach.**

6. **Take your time and settle into a slow and steady rhythm that feels comfortable.**

7. **Visualize the deep and long-lasting energy that each abdominal breath brings you.**

As you do the actions in steps 4 and 5, you should feel your abdomen expanding and contracting and experience the breathing movement all the way down to your pelvic area.

The deepness of the breathing in this exercise has a profound effect on your stamina levels; if you practise it regularly, your long-term and endurance energy levels rise.

Becoming happy and contented

In this section, you turn your attention towards your mind, as you seek to instil as high a level of contentment as possible.

Now, happiness is one of the main goals in life – for most people anyway; but it's also a vital part of becoming and staying healthy. If you aren't happy, your body suffers, but if you can raise your spirits, your body follows. Doing so enables you to deal with health issues and any bad habits much more effectively.

Exercises throughout this book help with happiness, particularly in Chapter 7, but you can't go wrong with doing the following simple exercise any time you want to lift your spirits (now and for weeks to come).

Spend the next ten minutes thinking about your future life, imagining that absolutely everything has gone as well as possible and visualizing how you've worked hard and succeeded at accomplishing all your life goals. Now grab a pen or pencil and a piece of paper and write down everything you just imagined. And that's it – visualization done.

Mental Flash Cards for Improving Your Health

Here are a few mental flash cards you can use to help improve your overall health and support your desire to stub out bad habits:

✔ **Running for joy:** Picture yourself running just for the fun of it. You're running fast and your feet are flying. The air's whizzing past you and every muscle in your body is pushing you on faster and faster.

✔ **Becoming a burning torch:** Imagine you're like the Olympic torch burning over the stadium. Kept alive between games, the fire never goes out and is carried to each event by top athletes. You're like that eternal fire, representing everything good about a strong healthy body and participating in athletic activities.

✔ **Ringing like a tuning fork:** Feel your whole self vibrating like a tuning fork, producing a single note. Every cell of your body is in tune with every other, all adding together to make a powerful sound that carries for miles.

✔ **Growing ten feet tall:** Picture yourself getting taller: first six feet, and then seven, and keep on going through eight and nine until you're ten feet tall and towering over everyone. You're taller than a truck, and can look over high walls. If you want you can grow even taller because you're fit, healthy, and full of energy.

✔ **Having a happy body:** Like the penguins from the movie, feel your happy feet, and then your happy legs and happy thighs, followed by your happy hips, happy stomach, happy chest, and happy arms. Now feel your happy neck and happy head with a happy brain inside. Smile.

Being eager to learn

When you develop new skills or build knowledge, you create new neural pathways in which your memories are stored. And when you want change (that is, to remove bad habits and be healthier), you also want to create new neural pathways. Studies show that people in the process of working towards a qualification (or who make a point of constantly discovering new things) are able to remember and recall information much more easily.

The more you learn, the more you're capable of learning.

Therefore, if you want to keep your grey matter as flexible as possible and compliant to your desire to be healthier, you can make the whole process much easier if you adopt an approach of curiosity towards life and always ask yourself questions about anything interesting. To help inspire your curiosity and thirst for knowledge, repeat out loud the following set of affirmations from time to time:

✔ I'm always keen to learn new things.

✔ I have an active and curious mind.

✔ I want to look up every new word I hear on TV or the radio.

✔ I wonder what the world is all about and why I'm here.

✔ I like to understand what makes people tick.

✔ I want to know the reasons behind decisions.

✔ I'm curious about how things work.

✔ I'm interested in other cultures and languages.

Of course, you may not consider that all these affirmations are true to the way you think, so choose the ones that fit you best. And make up new affirmations too, if you want to be more curious about something.

Quitting Smoking

When you give up smoking, you reap more rewards than with breaking any other bad habit. Your health starts to improve straightaway, in terms of losing any smoker's cough and reducing your blood pressure, the risk of cancer, and other diseases. In addition, you save a great deal of money and have many more years of life in which to spend it.

Smokers tend to spend a lot of time in denial. Many of them say that they like smoking, but you have to ask yourself whether that's really true or if they say that because they've spent a fortune on their habit and, rather than admit that it controls them, they pretend that they're controlling it.

I speak from experience, having started smoking at the age of 16 and then continued (up to two packs a day) until my 30s. Occasionally, I gave up for a few months, and even a couple of years once, but I stupidly got lured back into it. So I know exactly how addictive smoking is and all the thoughts that go through your head as a smoker. Fortunately, I was able to combine modern medication (smoking-cessation pills and nicotine patches) with positive visualization in my early 40s, and I've now been smoke-free for 10 years.

Scaring yourself

Being scared of something is definitely a good motivator, and so here are a few more facts. Smoking over a prolonged period can cause a number of serious diseases and illnesses, some fatal and others that don't kill you but leave you with a much poorer quality of life. Of course, the main and best known disease you can get is lung cancer, which may begin with coughing up blood, chest pains, and shortness of breath. The cancer often spreads to the liver, bones, and brain, causing weakness, vision problems, and seizures. Plus, you can develop a wide range of other cancers such as mouth, throat, stomach, and kidney.

Long-term smokers can also suffer from coronary heart disease, heart attack, stroke, and emphysema, the last of which may require you to take an oxygen tank wherever you go or, more likely, you find yourself bedridden. And I've touched only the surface here. Smoking is a nasty addiction, that's for sure.

One reason smokers continue the habit despite this evidence is that certain hand-to-mouth actions create an instant hypnotic 'shut-down' of the awareness of the fact that they are engaging in self-harm. This same hand-to-mouth shutdown trigger also applies to over-eaters, and bulimics during purging actions.

Looking at the good news

The good news – and boy do you need some if you read the scary information in the preceding section – is that your health starts to improve immediately when you quit smoking. Table 10-1 shows you what happens in the minutes, days, weeks, months, and years that follow giving up smoking.

Table 10-1	How Your Body Recovers After You Give Up Smoking
Timescale	*Recovery*
20 minutes	Your blood pressure and pulse return to normal.
8 hours	Your oxygen levels return to normal and your nicotine and carbon monoxide levels are halved.
12 hours	Your carbon monoxide blood levels are almost back to normal.
1 day	Your lungs start to clear out mucus and smoking debris.
2 days	Your ability to smell and taste properly begins to return and no nicotine is left in your body.
3 days	Your breathing becomes easier as your bronchial tubes relax and your energy levels increase.
2 weeks	Your blood circulation is improved and your lung functioning beings to increase.
3 months	Your coughing and wheezing are reducing, and your lung functioning is 10 per cent improved.
1 year	Your increased risk of coronary heart disease as a smoker has been reduced by a half, and it continues to decline thereafter.

Timescale	Recovery
5 years	Your risk of heart attack is now only half that of a smoker, and your risk of a stroke has returned to that of someone who never smoked.
10 years	Your risk of lung cancer is now half that of a smoker.
15 years	Your risk of lung cancer is almost the same as someone who never smoked, as is your risk of coronary heart disease.

Additionally, if you can quit before the age of 50 you halve the risk of dying in the next 15 years compared with a continuing smoker.

Concentrating on the many benefits to your physical health is key to stopping smoking successfully. Read on for visualization exercises that help you focus on these benefits.

Running up the stairs

Very soon after quitting smoking you find your breath returns and you're able to manage physical tasks such as brisk walks without needing to keep taking breaks. This improvement is because your lung capacity is increasing and you're able to take in more oxygen. As a consequence your muscles now get the energy they need to work properly. To emphasise this benefit to yourself try the following visualization:

1. **Think about the last time you ran up the stairs.**

   Remember how out of breath you were when you got to the top.

2. **Imagine that you're a non-smoker and see yourself running up that same staircase with ease.**

   When you get to the top, notice that you're breathing more deeply (because any exercise requires extra oxygen), but that you're not panting or waiting for your breath to catch up. You simply feel normal and after a couple of deeper breaths your breathing, pulse, and blood pressure are all back to normal. Note how good this makes you feel – a once-tiring task is now easy.

3. **Now imagine that you're standing in front of the Philadelphia Museum of Art.**

   That's right, you're at the foot of the steps that Sylvester Stallone ran up as Rocky Balboa in the *Rocky* films.

4. **Visualize yourself running all the way up them to the top with the greatest of ease, and then run down again, turn around, and run all the way back up to the top.**

   Look around and feel like Rocky, like a champion. Imagine that you're now a total non-smoker and think to yourself how easy this running is now that you don't smoke. You feel no loss of breath or coughing, and you're full of energy.

Tasting your food

The thing that many smokers associate most with food is the smoke they have after finishing a meal. Because eating a meal can take a while, the nicotine level in your blood lowers and the cravings therefore mount up, which is why an after-food cigarette is often so enjoyable.

Smokers forget, however, just how good food really tastes because their taste buds are clogged up with tar and other pollutants. One of the strongest sensations when you quit smoking is how amazing a good meal tastes. Use the following visualization to emphasise this benefit, which can help strengthen your resolve to give up smoking or continue to abstain:

1. **Imagine that you haven't eaten all day and you're anticipating your evening meal.**

   Feel how hungry you are, especially now that you've given up smoking. Savour the hunger and know that you're soon going to be rewarded.

2. **Visualize a plate of your favourite food in front of you.**

   Choose whatever you like: a juicy steak, a burger with melting cheese dripping off it, a crispy Caesar salad, or anything that you really enjoy eating.

3. **Smell the aroma of the food and then take a bite.**

   As you do so, notice the explosion of flavour that takes place in your mouth. Taste how wonderful the mouthful is and how it makes you feel. Note how the lack of a stale, smoky odour and dull, ashtray-like aftertaste make the food stand out as something special.

4. **Swallow the mouthful and imagine eating the remainder of your meal.**

   If you like, have your favourite dessert too. Treat yourself just this once, because the whole meal has zero calories!

Practise this exercise during the first few days of giving up smoking, when your taste buds haven't yet fully recovered. Doing so primes you and keeps your willpower strong for when your full taste sense does return.

And I know, people do tend to put on a few pounds when they quit smoking. But don't worry about it, because the benefits of not smoking far outweigh the downside of a few extra pounds. So use the food incentive to keep yourself going – food is strong motivator and the ability to taste it to the full helps you refrain from sneaking a cheat cigarette.

Living to a ripe old age

If for no other reason, you probably want to quit smoking in order to live your life to its full length, instead of having an abruptly curtailed existence. So try to think about all the things you plan to do when you retire, when you're finally free to do all the things you enjoy, with no need to go to work ever again (unless you want to):

1. **Visualize the future you aged 70, free of smoke and feeling fit and healthy.**

   Maybe you're walking in the park or sitting on a bench. The sun's warm and bright and the air clear and fresh – you can easily tell this with your keen sense of smell (untainted by smoking). Perhaps you're on a sunny beach instead, or taking a hillside walk, or even doing things you always wanted to do such as skiing, ice skating, or simply lazing on a chair in your back garden.

2. **Now see yourself aged 80 and 90.**

   Yes, you may be a little older and slightly more frail, and you may have to restrict your physical activity, but all things considered you're happy and well and your body's holding up.

3. **Compare that scene to what it may be like if you continue smoking.**

   You'd be short of breath, your skin would age and become wrinkled more quickly, your teeth would degenerate and fall out and you'd constantly cough and wheeze. No way would you be at all active, and performing even the simplest tasks would be strenuous. On top of that your chances of major and fatal illnesses would increase year on year, and that thought would constantly weigh on you. No, that's definitely not your future, you can feel it in your bones.

4. **Return to visualizing the non-smoking future you.**

   Think to yourself: 'This is how it's going to be; this is my real future.'

Reducing the addictive hold

When quitting smoking, anything you can do to ease the withdrawal symptoms of nicotine addiction helps tremendously. If you're the type of person prepared to go 'cold turkey' and do it alone, that's fine. But many people (myself included) have found support – from counselling to smoking-cessation tablets, nicotine gum to patches – helpful.

And creative visualization and positive affirmations, especially when combined with other kinds of support, can really help you curb those cravings.

Most of the medications available to help you give up smoking began life during research into new types of antidepressants. But when the volunteers in the studies were interviewed it was discovered that a very high proportion of them – over 30 per cent – had lost all interest in smoking. Think about that. What if they could work the same way for you?

Nicotine replacement therapy, such as patches, gum and inhalers, acts to reduce cravings so that the urge to smoke is greatly reduced. Over a few weeks the idea is to slowly reduce the dose until you're nicotine free. Again, in studies, the success rate of this type of treatment is around 30 per cent. When I gave up smoking I used both the medication and nicotine patches because I figured I then had a 60 per cent chance of it working.

And then, of course, there's creative visualization, which, even if it only works at the placebo level of 30 per cent, will still be a great help. And when combined with the other methods you should have over a 90 per cent chance of breaking the habit. Whatever methods you settle on, the important thing is to choose *something*, because giving up smoking will be the best thing you've ever done for your health.

Creative visualization works best when you apply it alongside tried and tested medical treatments. Let modern medicine help you all it can, and then add the power of creative visualization on top of that to hit smoking with a double whammy and finally free yourself from its addictive hold.

Use the following affirmations whenever you get nicotine withdrawal cravings; they help keep you on the straight and narrow. Say them out loud and mean every word. Your unconscious listens and takes action to achieve your desire, and the craving fades:

- ✔ I don't want a cigarette.
- ✔ Nicotine has no control over me.
- ✔ I choose to be healthy and fit.
- ✔ I refuse to feel any urge to smoke.

After a couple of weeks, and certainly after a month or more, you're well on the way to being a non-smoker and experience fewer cravings as each day goes by. But keep your guard up. I know from my experience when I tried to give up without also visualizing that a sudden craving can hit you between the eyes from right out of the blue; and if you're not ready for it you can succumb to temptation.

Therefore, I strongly recommend you also repeat the following affirmations regularly for the first few months and years of being smoke-free:

✔ I'm not a smoker and I'll never smoke again.

✔ I know that every day my lungs, heart, and body are healthier.

✔ I'm glad that nicotine no longer controls my life.

✔ I'm a new person and like it that way.

You may well experience strong pressure from peers who haven't stopped smoking. You must be strong and simply tell them that you've made your choice and no, you really don't want a cigarette thanks. Nothing reassures a smoker more than a non-smoker who fails and returns to the fold, thus showing how 'hard' giving up is and justifying the continuing smoker's not trying to quit.

Such peer pressure can sometimes be intolerable. Once, after being smoke-free for five years, I was at a party celebrating the birth of a friend's baby and the cigars came out. No matter how much I protested, the others made clear to me that I *had* to accept one. Believe me, I turned it down every possible way, but the offence taken by my friends was clearly evident.

In the end I accepted and I figured that I'd prevent myself getting hooked again by not inhaling. After all, the nicotine can only enter your blood if it first gets into your lungs. So I pretended to inhale and simply held the smoke in my mouth and let it out slowly as if I'd breathed it in. After a few minutes everyone was satisfied that I'd partaken in the 'ceremony' and no objection came when I stubbed out the cigar. Also, I received no further pressure when I refused to accept any more cigars.

So if you find yourself in a similar situation, and you absolutely have no other option, make sure that you don't inhale even the tiniest amount of smoke, or very soon you'll want more . . . and more.

If you do happen to give in and smoke, don't persecute yourself over it. Simply quit again – immediately. The period during which you didn't smoke made you much healthier, and so the damage of a few cigarettes can be quickly reversed.

For your own sake, move on, put the mistake down to experience, and continue with your visualizations and any medical assistance. Whatever you do, don't say to yourself 'that didn't work then', and give up on giving up. Your efforts did work because you stopped smoking for some time; just get back on track. And tell yourself that you know you're going to succeed.

You can also further guard against picking up the habit again by using *aversive conditioning*, in which you link the smell of cigarettes to something you detest. Then, instead of noticing a waft of smoke in the street as a smoker passes by and thinking 'Mmm, that smells good', you think 'Yuk, that smells disgusting'.

To do this imagine a smoker passing you in the street and make the trail of smoke that follows that person seem like the stench from a sewer, or some seriously rotting fruit. Or, if you have another strong smell you hate (for example, some people really dislike the smell of garlic) then imagine the cigarette smoke smells like that. It's a quick visualization you can practise every time you smell tobacco smoke and, over time, it'll lead to you really objecting to the smell and eventually to you finding the thought of smoking ever more unpleasant.

Reducing Alcohol Consumption

Like plenty of other things (such as chocolate and watching daytime TV talk shows), alcohol isn't bad for you in small quantities. In fact, numerous studies show that small amounts of alcohol help to keep you healthy and can prevent illnesses such as heart disease and stroke. For example, the Mediterranean diet, which includes red wine with many meals, is thought to be particularly healthy.

But you can have too much of a good thing and, unfortunately, in the case of alcohol you can very quickly start consuming too much without even realising it. The generally recognised safe upper limits for alcohol consumption are 21 units a week for men and 14 for women. As a guideline, the following drinks are very roughly equivalent to a unit of alcohol:

- ✓ A small shot of a spirit such as vodka.
- ✓ A small bottle, can, or half pint of regular strength beer.
- ✓ Two thirds of a small glass of regular strength wine.

Therefore, men can safely drink three small shots or three small bottles or cans of beer a day, or two small glasses of wine. Women should restrict themselves to a maximum of two small shots, or bottles or cans of beer, or about one and a third small glasses of wine a day. And indeed, at those levels you find the highest benefits for the circulation system.

Never consume all these units in one sitting, otherwise known as *binge drinking*, which can be very harmful indeed. For example, one study showed that binge-drinking patterns at the weekends in Northern Ireland led to higher blood pressure levels, and a higher incidence of heart attacks on Mondays and Tuesdays.

If you drink more than the recommended level of alcohol per week, you may want to consider cutting back on your alcohol consumption to reduce the risk of liver disease, increased blood pressure, stroke, damage to your immune system, and more. Limiting alcohol intake can also help to reduce excess weight, due to the fact that a unit of alcohol provides more or less 100 calories of energy, depending on the type of drink and its sugar/alcohol levels.

The following sections contain some ideas for visualizations to help reduce your alcohol intake.

Sleeping well without drinking

One of the biggest reasons people give for drinking excessively is that they have trouble sleeping or can't fall asleep without it.

I used to think this way too and regularly consumed up to 100 units of alcohol a week. Doing so didn't adversely affect my work, but come 5 p.m., I was ready for the pub, and spent much of my time (and money) there. Even after having children, I still drank several cans of beer during the evening at home, and mostly I told myself it was so that I could sleep well.

This conclusion wasn't surprising, because on the few days I didn't drink I was awake half the night (from alcohol withdrawal). Mostly, I wasn't drunk, I was just in a sort of subdued state in which I didn't get a lot done. And all I really ended up with was a beer belly and a headache every morning!

Well, eventually something had to be done. I didn't feel I was alcoholic, and so AA wasn't in my mind. Instead, for a while I tried swapping the beer for sleeping tablets (antihistamines or melatonin, or both), and that sort of worked, until I fancied a drink too. Hmm. Back to the drawing board.

The solution came when I discovered creative visualization and started to imagine the time I was wasting in my evenings just drinking. As I visualized more, I realised that I didn't like the beer very much and very soon, without using willpower or making any conscious decision, I noticed that I was only drinking a couple of cans a night – I was back within sensible drinking levels.

But as I visualized more about other areas of my life, I found that after a while I stopped drinking altogether, without noticing. Instead, as I took an interest in other things such as gardening, playing the guitar, spending more time with the children, swimming, or just watching TV, gradually beer simply edged out of my life.

Nowadays I still drink a little; perhaps a few units a week. And if you feel as if you're drinking too much, I believe you can achieve a similar reduction to mine through creative visualization. You may find the process begins naturally anyway as part of your overall visualization plans, or you can use exercises such as the following one to reduce your desire to drink.

Make a mind movie of an entire alcohol-free evening (flip to Chapter 9 for more on creating mind movies). You can keep it simple so that you don't have to invent lots of things to do; the point is only to see the movie through to the point at which you're asleep:

1. **Visualize yourself eating your evening meal and then watching TV.**

   If you prefer, see yourself tidying the garden or anything else you do in the evening.

2. **See yourself yawning.**

   You've had a busy day and you're tired.

3. **Start preparing for bed by following your normal routine.**

   See yourself going to bed, settling down under the covers, laying your head on the pillow, yawning again, and your mind starting to wander about as you drift gently off to sleep.

4. **Watch the movie run backwards all the way to the evening meal.**

   Now once more watch it play forwards again.

By repeating this visualization you prepare yourself for getting to sleep without the aid of alcohol. Then, when you choose not to drink (or it just happens), you find you can sleep more easily than you thought.

You may find that when you perform this exercise you can enhance its effectiveness by projecting the mind movie onto an imaginary screen outside of your body. This helps disassociate the movie from yourself and provides additional emotional distance, allowing you to better control the imagery.

One trick you can use to help with getting to sleep is quite simply to get up really early in the day to ensure that you're tired.

If you decide to use sleep medication, do so only for a short period while you re-establish your normal sleeping patterns, and always consult your doctor or a sleep therapist first.

Waking up healthy and hangover free

A powerful visualization that can help you to reduce alcohol intake is to imagine how good you're going to feel when you don't have a nasty headache and hangover in the morning. Excessive alcohol can also lead to needing to rush to the toilet in the morning (and sometimes throughout the night too), and you can be free of this hassle by reducing your consumption.

1. **Imagine that you're asleep in bed just before the alarm is due to go off.**

   Outside the sun is beginning to rise and the birds are singing.

2. **Hear the alarm, open your eyes, and turn it off.**

   Notice how clear your head feels. You've no headache and you actually feel good. More than that, your throat is moist (not dry), your vision is clear (not blurred), and you're in no rush to go to the toilet.

3. **Visualize how wonderful this feeling is.**

   Today is going to be excellent!

4. **Compare that feeling with a nasty hangover morning and notice the huge differences.**

   You even feel appetisingly hungry and ready for a good breakfast (and not nauseous). Boy are you glad that you didn't drink last night, and no way do you want to tonight either.

Building your mental pile of cash

How much does the alcohol you buy cost? I know that when I was drinking heavily I was spending the equivalent of about $75 a week or more (about £45 or €55), which was getting on for a yearly total of about $4,000 (approximately £2,500 or €3,000). Now I'm saving most of that cash (because I do drink a little). Try the following exercise as an additional incentive to reducing your alcohol consumption:

1. **Calculate how much you drink on a typical day and what that costs you.**

2. **Visualize that total as a pile of cash on the table in front of you.**

3. **Add another equal pile next to it, and another, and another, until you have seven of them, which is a week's worth of drinking.**

4. **Imagine stacking the cash up into a single pile and then place another beside it; that's two weeks' worth.**

5. **Place another two beside those piles and you have four weeks' worth of savings.**

6. **Merge all the cash so far into one heap and place another equal-sized one next to it; that's two months' worth of drinking.** ·

7. **Add another, and another, until you've added 12 more heaps.**

8. **Stare at the 13 heaps of cash piled up in front of you, a full year's worth of money saved.**

9. **Think about what you're going to spend all that money on.**

By the way, this exercise also works well with quitting smoking (not a cheap habit by any means), and cutting back on the amount of food you eat.

Replacing your cravings

One method I used to cut back on drinking was to replace an alcoholic beverage with a popsicle (or ice lolly as they are called in the UK). Because they are cold they can take quite a while to finish, and keep both your hands and mouth busy. If you choose the right variety (more fruit juice and less sugar), these treats can also contain far fewer calories than beer.

Substitution is a tried, tested, and successful technique, so you may find that creating a mental flash card of you eating a popsicle (or something similar) is beneficial each time you think of drinking alcohol. You can also use the pattern interrupt visualization technique (which I describe in Chapter 9) and actively imagine that you're reaching for a drink, only to switch to grabbing the alternative at the last minute. Simply choose an alternative food, drink, or action that you prefer and visualize on it.

Making it boring

When you think about it, alcohol is really quite boring. People who've been drinking may seem funny up to a point but then they can get on your nerves (especially if you aren't also drinking). And when you drink, all you're doing is taking a sedative drug that slows down your brain synapses, clouds your thoughts, interferes with your motor abilities, and messes with your memory. Yes, drinking can be quite boring indeed, so you may find that visualizing on these aspects helps you negatively reinforce against your desire to drink.

Eating Less

Losing weight is about more than eating less – it's also about eating healthier, lower-calorie foods. For example, you could eat the same amount of food as usual but change the kinds of food you eat and lose weight. Also, you could lose weight by eating smaller amounts of unhealthy foods – for example, two cheeseburgers a day and nothing else – but this clearly isn't good for your health.

So, as you've probably discovered by now if you've ever dieted, weight loss is complicated. Therefore in this section I address only the aspect of losing weight that is easiest to control with creative visualization, which is simply eating less. For a more comprehensive guide to weight loss, including eating more healthy foods, you may like to refer to Dieting For Dummies by Jane Kirby RD.

Although I succeeded in changing many things in my life through creative visualization, I have to hold my hands up here and admit that my weight is still a work in progress. That said, I have managed to drop a reasonable amount of weight over the last few years, and that amount looks like it's off permanently. However, I still have a fair bit more to go before I'm back to a sensible weight.

In life, some people do some things better than others, and I guess weight is my hardest thing to change. Nevertheless, I'm making progress, and you can do the same.

Feeling completely full

The stark truth is that the amount of food you eat is what makes you put on weight. Of course you can exercise to work off the calories but at the levels at which many people eat, you'd have to exercise most of the day to burn the calories off.

For example, each pound of weight comprises 3,600 calories. This means that a person weighing around 170 pounds (77 kilograms) burns off about 410 calories during a 30-minute, 6-mile run. In other words, to lose just 1 pound of weight, that person would have to run over 50 miles (80 kilometres) during the course of nearly 9 hours!

A typical quarter-pound burger contains about 515 calories, so just think how much easier eating 7 fewer burgers is than running 50 miles. I know which I'd rather choose. Therefore, whenever you can make yourself feel full, and consequently eat less, you're actually taking the easy route. If you don't and you over-eat, you have only two options: get fatter or exercise (a lot!).

Here's a visualization exercise you can practise after a meal to make yourself feel full more easily and avoid snacking:

1. **Think about the meal you've just eaten, now waiting to be digested in your stomach.**

   Realise how it contains all the calories that you need for the moment to be strong and full of energy.

2. **Place your hand over your stomach and rub it around.**

   Feel how you're completely full up and simply couldn't eat anything else. If you were to take even one more bite you would be bloated and feel fattened.

3. **Consider that many hours are going to pass before you become hungry again.**

   Know that you can continue until the next meal without feeling hungry and wanting to snack.

Savouring every bite

You can prepare yourself to eat less by making sure that you take your time and enjoy every bite. As you eat a meal, think about each mouthful and how enjoyable it is. The Mediterraneans are well known for spending a very long time over their meals and also for how healthy they are.

When you eat, 20 minutes is needed for the proteins to signal to your brain that you're starting to get full.

Make your meals last at least 20 to 30 minutes and you may well find that you can even stop before your plate's empty. Every bite uneaten is calories you don't have to burn off.

Viewing a slimmer you

Creative visualization is all about positive thinking. Don't burden yourself with the thought that you feel overweight; instead, whenever it comes to mind, instantly switch the thought to think, 'Yes, but I'm going to be slimmer'. Then visualize yourself into the future and imagine how great you're going to feel when you're slimmer. Know that being slimmer is the real you inside, and make sure that you have high positive expectations of being that way.

Every time you switch thoughts in this way, you help reinforce the neural pathways in your brain that lead to the actions you must take to achieve your goal of becoming thinner.

When you think about the future slimmer you, also visualize others noticing it too. Feel their appreciation that you managed to lose some weight and enjoy the fact that the effort was worthwhile and worked well enough so that even other people can tell.

Avoiding yo-yo dieting

You probably spent many years building up to your present weight (rarely does it happen overnight – that would be one huge midnight feast!). Similarly, losing this weight effectively is also going to take time to achieve; and half-starving yourself to death doesn't work.

Evidence suggests that fat cells have a kind of 'memory' and know how long they've existed, so that the newest ones go first and the oldest ones are the last to disappear. When you lose a lot of weight quickly, your body seems to go into a sort of shock (or famine) mode, and as soon as you start to eat normally again it piles on the pounds because it thinks you have to get back to your previous weight.

The problem is that when you initially lose fat, the cells that held it remain in place for a while in case they're needed again. Current research suggests that some time is needed before the unused fat cells are reabsorbed into the body, along with any memory of your previous weight. Only then, do you not balloon back up to a previous weight all too easily.

Therefore, imagining a long-term and sustained weight-loss programme is the only way to go, in conjunction with constant visualization. If you took ten years to put on the weight, would it be so bad if it took a similar amount of time to lose it, as long as you could be sure you wouldn't pile it on again?

This is the view I now take. I've lost 30 pounds (almost 14 kilos) of my more recent weight gain and I'm now trying to work on the older fat that's been there for some time. Little by little I'm pushing back the age of my fat. And so far, so good. The progress may be slow, but it's happening.

Chapter 11

Overcoming Fears and Phobias

· ·

· ·

*W*ith well over 500 different phobia names listed at The Phobia List website (www.phobialist.com), you may think that human beings are a highly neurotic species, and perhaps you're right! People certainly have a knack for getting into a 'to-do' over the seemingly smallest of things. Here are ten of the most common fears and phobias:

- ✔ Dentists
- ✔ Lifts
- ✔ Enclosed spaces
- ✔ Flying
- ✔ Germs
- ✔ Heights
- ✔ Injections
- ✔ Open Spaces
- ✔ Public Speaking
- ✔ Spiders

This list is quite long, and so you've probably been affected by at least one of these phobias – certainly I'm familiar with a few.

This chapter helps you come to terms with or get over any fears or phobias that are holding you back from enjoying life to the full. Through the power of creative visualization, you can minimise or even completely cure a phobia, and prevent it from bothering you again. The chapter introduces various techniques, and if I don't cover your specific phobia from clowns to teapots (or teapot-wearing clowns), you can easily modify one or more of the exercises to suit your personal situation.

Using the Anxiety Meter

The first step towards curing a fear or phobia is to acknowledge that you have it.

If dentists frighten you but you're in denial and 'never get round to going', this chapter isn't going to help you. But if you're prepared to admit any phobias to yourself, you can certainly work on relieving them.

Once you've admitted to having a specific fear or phobia, you need to ascertain just how bad it is.

Select a fear or phobia that's giving you concern and then quickly visualize about how it makes you feel. Now look at the meter in Figure 11-1 and decide where the needle is when you think of the fear or the phobia. The figure shows a VU meter, more commonly used to measure the volume level of sound in recording studios and radio or TV stations (with VU standing for Volume Units). But in this case, the meter measures your level of anxiety brought on by a phobia, from –20, which is the least anxious and indicates that you aren't at all concerned, to +3, which is the most anxious you can be. Imagine that the far right section is red, indicating that a fear is causing you a problem, and that the rest of the meter to the left of the 0 is white.

Figure 11-1:
An anxiety meter for measuring the effect of a phobia.

When you decide where the anxiety needle is pointing, make a mental note and keep that level in your mind's eye. This reading is the baseline against which you can test the effectiveness of the exercises in this chapter.

Most people who are bothered by a phobia, register their anxiety level as somewhere between about –2 and +3. Any less than that and you're probably not that concerned, but you do find the phobia a nuisance. Your main goal, however, is to move the needle out of the red (that is, to a position below 0). If you can succeed in that, you've minimised your fear or phobia. Then you simply need to see how much farther to the left you can move the needle to continue alleviating the problem.

Preparing to Do Battle with Your Fear

Before you can rid yourself of a fear or anxiety you first need to acknowledge its existence. If you have a phobia, for example, but try to ignore the fact as part of your strategy for dealing with it, how can you attack it head on and permanently remove the problem?

Therefore, in this section you examine your fears and phobias and select any that are causing your problems. You then accept the fact that they are interfering with your life, and choose to vanquish them.

Having taken the two steps of acknowledgement of a problem and having the desire to be rid of it, you then discover the good news that you can address your fears through creative visualization, and I introduce some powerful techniques to help you do this.

Wanting the problem gone

If you don't like suffering from a fear or phobia, simply getting upset or angry doesn't help you; instead, you must actively want the problem gone from your life. This firm desire for riddance plants the seed of recovery and provides the motivation to increase that desire until the problem is no longer an issue.

To help get this idea fixed in your mind, repeat some of the following positive affirmations, filling in the blanks with your own problem (and yes, I've deliberately made you mention the problem several times because first you need to acknowledge the problem, and then you can focus on solutions):

✔ I acknowledge that I have a fear or phobia.

✔ I no longer want this fear to unduly affect me.

✔ I hate being held back by my problem.

✔ My fear isn't rational and I want it gone.

✔ I intend to rid myself of my phobia.

Knowing that you can be free from the fear

To be rid of your fear or phobia, you need to make yourself clearly aware that this aim is, in fact, achievable. Recall a time when you didn't suffer from the problem. You know the fear or phobia didn't always exist, and in the same way you know that it can (and will) be gone, if you visualize on it.

Try some of the following affirmations:

✔ Having a fear/phobia isn't my natural condition.

✔ I know that I can be rid of my problem.

✔ Reducing and removing fears and phobias is proven to work.

✔ Millions of others have quashed similar problems.

✔ Getting rid of my fears is easy with creative visualization.

Repeat the affirmations in this section and the preceding one frequently so that they become integrated into your psyche and you and your unconscious mind believe them. You're preparing yourself for actively dealing with the fear or phobia.

Seeing how you feel when the fear is gone

Take a moment to consider how you're going to feel when you're rid of your fear or phobia.

Imagine how being free of the fear or phobia is going to benefit your future life. For example, if you diminish any phobia of spiders or other such creatures, you can take up gardening, clear out the garden shed or dirty garage, take walks in the country or woodland, and perhaps even go camping. If you're afraid of driving, losing that fear enables the world to open up to you and you can go anywhere without taxis, public transport, or relying on friends and family to drive you. And losing a fear of heights lets you visit high-rise sky-scrapers, stand next to the railings and take in wonderful views while sightseeing, and so on.

Whatever your problem, visualize all the things you can (and will) do when the fear's gone, and feel how much you enjoy your new freedom.

Turning the Issue into a Non-Issue

To vanquish a phobia or fear you need to make it insignificant, to remove any importance it has for you. Doing so is far stronger psychologically than trying to use brute force to confront the fear while it still seems huge to you. This section provides several exercises for diminishing the importance of your fear.

Creating positivity points

You can use a combined physical and mental visualization approach to instantly draw in inner help whenever you become anxious. This technique involves assigning emotions and feelings to parts of your body, which you then touch in order to recall them.

Figure 11-2 shows the palm of a left hand upon which four positivity points (A to D) are highlighted. Sometimes therapists also refer to these as anchors. In the following visualization exercise you assign positive feelings to these points (most people are unlikely to touch locations such as the first segment of each finger very often, making them ideal points to focus on):

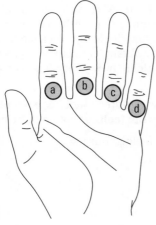

Figure 11-2:
A hand showing four positivity points for quickly recalling feelings and emotions.

1. **Touch your right pointing finger to position A – or gently squeeze it between your thumb and finger – and think of something that gives you a great sense of calm.**

   It may be a piece of music, a location such as a church or a wilderness, a poem you love, or anything else you like, as long as the feeling is strong. If you're *claustrophobic* (afraid of closed spaces), imagine somewhere with plenty of space. If *agoraphobic* (afraid of open spaces), maybe think of a place you feel secure, and so on. Remain focused on that feeling for a while and all the time notice your finger touching the positivity point.

2. **Forget that feeling, clear your mind, and touch positivity point B while you think of a situation in which you feel totally in control and fully competent.**

   The place may be in the kitchen preparing a meal, in front of a computer programming or typing, behind the wheel of a car driving, or chairing a meeting (although all these can also be phobias for some people). Choose your best control situation and think of how it makes you feel, and the way you lose any anxiety and are able to make decisions easily and act decisively. At the same time, be well aware of your finger touching the positivity point.

3. **Empty your head of thoughts, move your finger to touch point C, and think about a time when you were at your most creative.**

   Perhaps you wrote a poem, song, or piece of music of which you're proud. Or maybe you won a cookery or photography contest. Then again perhaps you're in the zone while sketching. Even if you don't think of yourself as a creative person, you are. Humans are creative beings. Just think of something you like to do and are good at. And keep concentrating on what makes you proud for a few moments while feeling your finger touching the positivity point.

4. **Clear your mind again and move your finger to point D as you recall something or someone that makes you smile.**

   It may be a joke you recently heard, a television show you enjoy, a particular comedian, or simply spending time with friends. Or you may find that participating in a sport or activity brings on a smile, or playing a musical instrument does it for you. Again, concentrate on whatever easily comes to mind while also noticing how your finger is touching the positivity point.

5. **Empty your mind and spend a few minutes touching each of your positivity points and recalling the specific feeling that each brings.**

   In the case of this exercise, you're feeling four Cs:

   - Calmness: position A
   - Control: position B
   - Creativity: position C
   - Comedy: position D

6. **Keep touching each point until you can easily recall the feelings on demand.**

Thereafter you can touch whichever point you need to quickly induce the response you want to deal with the anxiety caused by confronting your fear or phobia. You can use these positivity points in a wide variety of other situations as well.

You have eight more finger segments on your left hand to which you can attach other feelings and emotions, such as love, motivation, and so on, along with two more segments on your thumb and the centre of your palm. And your right hand contains another 15 points. With both hands, that's 30 different feelings and emotions you can train yourself to recall on demand. Because this book is about creative visualization, I leave it up to you to use your creativity to allocate these associations yourself according to how you feel that they're likely to benefit you the best.

Making your fear ridiculous

The behaviour therapist Joseph Wolpe was famed for his research on reciprocal inhibition, in which fears can be substituted with sexual arousal, relaxation, hunger, thirst, and even laughter. The idea is to evoke a feeling or response that is incompatible with a feeling of anxiety, which results in inhibiting it.

For example, being afraid of something ridiculous isn't easy; you're more likely to laugh or be scornful. You can employ creative visualization to help make fears and phobias seem ridiculous, and so diminish the effect that they have on you.

The idea is to make the fear seem stupid, senseless, or ridiculous. For example, you can visualize a spider as being dressed in a clown costume with crossed eyes, or a snake being like the hapless reptile in the Disney animated film *Robin Hood*.

In ancient times, people believed that angry gods caused thunder and lightning, so if storms scare you, imagine a feud between two such deities (say Thor and Zeus – the fact that one's Scandinavian and the other Greek simply makes the whole situation even more ludicrous!). Visualize them fighting over something as stupid as one having thrown a custard pie in the other's face.

Harry Potter fans will recall the boggart, a shape-shifting being that takes on the form of its intended victim's worst fear, and which can be vanquished by imagining it as something ridiculous, while saying the charm, 'Riddikulus.' If you like you can try visualizing your fear as a boggart and then disposing of it in the same way.

Not all phobias can fit into the 'making them ridiculous' category (the following section may be more helpful for cases in which the fear looms large in size to you). But if you can make a fear seem silly, meditate for a while on just how dumb you can make the fear appear. And give yourself an anxiety meter check afterwards to see whether the needle has moved more to the left (check out the earlier section 'Using the Anxiety Meter').

Reducing the size of the fear

Many fears and phobias can seem large in size to you, which makes them appear more frightening and harder to tackle. By reducing the fear in size in your mind's eye you can diminish its effect on you. This technique doesn't work on every fear and phobia, but can help you with many.

If you fear injections, visualize that the needle on the end of the syringe is very small already. Now imagine it becoming thinner and thinner until it's only a few molecules wide. Then make it smaller still, until it measures only a few atoms in width. At that size, when the needle's inserted it easily squeezes past all the other atoms in your skin, gently pushing them to one side without hurting.

Research into injection (and blood taking) phobia shows that you don't diminish the fear by looking away. I know that this finding seems counter-intuitive, but in fact you have the most anticipation and anxiety when you can't see what's going on. So instead, visualize yourself looking down at a part of your skin near the site where the needle is going to be inserted, but not so near that you can see it directly. Focus on that area of skin and imagine seeing the syringe only out of the corner of your eye. You can't see what's going on in detail, but you can tell when the needle is inserted and when it's removed – all the time remaining fixated on your chosen area of skin.

Now, when you have to go for a blood test or injection in real life you can use these same two techniques to minimise your anxiety levels substantially. Take a look at your imaginary anxiety meter from the earlier section 'Using the Anxiety Meter'; perhaps it's moved farther to the left.

Imagining that you like what you fear

Imagining that, in fact, you like the thing you fear can help tackle some phobias.

If you're afraid of cats or dogs, you may think that they can sense this fear (and sometimes they can). But by liking them, they don't pick up any bad vibes from you and tend to leave you alone.

Of course, you can't use this technique on all phobias – you don't want to like cancer, for example. But you can choose to like (or imagine that you like) things such as animals and insects, dentists, and public speaking.

Combine a little willpower, a strong imagination, and your hand positivity points (see the earlier section 'Creating positivity points'), and you really can visualize your problem as something you like. I leave the details to your creativity and specific fear, but after a few times of doing this exercise, you can find that you've reduced your fear.

After trying this exercise, check your imaginary anxiety level (from the earlier section 'Using the Anxiety Meter') afterwards. The needle may well have moved to the left. Continuing to repeat the exercise and checking your meter level each time, sees the needle moving even farther left.

Visualizing the fear already gone

In the earlier section 'Seeing how you feel when the fear is gone', I suggest that you visualize all the things you can do when your fear or phobia has disappeared. In this section, you visualize that your problem actually has gone and that it no longer affects you.

Briefly recall the problem you want to tackle, and then visualize that you've just realised that it's no longer an issue. Use your imagination to the full, and deeply experience how the fear doesn't affect you any more. Doing so is quite easy because you're not in the presence of your fear or phobia right now – it's only in your imagination, and therefore your imagination can choose not to see the imaginary fear as a problem at all.

Doing this exercise helps your unconscious mind to draw encouragement and know how to help you when you encounter the problem in real life. Your unconscious does its best to bring you the same feeling of the phobia being a non-issue as you consciously imagine it to be.

Use your positivity points to aid this visualization (flip to the earlier section 'Creating positivity points' for more details).

After completing this visualization, take a moment to see how your anxiety meter is doing. I hope that the needle has moved over to the left, but how far? Compare it to your baseline reading from 'Using the Anxiety Meter' earlier in this chapter.

If your reading is still in the meter's red zone, don't worry. Keep working through this chapter's exercises, repeating them again and again until you get the needle as close as you can to the meter's white zone.

That's your first major hurdle, and after you achieve it you simply have to keep on pushing the needle leftwards until it slips out of the red and into the white zone.

Overcoming the Problem

The previous sections guide you through acknowledging your problem and visualizing turning it into a non-issue. When you feel adequately prepared, you need to dig a little deeper to weed out and remove the fear or phobia from your life. In this section, you aim to get your anxiety meter's needle right out of the red zone (read the earlier section 'Using the Anxiety Meter' if you haven't already).

Confronting the problem head on

The reason people acquire phobias so easily is that they perform a useful function. For example, in parts of the world where spiders and snakes are poisonous, a phobia ensures that you try to keep well away from the beasties to avoid harm. But a phobia can become too strong and prevent you from functioning properly, particularly when it's about something relatively harmless or even benevolent, such as dentists.

One way of dealing with such a problem is to visualize around your phobia and understand that you have it because your unconscious mind thinks that you need protection against something. Generally, your unconscious mind works to protect you and is always looking out for your best interests. But it works at quite a basic level and doesn't have the reasoning ability of your conscious mind.

Visualize thanking your unconscious for bringing this problem to your attention and guarding you from potential danger. Then imagine telling your unconscious that it's done a great job, but now it doesn't need to maintain the phobia any more. Tell it that you're going to be mindful and take control over the problem yourself, and promise that you'll be careful. Mean what you say so that your unconscious believes you.

Now visualize confronting your phobia. Imagine telling it that its job is done now and you're letting it go. Say that you're releasing it immediately and that it can leave and go elsewhere. Now turn your attention away from the phobia and leave it to go away in its own time.

So, how's your anxiety meter doing? Is the needle now out of the red zone? In some cases the preceding exercise is sufficient to shift the needle more than halfway to the left.

Imagining the fear never existed

What if you never had the phobia or fear in the first place? Wouldn't that be the best of all possible worlds? It never bothered you or held you back, and you don't have to work at making it disappear.

Visualize yourself in the past, present, and future, and in all cases without the problem. See yourself in a short life-movie from being a baby, through growing into a child, a teenager, a young adult, middle age, and retirement. Note that at all times the phobia was never present. In fact, you're noting nothing. I know it's like saying 'Don't think of Donald Duck' (because that very sentence causes you to do so), but as you visualize, note that your fear is not there in your movie – because it's your movie that you just created and so the fear really doesn't exist in it. Realise that you're problem free, have been all your life, and always will be.

Watching the scary thing run away

Instead of being afraid of something, try letting it be afraid of you.

Small creatures such as cats and dogs, insects and spiders, are generally a lot more scared of you than you are of them, and are used to running away from potential danger (at least the undomesticated ones anyway).

Visualize the root cause of your problem running away from you whenever you approach it. If the fear is of a creature, see it scrambling away from you as fast as possible because it's truly terrified of you. If the fear is something like germs or cancer, visualize them trying to get away from you because your body is too strong. Or imagine thunder and lightning heading off away from you in another direction to terrify someone else who may be scared of them (unlike you).

You can't apply this exercise to all fears and phobias, but you can address many in this way. And each time you see your fear running for the hills in your mind's eye, you have one bit less anxiety to feel in the future.

Denying your fear any nourishment

If you deny your fear any sustenance, it may well simply give up and die on its own.

Imagine that the root of your problem is like a nasty, stubborn weed that you want rid of but whose roots go way down so that you can't easily uproot it. You can, however, deny it any food, water, and sunlight by putting a dark plastic box over it for a week or two. Visualize your phobia withering away and then lift up the box and see that it's shrivelled up into a mass of brown and grey. Now, simply pull it up with a pitchfork and drop into the bin.

Your fear or phobia is now a thing of the past and it can't bother you again.

Finding the positive in what you fear

One effective way of dealing with a phobia is to turn it upside down and examine its possible positives.

Spiders eat flies and other irritating insects. Dentists perform an important health role, lifts take you quickly to different floors, planes to different cities and countries, and even vomit is good because it removes contaminants and irritants from your system.

Consider for a minute whether your problem has any positives. To see that you can find a positive aspect for almost everything, I select one of the most common and deepest phobias: the fear of death. Even death has positives, because otherwise far too many people would be in the world and everyone would starve. Also, religious people can visualize the afterlife they can expect. From an evolutionary point of view, without death, species wouldn't develop and humans wouldn't exist. You can find positives about any fear or phobia, if you think them over.

Take a look at your anxiety meter (that I describe in 'Using the Anxiety Meter' earlier in this chapter) and see where the needle points. I hope that it's noticeably within the white area now, possibly even to the left of the −1 position. But if you're still in the red, that's okay. Keep on using the techniques in this chapter to work on your fear. If you do, I'm convinced that you *will* succeed.

If the anxiety needle is on the boundary between red and white, visualize giving the meter a quick tap and nudge the needle over. Go on, you can do it.

Using the exercises in this section, you can take the anxiety meter out of the red zone so that your fear or phobia is no longer a problem to you. Even though the fear may still exist and even feature in your mind, the problem aspect of it is now vastly reduced.

Focusing on the Future

Working through the visualization exercises in the preceding sections helps you to reduce the intensity of your fear or phobia problem down to a manageable level. The object of this section is to reduce that intensity even further, and to prevent the fear or phobia from ever recurring in the future.

To do so, you travel backwards and forwards in time to see your before and after feelings regarding the problem, and you set up your own mental department of immigration and border guards to keep the phobia from ever returning.

Going forwards in time

Take a trip into the future with the knowledge that you're working on beating your fear or phobia.

In this visualization, you use a mental time machine to go forward to the next time you visualize on your phobia, whether that's later today, tomorrow, or next week:

1. **Think about how much less the fear affects you now.**

2. **Imagine the needle of your anxiety meter (from the earlier section 'Using the Anxiety Meter') moving a notch to the left.**

3. **Jump ahead to the session after that and see how much better you then feel.**

4. **Visualize that the needle is yet another notch leftwards.**

5. **Keep on going until the needle is all the way to the left and you see that you no longer have any thoughts about the phobia; the fear has entirely evaporated and absolutely nothing bothers you about it.**

Make sure that you perform these additional sessions so that your imagined future becomes your true future. If things go well, move the anxiety meter needle two or more notches to the left each time (if you can), so that you don't have to perform more exercises than necessary.

Looking back and laughing

Laughter is always a good cure for any problem: it reduces anxiety and releases feelings of relief. So get in the mood for a good laugh as you prepare for the following exercise:

1. **Use your time machine from the preceding section to move yourself forward to a point in time at which your fear or phobia is completely gone.**

2. **Make that time point your 'now', and pause for a few seconds.**

3. **Use the time machine to travel back into the past to the time when the problem affected you.**

4. **Feel how silly the fear seems as you get closer to it, and how ridiculous you were being hung up over such a stupid thing.**

5. **Laugh out loud (with, not at yourself) at how foolish you were, and at how glad you are that the problem no longer affects you.**

6. **Bring yourself back to your future and continue to laugh as you reflect on how the whole situation was a big to-do over nothing.**

7. **Let go of your adjusted timescale and allow yourself to return back to the real now.**

This exercise may seem a little confusing (but probably no more so than the *Back to the Future* films!), but it serves the purpose of letting you laugh at your problem from a detached viewpoint in which the issue doesn't exist anymore. You've now integrated this feeling into your psyche and your unconscious mind is primed to take things from here.

Seeing all you can now do without the problem

When you feel that fear is no longer an unmanageable problem (after working through the exercises in the preceding sections), you can actively start to look at yourself, your life, and what you're able to do now.

All you need to do is relax and consider all the things you can now do without the problem on your back or in your way, and how these things are going to become ever easier and more enjoyable from now on.

If you were scared of public speaking and have a wedding coming up at which you must speak, just think how much easier that speech is going to be to give. You're going to be able to enjoy it and deliver it well, so that the wedding dinner is enjoyed and remembered (for good reasons) by all.

If your fear of failure has been holding you back from starting out on a major project, now you can undertake it – and enjoy when it comes to fruition.

Mental flash cards for minimising fears and phobias

Here are a few mental flash cards to help counter fears and phobias, and so limit their effect on you:

✔ **Dressing it up absurdly:** Dress your phobia or the thing that causes it in strange clothes. Maybe as a clown, in a mankini, or another bizarre item of clothing. Doing so helps to ridicule it so that you laugh and are less afraid.

✔ **Making it irrelevant:** Turn your phobia or its cause into something entirely unrelated and irrelevant such as a fish, golf ball, or a sneeze. The weirder and stupider the thing, the less of an adverse effect it can have.

✔ **Wearing an invisible force field:** Switch on your invisible force field through which only light and air can pass. The field is so strong and supportive that bullets can't even get through, and yet it's so light that if you fell off a tall building you'd just float gently to the ground. With the field on, the cause of your phobia can't bother you in any way.

✔ **Smiling whenever you think of it:** Just smile. That's all. Whenever the phobia or fear comes to mind, simply smile and your anxiety decreases.

✔ **Feeling as powerful as a superhero:** Be Superman or another superhero. You're almost infinitely strong and capable of anything. No puny phobia can have any effect on you.

Denying your fear a visa

When you feel that your fear or phobia is so well managed that you've pretty much eradicated it, you may want to use the following exercise and the one in the subsequent section to build a block in your mind against it ever returning.

Imagine that all ideas and thoughts can only get into your mind if you let them. Your positive thoughts are like the US and the UK and you have a reciprocal agreement whereby an advance visa isn't required for citizens of each country to travel to the other. But fears and phobias are from a non-friendly country and they absolutely require a visa before you let them in.

Yes, the exercise seems far-fetched, but the unconscious mind loves weird and wonderful stuff and takes notice of these kinds of ideas because they're so out of the ordinary. That's why I like to include highly creative exercises now and then; your unconscious mind appreciates and makes use of them.

Maintaining a border patrol

The preceding section helps you set up a 'legal' method for banishing fears and phobias. Now you need to stop any of those pesky negative thoughts from sneaking into your mind 'illegally'.

Visualize that your unconscious mind is like a big brain-shaped island, surrounded by the sea, and with border patrols and guards spaced out at frequent intervals around the island. Now imagine any fears or phobias that try to swim ashore or pull up in boats are taken or towed away by the coastguard back to their own islands far, far away. In your mind's eye understand that you have the most effective border agency that's ever existed, and not a single problem thought can ever get through.

Testing Your Cure

When you feel that you've carried out all the necessary preparatory visualization work on tackling your fear or phobia (as I describe in the preceding sections), you can start mentally practising dealing with it.

This section uses the example of someone who's afraid of lifts. But whatever your issue, adapt the situation as necessary and use the following exercise as an illustration of how to encounter your banished problem in visualization form, so that you can later do so in real life:

1. **Imagine that you're with a friend you know and trust, and you're both about to enter a skyscraper where you need to get to the top floor.**

   Stand outside the building with your supportive friend and take a couple of deep breaths.

2. **Touch your four positivity points in turn (see the earlier section 'Creating positivity points').**

   Each time, feel the sensations of calmness, control, creativity, and comedy well up as you do so. Know that you can instantly bring any of them to the forefront of your mind whenever you touch its positivity point.

3. **Enter the building and, as the pair of you head towards the lifts, call up your anxiety meter (which I describe in the earlier section 'Using the Anxiety Meter').**

   Note where the needle is pointing. While you try to feel calm and unstressed (and use your positivity points), visualize pushing the needle leftwards as far as you can. Wait until the needle is out of the red zone.

4. **Press the button in front of you to call the lift, and when the doors open quickly enter with your friend and press the top-floor button.**

   Keep calm and continue to use your positivity points as necessary. As the lift starts to move you can chat with your friend if you like, or be silent. Your friend knows your problem and is simply there to support you. Feel how the lift moves swiftly and steadily and how it doesn't bother you, and notice how your anxiety meter is to the left, way out of the red zone. All the time continue to think calm and happy thoughts and use your positivity points whenever you need to.

5. **Allow your friend to get off when you get to the top floor, but remain inside yourself, press the street-level button, and travel down.**

   Notice how the journey's even easier than with your friend beside you because you're travelling in an lift for the second time in a few minutes, and your anxiety meter has moved farther to the left of the dial.

6. **Wait for your friend to follow you down when you get to the bottom, and imagine how your friend feels in there.**

   The answer is: he feels absolutely nothing. No phobia. No fear. Just like you. Notice that your anxiety meter's needle is floating all the way over to the left.

By imagining a friend, you have somebody you can turn to if you feel too anxious. But friend or not, you're now ready to beat whatever your phobia is in real life, and you need to perform the visualization exercise for real.

You may not even need a friend with you, having visualized one so successfully, but if you have a willing friend, by all means take him too.

Chapter 12

Fostering Strong Relationships

Getting on with other people is sometimes the easiest and sometimes the hardest of things to do. But easy or difficult, relationships are vitally important. Humans are social creatures who love to live in tribes, whether in the forest or desert, or in towns and cities. All cultures feature hierarchies of power and social formalities, from the smallest tribal unit – the family – all the way up to huge organisations such as the European Community and the United Nations.

Wherever you go and whatever you do, you interact with people: those you have power over and those who have power over you; those you teach and those who teach you; those who guide you spiritually and those who entertain you; those you work with and those who work for you; and so on. And you build relationships with all the people you come into contact with most frequently, or with whom you choose to spend your time.

For some people, fostering strong relationships comes naturally, but for the rest the process takes a little work, particularly if you're shy or of a nervous disposition. So this chapter discusses a range of things you can do to help improve your relationships with other people and enjoy life more fully when spending it in their company.

Avoiding and Handling Conflict

Conflict often occurs when one person wants to do one thing and another wants to do something else. It can happen when people have differing points of view about something or someone, and also arises when people have something on their mind that interferes with their ability to think rationally.

More precisely, conflict can result from a perceived breach of faith or trust, an unresolved disagreement that escalates to an emotional level, a miscommunication leading to unclear expectations, personality clashes, ego problems, and so on. Conflict may also arise when one person has a clear strategy and another doesn't but attacks the strategy to boost her own image. This is known as an *envious attack*, a commonly used therapeutic phrase.

But whatever the reason, being able to manage conflict well allows you to progress with your own plans with the minimum of obstruction. Reducing the negative effects of conflict in turn reduces your stress levels and in this section I provide strategies you can adopt for handling conflict effectively.

Knowing that arguments seldom solve anything

The end result of argument – as opposed to rational discussion and debate – is usually nothing more than raised blood pressure, anger, hurt feelings, and animosity. Very little else is ever achieved through arguing. So why do people do it so much? The main reason seems to be that people are adamant about getting their point of view across, and they honestly think that they're trying to achieve something positive.

When you argue you have an overwhelming sense that you're right and the other person is wrong, and therefore that somehow gives you the right to continue arguing and escalate the row further. You feel that you have an overriding mission to beat the other side over the head until the person submits which, of course, rarely happens – because you both feel the same way! And on it goes until one or the other side loses his or her temper and things are said that really shouldn't have been said. Sometimes, objects are thrown, violence ensues, along with melodramatic exits and door slammings.

Not only does this process apply to individuals, but also to groups and even entire nations, where arguments over border territory and the like have led to many a bloody war. At the end of which, after all the fighting is over, the borders often remain as they were initially.

Tact, diplomacy, and negotiation easily beat arguing when you want to achieve something concrete. When tempted to argue, the sooner you remember that fact, the quicker you resolve a difficult situation and prevent it from escalating and potentially getting out of hand.

If you find yourself seemingly unavoidably drawn into arguments, you can help prevent this happening and mitigate the results by practising the following visualization exercise, which emphasises the futility of arguing:

1. **Imagine a situation in which you've argued with someone else enough that one or other (or both of you) raised your voice and started to get angry.**

   Hold that thought. Freeze-frame the pair of you in your mind's eye and take in the situation. Both of you are cross and you both feel equally justified in your side of the argument.

2. **Fast-forward to a point after this moment where you're both getting along just fine.**

   Freeze-frame that moment.

3. **Flick back and forth between the two scenes. What can you notice that's different?**

   In the second scene, was the subject of the argument resolved one way or another? If not, what happened? Most likely you both cooled off over a period of hours or days and let the topic slide. You also probably both still hold the same views and therefore they may become a bone of contention in the future and lead to another pointless argument. So the difference between the two situations is probably only that in one you're arguing and in the other you're not. You wasted your time, and both of you became upset but to no effect.

Avoiding quarrelling

Obviously, the best thing is to avoid arguing in the first place, and you can achieve this aim in a number of ways.

You can use the following visualization exercise to prepare yourself for when your hackles may be raised so that you don't immediately fall into the knee-jerk argument response and, instead, take a more logical and relaxed view of the situation:

1. **Imagine that someone makes you angry.**

   Perhaps the person says something to you with which you strongly disagree, or makes a disparaging comment about you, someone, or something you like, or is rude to you or another person. Sense how this behaviour makes you angry and that you simply aren't going to put up with such aggression, rudeness, or nonsense. Note that your blood pressure rises along with the feeling in your head that says you must assert your opinion.

2. **Take a deep breath in and then breathe out as slowly and steadily as you can.**

   Visualize telling yourself that you choose not to be angered or engaged by this person. The other person expects you to respond by arguing and you're going to do just the opposite. A quarrel achieves nothing, even when you feel that you've been offended or slandered; and now is definitely *not* the time to do or say anything rash.

3. **Hold that feeling, or collection of thoughts, as you breathe slowly in and out.**

   Visualize placing the fingers of one hand over your other wrist and feel your pulse starting to slow back down. Understand that better and more effective ways exist of dealing with whatever got your goat, and that in due course you're going to make a decision about how to approach the issue.

4. **Try the exercise with a different person you may argue with and about a different subject.**

   Cover the main situations, subjects, and feelings that may draw you into an argument and perform the same calming exercise for each.

This exercise is very useful for preparing yourself for when an argument suddenly arises out of the blue, and for dealing with or minimising it. But you can often avoid the possibility of a quarrel happening altogether by taking appropriate steps.

To help with this aim, visualize you and the other person in this pre-discussion meeting, with your inner self out of your body watching the two of you. Sense the tension and difficulty, but also note the intention of you both to resolve the conflict. See how you both manage to discuss things rationally and come to an agreement about how you're going to approach discussing the bone of contention. Imagine a positive outcome for both sides and feel the relief in all concerned.

Managing opposing views or interests

So how do you manage views that are so opposite as to cause arguments? Well, the simplest solution is to try to find some common ground and work from there.

In life things are rarely as cut and dried as they appear and you can almost always achieve compromises. But seeing what these compromises may be isn't always easy. Examining the objectives of two people with differing viewpoints, however, allows you to determine one or more mutual goals and then use them as starting points for discussion.

For example, in Figure 12-1, Alice and Bob are two jigsaw puzzle pieces that are compatible with each other. The pieces would slot into place if only Alice's and Bob's objectives weren't incompatible. Their opposing objectives are causing conflict between the two of them, and so the two pairs of jigsaw pieces can't be connected.

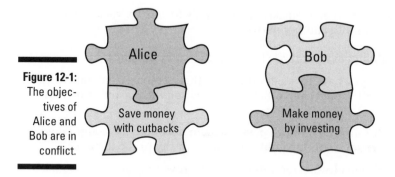

Figure 12-1:
The objec-
tives of
Alice and
Bob are in
conflict.

Alice is of the opinion that she can help her company through the current dif-ficult economic climate by making a number of cutbacks that save money. Bob, on the other hand, wants an increase in expenditure to fund some opportuni-ties he's identified that may result in greater revenue for the company.

These two goals are difficult to reconcile, until the common goal of greater efficiency is identified (as shown in Figure 12-2). They discover that the money Alice wants to save the company is achievable by, for example, increasing the efficiency of the production line by 10 per cent; and buying in some new machinery that Bob sourced can accomplish this aim.

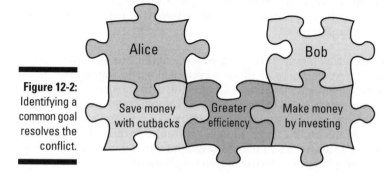

Figure 12-2:
Identifying a
common goal
resolves the
conflict.

All right, this analogy is highly simplified, but it illustrates the point. If you and another person have a conflict of interest or any other disagreement, work together on finding common goals on which you agree, and then work back from these goals to find acceptable compromises. Sometimes this type of collaboration results in the surfacing of brand new ideas, which end up being optimal for both of you – a genuine win-win situation.

To help this process come quickly and naturally to you, try visualizing the conflict you have with another person:

1. **Think about your point of view, and the other person's.**

   Neither of you have to accept that the other person's right, but you *do* have to understand each other's opinions and the reasoning behind them.

2. **Reflect for a while on both positions and now imagine a mutual goal in the form of a shining gold star, far, far away in the distance.**

   The star's minute and yet it dazzles you, preventing you from seeing it clearly. But it continues to come slowly towards you, and you know that you're soon going to see the true nature of the goal.

3. **Feel reassured that you now have an answer to the problem, even though you don't yet know precisely what it is.**

   The important thing is that the solution exists.

4. **Allow the golden glow of the solution to begin to envelop you and feel the power of creativity well up inside yourself.**

   Tell your unconscious mind that you're ready for the solution to be revealed, and relax.

By practising this exercise a few times, you build the required neural pathways in your brain for general problem solving around conflict areas, and are ready to come up with compromises and alternatives that may be acceptable to you and the other person.

Sometimes, however, you may have to agree to disagree. For example, consider the stances that members of opposing political parties often take. Rarely do you see politicians from the left agreeing with those on the right, because their viewpoints seem irreconcilable. As a consequence, politicians have to agree to disagree. They make their points to the voters and let them decide. The politicians are then judged by how they perform and voted into or out of office (or at least that's the theory behind democracy – in practice, as in life, things are always somewhat more complicated).

Therefore, if you can't find a way to agree, be prepared to respect another person's choices and opinions when they're different to yours. Okay, you may have a long-term goal of trying to persuade someone (or people who follow that person), but arguing gets you nowhere. So try repeating the following affirmations from time to time to guard against getting het up:

- ✔ I may disagree with them, but other people are entitled to their opinions.
- ✔ I have my opinions but other people's viewpoints are as valid as my own.
- ✔ I'm not offended by anyone's thoughts but my own.
- ✔ I choose not to be negatively affected by anyone else's opinions.

Additionally, you can become more secure about yourself and your thoughts with the following affirmations:

- ✔ I don't need other people to think the same as me.
- ✔ I don't need to change anyone else's mind.
- ✔ I accept that my opinions and beliefs may not always be correct.
- ✔ I know that life would be boring if everyone thought the same.

Affirmations are processed by the speech and language portions of your brain. Creative visualization works best when many different parts of your brain are brought into play – so affirmations provide positive enhancement for visualizations.

To best enhance your affirmations, imagine yourself from a third person's point of view, and see how completely you mean every word that you say. Just by looking at yourself you can see, for example that you truly aren't offended by other people, and that you wholly understand that you don't need to always be correct.

Be creative whenever you repeat your affirmations, and try to accompany the words with matching imagery, and even other senses if you can, such as smells or sounds. That way your unconscious mind will pay even greater attention and you'll remember the affirmations for longer and the results will be stronger.

These affirmations lead directly on to the next section, in which the goal is to let go of needing always to be right.

Reducing your need to be right

You don't always have to be right – even when you are! Being right isn't that important really. In fact, getting on with people is much more important than being right about something, don't you agree?

Think back to the last few arguments you had. What was the most fundamental thing about them? If you're like me, and probably most people, you were trying to prove a point. You probably started by saying something that the other person objected to or disagreed with, or the other person said something to which you took exception, and one or the other of you simply tried to correct what you saw as the other person being wrong. But then the other person felt the first person was wrong for responding in this way, and so it escalated.

But if you don't feel the need to be right, these kinds of spats don't occur because you simply don't rise to the bait. If you're happy to be wrong (and probably to admit so), or you don't care that the other person thinks you're in the wrong when you believe you're in the right, you can shrug off a comment.

You can almost always ignore what someone says or give a non-committal response; just don't say the disrespectful and antagonising 'whatever' – whatever you do! It's one of the most enraging and argument-inducing things you can say, because you're effectively dismissing absolutely everything the other person has to say as being completely inconsequential. If you do say it, be aware that your unconscious intention is actually to antagonise and provoke further quarrelling.

Changing the subject is always a good way to divert a potential tiff. Think of a subject about which you hold similar opinions and say something like, 'Oh, by the way, did you see that. . .' or something similar.

To help you get into this habit of changing the subject, practise the following exercise (which uses the interrupt visualization technique from Chapter 9):

1. **Imagine a situation that would normally lead into an argument.**

   Feel that initial adrenaline rush that causes you to raise your voice and want to start arguing your point of view.

2. **Visualize that whatever was said or done to get you cross suddenly evaporates in a white puff of smoke.**

   The source of the conflict has vanished – completely gone. The trigger is nowhere to be seen and consequently you feel nothing. You aren't bothered, and have nothing to justify, explain, or argue about.

3. **Think of something that you and the other person have in common and imagine bringing that up as a replacement topic of conversation.**

   Perhaps you agree on an item of news, or both need to consider buying presents for an upcoming birthday. Maybe you heard that the weather tomorrow is going to be better. Simply think of something on which you both can agree.

Practised frequently, this exercise helps retrain your brain to take a different, more sensible approach whenever it gets the urge to argue.

Respecting opinions and beliefs

A good philosophy for life is to respect the opinions of others, in the same way that you want them to respect yours. The more you listen to and accept other people's positions (even if you don't agree with them), the more open-minded you become and the more people respect you. Nobody says that you have to agree on everything; all you need to do is accept other opinions as being equally valid to the other person as yours are to you.

When you practise this philosophy, you sometimes change your mind and accept another idea, which therefore enriches your life. And at the same time other people are more likely to adopt some of your ideas and opinions, because you're not dogmatic or narrow-minded. Getting along with people is a case of give and take, being flexible, and welcoming a wider variety of experiences, values, and opinions into your world.

Overcoming Shyness

Shyness (or social anxiety) – which is usually caused by an overblown awareness of self, in which you think that other people are watching you a lot more closely than they actually are – can be debilitating when trying to participate in peer activities.

If this experience feels familiar to you, tell yourself that most people are far more concerned with themselves than with other people. In any given group setting, many of the people are equally as nervous as you, or even more so.

Now, fear of public speaking is understandable; you're expected to say something and all ears are on your words. But in normal group circles everyone usually takes turns to speak, and nobody's judging you (at least, not in the way you think they may be).

Read on for more pointers on combating shyness.

Surprising yourself

Go ahead and give yourself a pleasant surprise as part of combating your shyness. Next time you're in a group situation in which you'd normally keep quiet, say something; even just a single sentence, repeating and agreeing with something that someone else just said.

To prepare for joining in with a conversation, carry out the following visualization first:

1. **Imagine yourself in a group, such as with a bunch of friends at the pub.**

2. **Visualize yourself as just one of many participants, each with equal value and opinions to the others.**

3. **Hear somebody say: 'I've heard there's this great new film called such-and-such coming out'.**

4. **You quickly drop in 'Yes, isn't so-and-so in it?'.**

Obviously you can adapt the actual situation and topic as you feel the need. Perhaps change the dialogue to something that you know about, so that you can easily drop in the odd participatory sentence.

If your shyness is a problem at work, imagine someone saying: 'I understand sales were up in the Far-East division last quarter' and you quickly say: 'Yes, 11 per cent wasn't it?'.

After you practise doing this in visualizations, you're ready to participate in real life. To start, drop in just one or two sentences per gathering. By doing so, you increase your level of confidence and other people rate you as having been a valid participant, even though you added very little to the proceedings.

After you get the knack of this exercise, you begin to lose your inhibitions and when you do have something important to add, it comes easily: you say your piece, people listen and respond, and you take part as fully as everyone else in the group.

Taking note of what people say

Shyness can cause you to shrink into your shell.

Don't let yourself get bored in a group, or spend too much time in self-contemplation. Instead, listen to what other people say and remember it. Pay particular notice when you see other people nod in agreement or say 'yes' to something and make a note of the type of thing that was said.

To get used to this, try visualizing a meeting or a social get-together in which you're a participant, and imagine listening intently to everything each person has to say. See yourself nodding in agreement or shaking your head in sympathy, and smiling when you're smiled at by someone. Feel yourself actively involved and practise taking a mental note of everything that is said, rather than simply waiting your turn to say whatever is on your mind.

By doing this you practise paying careful attention, so that when you participate in an actual discussion you stay on-topic and further the conversation flow.

When you've made mental notes in a number of group situations, you've begun forming the mental pathways to prompt you to formulate what you have to say in a similar style and to present it in a similar manner to the things other people say that get general agreement from the rest of the group.

Breaking the routine

If you want to reduce your shyness, try breaking out of your routine. Do something totally different to the usual and put yourself in a situation where you must improvise. Pretty soon you find that your shyness evaporates because your brain's too busy processing all the new things going on.

Suppose that you're keen to get to know someone at work better but are too shy to take the first step. Perhaps you can find some project that requires the pair of you to work on. The chances are that when busy on the project, you forget about your shyness and find yourself communicating normally. You've then created the option of whether to take things any further outside of work.

To practise this, visualize a situation in which you're normally shy, and then change it so that you have several new and different things to do. See how busy they keep you and that as a part of this busyness, you talk to other people quite normally and without fear or shyness.

For example, imagine that you have to collect your son after school each day and are generally fairly shy when it comes to chatting with the other parents. Now imagine that your son loves a particular sport and really wants to play in a team but that there isn't a local league, and so you talk about this with some other parents and discover that their children are also interested; between you, you decide there are enough interested children to form at least two teams, and maybe more.

Now imagine that the school allows you to use its sports facilities if you form some teams, which spurs you all to action, and see yourself arranging with the other parents to put a league together. Now you all have something in common to unite you and which makes it easy for you to chat with each other, as you busily arrange teams and schedules.

Taking the initiative

If you want to get over your shyness with other people, sooner or later you're going to have to grab the bull by the horns and take the initiative in certain situations. If you don't, you may be destined to be a wallflower or to never express your valid opinions to others.

You can practise such actions beforehand using creative visualization, and so get the hang of it without feeling like you're jumping into the deep end:

Pick a situation in which you're shy, in a group, or with just one other person, and in which participating actively is important. Now simply go ahead and see yourself speaking. Do so clearly and confidently and then when you finish, note the positive response from the others having noted what you said. Now imagine adding a further item of information to the topic of conversation, followed by another person replying to it, and so on. There you go: you've started a conversation and it was as easy as anything.

Try this exercise a few times, covering various situations in which you normally hold yourself back from getting involved; simply see yourself engaging with other people on the same level. You're an important member of any group or pair and you're sharing with others without anyone jumping down your throat – possibly the main worry many shy people experience.

Sharing your passions

Nothing removes all hints of shyness like feeling passionate about something, particularly when other people share the same interests.

Take a moment to consider the things that really interest you and visualize that you're in a group situation with other, similar-minded people. Feel the vibe that you all share about your hobby or interest and how each of you has something unique and interesting to offer on the subject.

Whether the subject is a sport, photography, the environment, gardening, or anything else, that common bond draws you together and helps you to participate in group activities and discussions. Feel this bond emotionally. Each one of you is enjoying the experience of sharing a favourite activity in common with other people, and it's a great feeling.

Take that generated, passionate feeling with you whenever you're in a setting that causes your shyness. Feel how, when the time comes for you to participate, your strong interest overrides your acquiescence and you bring it to the front of you mind, even when the discussion isn't related to your passion.

Mental flash cards for improving your relationships with other people

The following mental flash cards help you to overcome shyness, increase your confidence, and strengthen your relationships with others:

✔ **Smiling at everyone:** By simply smiling as often as possible, people naturally like you, so imagine yourself smiling when you can and then let this action turn into real smiling.

✔ **Shaking hands firmly:** If a handshake isn't suitable for any reason when you meet someone (perhaps your hands are full or you're in a car and the person is outside), perform the handshake in your head anyway. Doing so strengthens the greeting in your mind.

✔ **Embracing or cuddling:** When you're with your close friends, visualize cuddling or embracing them in a way compatible with your relationship. This thought engenders warm feelings that your friends pick up on.

✔ **Acknowledging how good you are together:** Simply think to yourself how good you feel with someone and understand how that person feels the same. Acknowledging this feeling helps grow the relationship.

✔ **Having the time of your life:** When you're with people whose company you enjoy, realise that companionship is one of the main things that life is about and think to yourself that you're having the time of your life – because you are.

Building Mutual Trust and Respect

Getting on well with other people and building strong relationships requires you to foster mutual trust. *Trust* is the willingness to be vulnerable to the actions of another, while having a reasonable expectation that the person is going to behave in a manner beneficial to you. Trust is earned over time as you keep confidences, stick to your word, stand up for someone, provide help when needed, and so on.

At the same time, people who trust you respect you, and vice versa. *Respect* is a positive feeling of esteem you hold for another person's viewpoint, conduct, and actions. As you can see, respect and trust are important attributes that act as a strong glue in interpersonal relationships.

To participate well in society, you need to engender these feelings about you in other people, and also feel them about others. As the poet John Donne famously wrote, 'No man is an island'. Humans are sociable creatures and benefit when they have trust and respect for one another, so that they can work together to the benefit of all.

Being loyal

If you want people to be loyal to you, you need to be loyal to them. For example, because almost everything you post online has a habit of getting back to people, berating your employer on your Facebook page isn't going to help you if you later encounter personal difficulties at home and ask to take some time off work. And if you want to keep your friends, you need to stand up for them when they're criticised because the favour will be returned. What's more, you become known for being a positive supporter of people and gain plenty of respect.

Like respect and trust, loyalty is earned over time and so you can't expect others to be loyal to you immediately. Having said that, giving people a chance before you get to know them is a good idea. But if they end up not earning your loyalty, don't be disloyal to them, because that reduces your worth in the eyes of others. Instead, I recommend either being neutral towards someone or loyal to her, according to the extent to which you think she's earned it.

The following affirmations are worth repeating out loud to yourself from time to time to reinforce the way you feel about loyalty:

- ✔ I know that loyalty is a quality attribute to possess.
- ✔ I want other people to be loyal to me.
- ✔ I choose to be loyal to people who deserve it.
- ✔ I give anyone a first chance with my trust.
- ✔ I earn loyalty from others by being loyal to them.
- ✔ I positively seek relationships in which I'm mutually loyal with another.

As with all other sets of affirmations, you can enhance the results by imagining yourself and another person with whom you feel loyalty as you speak. You can do this either as a third person looking at the two of you, or from your own eyes, looking at the other person looking at you. Try to feel strong and firm in your body too as you speak to further convey the message to your unconscious mind.

Being honest

People often say that honesty is the best policy, and the saying's (mostly) true. When you're honest, you share real facts and feelings without deceit. But when you lie, you fabricate an alternative reality in your head that you then have to maintain and which usually leads to yet more lies.

Humans are fairly good liars but don't enjoy it. For example, when someone lies and answers 'yes' to a question, you may often see a slight shake of the head at the same time. This giveaway action is because the unconscious mind wants to be truthful and its desires come to the surface. So, often, you can tell when someone is lying but not put your finger on precisely why you know it – something about her body language or facial expression gives her away.

Like the disloyal (see the preceding section), known liars go down in people's estimation – telling lies isn't an admirable trait. So, on the whole, good friendships are built on a lot of honesty, because honesty leads to trust, and trust to respect.

At times, however, you can't easily be honest because it conflicts with your loyalty to someone. Generally the best thing in these situations is to keep your head down and try not to get involved. If you need to lie to protect company or national secrets, for example, you must make a judgment call on your conflicting priorities. You may also decide that lying is the best action for preventing hurt feelings, in which case society recognises the special circumstances and calls it a white lie.

On the whole, strive to be as honest as possible with other people because they then behave the same with you and you can build strong relationships. But if you find you have a tendency to lie when you don't really need (or want) to, try repeating out loud the following affirmations from time to time:

- ✔ I value honesty as being an important part of a strong character.
- ✔ I choose to be honest whenever I can.
- ✔ I don't enjoy telling lies and refuse to unless I absolutely must.
- ✔ I admire and respect people who are honest.
- ✔ I want people to know that I'm an honest person.

Respecting other people

When you respect people you pay attention to what they have to say because you trust their judgment and honesty. You also know where their loyalties lie and what and who they respect.

Respect isn't *tolerance*, which is merely the use of self-restraint to put up with differing values and opinions, and is all too often related to contempt. No, *respect* is more than that: it's a positive feeling you have for someone you like and can personally relate to.

When you think hard about people you disagree with and try to understand why they're like that, or what brought them to hold their beliefs, you can turn tolerance into respect. Having respect doesn't necessarily mean that you agree, but it does mean that you understand why and how a person holds a view. You can respect the process and the fact that the person arrived at this position through living life, making choices, and fact-finding and decision-making processes.

In other words, take the time to understand what makes other people tick: their backgrounds, and educational and vocational training. By doing so, you can better decide whether you choose to respect, rather than merely tolerate, them.

The more often you take this time with people, the more natural it becomes, and the more you start to like and get on with them.

Understanding and respecting the opinions and values of more people (and the people themselves) allows you to earn more respect from them. To help you achieve this aim, here are some affirmations that feed your unconscious mind and encourage you to better and more positively evaluate and respect other people:

- ✔ I choose to see the best in other people.

- ✔ I want others to respect me for who I am and what I believe.

- ✔ I'd rather respect than merely tolerate differing viewpoints.

- ✔ I take the time to better understand why people are the way they are.

- ✔ I want to live in a society built on mutual respect.

To visually enhance these affirmations imagine yourself nodding at someone else explaining something you disagree with, but for which you respect that person's opinion. You can also see yourself holding your chin between your thumb and fingers as you listen intently to another person and attempt to completely understand what is being said.

Standing up for someone

Being a good friend means having respect and displaying loyalty, which can entail standing up for someone in times of need.

When I used to volunteer at a hospital radio station, a fellow DJ (I'll call him Robert, but that's not his real name) was called up for disciplinary action at an extraordinary meeting because a complaint was received about his over-the-air language on a particular afternoon.

Unfortunately, no archived tape of the particular show existed, but I was at the station at the time and was able to vouch for the fact that Robert's language was entirely appropriate for the whole period. An elderly patient had complained and I assume that he had listened to a different radio station or his hearing was failing. A few other members of the station, however, had it in for Robert. He was a long-term broadcaster with many shows that others wanted to take over for themselves (the office politics and backstabbing that can go on in even the most innocuous of places is truly amazing).

So I attended the meeting to speak up for Robert and state that he'd said nothing untoward on air, even though I was warned in advance that consequences were likely if I did. Because the station was operated as a volunteer group run by a committee, what the committee said went, and so it turned out that my evidence was ignored and I was asked to leave the station immediately, along with Robert.

I hadn't known Robert very well before this event, but as a consequence we soon after collaborated on creating the UK's first Internet radio station licensed by all the music copyright holders. We quickly built up a weekly audience in the tens of thousands, and as a result we were ourselves featured on many radio stations throughout the UK, and also on BBC television. Interestingly, none of this would probably have happened had I kept my head down and ignored a friend in need so that I could retain my volunteer job.

So, yes, standing up for other people can have consequences, but surely they're no worse and probably a lot better than *not* standing up for them. And when your hour of need comes, you can be sure that someone's there to support you.

Say these affirmations to support your grit and determination, and help you stand firmly alongside your friends:

- ✔ I believe that my friends are very important to me.
- ✔ I choose to stand by my friends when they need it.
- ✔ I trust that my friends will stand by me.
- ✔ I know that standing together strengthens our friendship.
- ✔ I do what's right for my friends despite the consequences.

With these affirmations, try to imagine you and a friend standing firmly with each other, resolute and supportive.

Keeping confidences

Everyone loves to hear a good rumour – that's why the gossip and celebrity magazines sell so well. The problem is that so many rumours start out as confidences that someone breaks, usually with an end result far worse than the person breaking it imagines. Usually the friendship of the two people is the first thing to suffer, and then respect goes out the window and, more often than not, the confidence breaker ends up distrusted and disrespected.

When people share confidences with you, they do so because they need to get something off their shoulders and are giving you the high honour of their trust. Or maybe they simply think that you may be interested to know something and are certain that you aren't going to pass the information any further. That's friendship.

If you want to be able to share confidences with friends and not with the world, and you also want to know some of their secrets, you have to make sure that you're really good at keeping them, no matter how tempting passing on a juicy piece of gossip may seem.

The reward of a confidence kept is far greater than the fleeting delight of passing on a secret; it's long-term reliable friendship.

Use the following affirmations to reduce the urge to spill the beans and help keep your mouth firmly sealed when it comes to confidences:

- ✔ I'm a trustworthy person who never reveals confidences.
- ✔ I share my confidences with those who share theirs with me.
- ✔ I find that keeping a secret is easy.
- ✔ I expect others to keep my confidences secret.
- ✔ I'd never break a confidence shared with me.

To visually enhance these affirmations, as you speak them imagine someone whispering an important secret in your ear. And then know that there's absolutely no way you'll ever tell another soul.

Growing Your Friendship

You can do several things to encourage friendships to grow, such as being a good listener, sharing your thoughts and interests, and providing support and help. The following sections cover these areas, with some useful visualizations and affirmations you can try.

Being a good listener

Being a good listener isn't always easy, but is essential to building a strong friendship. You can tell that someone isn't paying attention to what you say when she interrupts and continues with her previous train of thought, or says something unconnected with what you're talking about. Such people are too busy listening to their own thoughts, which can, unfortunately, happen with even the most mindful of us.

You see, the thoughts you have in your psyche are programmed to think that they're the most important ones ever, and if you're lazy or inattentive you filter out much of what other people have to say. Conversely, of course, the person that you're talking to thinks the same. So who has the most important stuff to say?

The answer is, both of you. By deliberately trying to play down the importance of your own thoughts and raise those of another person, you can slightly redress the balance, and find that others often have a lot of interesting stuff to say that you may have been missing out on.

The following visualization exercise makes you more receptive to what other people say and helps you to pay attention more. Consequently, your conversations and interactions with them improve as does your overall relationship:

1. **Imagine that you're talking with someone.**

   You both have a lot to say.

2. **Visualize that the other person's thoughts have a relevance to you of 20 per cent, while your own are 80 per cent relevant.**

   Clearly you're going to pay a lot more attention to what you have to say and want to talk about your own ideas rather than the other person's.

3. **Decrease the 'interestingness' of your own thoughts to 55 per cent, and increase those of your friend to 45 per cent.**

   Yours are still 10 per cent more interesting (because you almost never believe that what you think is less important than what others do), but at 45 per cent 'interestingness', what your friend has to say looks quite good too. So imagine listening to her thoughts and nodding in agreement.

4. **See yourself digesting that thought and responding with a further one of your own that it provokes.**

   Get a good feel for how all your thoughts are only a little more interesting than the other person's.

5. **Imagine a few ideas coming from the other person that suddenly register 70 per cent or more.**

   Think 'wow', that's a great idea.

6. **Allow your friend to perceive a couple of your thoughts at the 70 per cent level too.**

   See your friend's positive reaction and think what an interesting, balanced conversation you're having.

Having practised this exercise a few times, recall it when you're actively discussing something important. You may well find that you're more inclined to listen to the other person, and yet still easily get your own points across. In fact, you probably notice that a greater flow of ideas is going back and forth between you than normal.

Sharing your thoughts

Don't throttle your thoughts by assuming that they can never be of interest to someone else. Quite often your thoughts *are* novel and other people are glad to hear them, which helps build a friendship.

If you're sometimes shy about sharing your ideas, try visualizing yourself thinking something and then saying it straightaway to a friend. Don't worry about speaking, because the statement's only in your imagination. Now pretend that you're not imagining but doing it in real life; say something like 'Have you ever thought that. . .?', and tell the other person your thought.

Asked that way, the question leaves things open for your friend to share her small thoughts too. Over time, this type of visualization helps you value your lowest esteemed thoughts more highly so that you can share them.

Offering support or lending a helping hand

A good friend is always glad to help another in times of difficulty – whether picking up children after school, giving a lift, providing a reference, or any of a multitude of things. But good friends also don't like to impose and may never ask you, so letting others know that you're happy to lend a hand whenever necessary is a good idea. They may well reciprocate and you both benefit from each other's mutual support.

The following affirmations are helpful to repeat to make you more mindful and happy to help in times when you're tired or busy, or otherwise less inclined to offer your assistance:

- ✔ I'm always ready to help others when they need it.
- ✔ I know that my friends can depend on me for a helping hand.
- ✔ I know I can turn to my friends when I need support.
- ✔ I'm pleased to assist a friend even when tired or busy.
- ✔ I encourage friendships in which people support each other.

When saying these affirmations you may wish to imagine shaking the hand of a strong acquaintance, or hugging a close friend. Other visualizations include holding the door open for a friend, driving someone to the airport when a taxi is late, or any other ways of lending a hand that come to mind.

Enjoying mutual interests

Common interests are some of the best things for binding friends together. After all, when you're with your friends, everything's more enjoyable when you actually like the activity! Therefore, sharing your interests with other people makes great sense and, over time, the friendships that blossom the most are likely to be those in which we have shared interests.

Sometimes you come across new pastimes and activities that you didn't think you'd like, and yet via your friends you find yourself participating in them with great enjoyment. So the following affirmations are useful for helping you to keep an open mind and take an interest in the things other people do, and encourage them to participate in your activities:

- ✔ I have a wide range of interests and hobbies.
- ✔ I'm interested in the activities my friends participate in.
- ✔ I like to share my interests with other people.
- ✔ I enjoy finding new things to do with my friends.
- ✔ I like it when people invite me to join in new activities.

You can further enhance these final affirmations by imagining that you're with some of your friends at a social gathering. Everyone is laughing and smiling, having a great time as you discuss some of the interests you have in common.

Part IV

Using Creative Visualization to Achieve Success

The 5th Wave   By Rich Tennant

"I've used creative visualization to attain many good things in my life. Like right now, I'm visualizing you getting the heck out of my office."

In this part . . .

You'll learn how to increase your levels of self-confidence and feelings of self-worth, including how to speak in public, use positive body language and deal with setbacks in a constructive way. Techniques for improving your leadership skills are included as well as exercises for increasing your sporting ability and achieving success in both education and your career. This part also features exercises to help release the creativity within you.

Chapter 13

Cultivating Confidence: Strengthening Your Self-belief with Creative Visualization

In This Chapter

▶ Recognising your value as a person

▶ Practising good eye contact and body language

▶ Speaking in public with conviction

▶ Handling past mistakes and moving on

*O*ne single issue seems to underlie all the problems that many people experience on the path of personal improvement: lack of self-confidence. This affliction so often holds people back from behaving in ways that can enrich their lives.

Usually you develop confidence in response to the skills you acquire. For example, when you first learn to drive with an instructor or parent, you drive slowly and hesitantly because you don't yet have a feeling for the dimensions of the vehicle, and therefore you don't know what you can and can't do with it. But after a few lessons you almost feel that the car's exterior is an extension of yourself, and you become more confident with your speed and steering.

The same system of confidence coming from practice applies to all new skills you acquire: your initial lack of confidence is a natural self-protection mechanism that you release only when you feel safer and more in control.

Problems arise in these activities (and in life in general), however, when you don't get over that lack of self-confidence; sometimes, even though you've acquired the necessary skills for an activity, you remain timid and afraid of properly participating. To confuse matters further, you can also overestimate your abilities and rate them much higher than they really are.

Simply by deciding to work on your self-confidence, you're already evaluating your abilities, and the chances are that you're probably more capable than other people who appear far more confident. This acknowledgement can help you to navigate this minefield of real or unrealised, false or imagined, abilities. And this chapter helps, because by evaluating, understanding, and acknowledging your abilities, you naturally become more self-confident as a result of visualizing something (for example driving), in the same way as if you actually experience it.

Improving Your Feeling of Self-worth

A good place to start working on your self-confidence is with your opinion of yourself. You may not realise it, but you do have such an opinion, even if you express it implicitly through a general feeling of your value or self-worth rather than explicitly.

People with low self-confidence often find themselves in that situation because their feeling of self-worth is also too low and, for one reason or another (such as domineering parents, just wanting a quiet life, or lack of belief in yourself), this evaluation is so strong that developing a greater sense of self-worth is very difficult.

Creative visualization allows you to gain valuable distance and place your consciousness 'outside' of yourself, and so better judge the pros and cons of your psychological makeup, In a 2011 study by Polman and Emich at New York and Cornell Universities, two sets of people were asked to solve a puzzle in which a prisoner is in a high tower with just a metal bed firmly bolted to the floor and a rope only half as long as the drop from the window, yet he still manages to escape.

Both groups were asked to work out how the prisoner escaped. One of the groups were asked to imagine that they were the prisoner, the other group were asked to view the problem externally – as if happening to an unknown third person. It turned out that just under half of the first group were able to work out the solution, however two thirds of the second group got the right answer (an improvement of almost 40 per cent), showing that the detachment of a person working on a problem from the problem itself releases additional creativity with which to solve it.

The answer, by the way, is that the prisoner separated the rope into two by splitting it lengthways and then tied the two together which he then tied to a leg of the bed, threw the rest out of the window, and climbed down. Did you guess the same?!

The simple fact that you're reading this book shows that you have a desire to improve yourself and therefore your character is already proven to have positive traits such as willingness to change, flexibility, and the desire to better yourself. With the help of the exercises in this chapter you can develop the internal value of your self-worth, which in turn acts as a great platform for boosting your confidence.

Re-affirming belief in yourself

Belief in yourself is critical to maintaining a healthy level of self-worth. Without self-belief you're going to have difficulty convincing yourself (and your unconscious mind) that you truly are of value.

You can develop greater belief in yourself in a number of ways:

- Re-evaluate your abilities and past achievements in the light of your greater maturity, as well as your increased ability to understand what you've achieved. In other words, you're older and wiser than you were and can see your past achievements in a different way from before. Until now you may not even have thought too much about what you've achieved. But if you look at things from your current perspective you may appreciate the fact that you've actually achieved a lot.

- Change your viewpoint and choose to look at yourself (and the world) from a different and fresh point of view. This change often also throws up things about yourself that you previously hadn't considered. Just as with the prisoner puzzle earlier in this chapter, by shifting your viewpoint you may gain different insights and perspectives.

- Demonstrate a greater belief in yourself and your potential by using the exercises outlined throughout this chapter.

Take a note of the following set of ten affirmations, which when repeated regularly help to increase your self-belief:

- I have values and principles that I'm prepared to defend.

- I always try to make the right choices in life for all concerned.

- I don't feel guilty when others disapprove of my choices.

- I'm not worried about mistakes in my past; I've learned from them and moved on.

- I have the ability to solve any problem and I'm not stopped by temporary failure.

- I'm an interesting and valuable person who's responsible, reliable, and a good friend.

- I'm sensitive to the feelings and needs of others.

✔ I choose never to prosper at the expense of others.

✔ I enjoy a wide range and variety of activities and friends.

✔ I choose always to adopt a positive outlook on life.

As with all affirmations, if you write them down or speak them aloud you emphasise them more fully and your unconscious mind takes greater notice. After a while they become absorbed into your psyche and begin to form a part of your personality. (See Chapter 1 for more on the power of repeated affirmations.)

Although affirmations are not visualizations, insofar as that you're not thinking visually, they are the auditory equivalent.

When you read affirmations or say them out loud, you're exposing your brain to another kind of imprint just like a visualization, but it is processed through the audio sections of your brain. The same goes for writing affirmations down. This requires yet another part of your brain and so adds to the overall objective of using as many senses as you can in creative visualization.

When you write, read, and repeat your affirmations you can enhance them by trying to also see any symbols or pictures they evoke. For example, when repeating the preceding affirmation, 'I always try to make the right choices in life for all concerned', you can imagine a difficult situation such as a sacrifice you've made, like not purchasing something you really wanted in order to buy a pretty dress your daughter wants. Or when repeating the affirmation, 'I'm an interesting and valuable person who's responsible, reliable, and a good friend', you can see yourself shaking hands with a friend or hugging a child, partner, relation, or close friend.

Recognising your own value

Low self-worth is often caused by not appreciating just how much value you bring to the world. If you're a parent, for example, you're performing one of the most valuable services possible in bringing up a child safely, educated, and with good morals and values.

The work you do at home is especially important for your family and, although you may rarely hear appreciation from them, they do value everything you do for them and would sorely miss it if you didn't.

If you do paid work – whatever your level within an organisation – you're fulfilling an important role, and your interactions with your co-workers/clients/suppliers and so on contribute towards the running and the subsequent success of that particular business.

If you participate in any volunteer, church, or other group activity, your input is surely welcomed by everyone, and you're helping to make the group (and the world) a better place. And the same goes for the time you spend with your friends. Your sense of humour and quirkiness may not seem that evident to you, but you surely have them and other people have certainly noticed and appreciate them.

To highlight the things you do that provide value and help to others and of which you can be proud, check out the following visualization exercise:

1. **Settle yourself comfortably in a chair and start regular, relaxed breathing (as I describe in Chapter 1).**

   Continue until you're calm and collected.

2. **Visualize moving your consciousness out of your body.**

   See it floating a few feet behind your body.

3. **Imagine that you're a being made of pure energy, self-supporting and invisible, unconnected with the world.**

   This being has existed forever.

4. **Imagine that the body in front of you, that is you, was never born.**

   Watch as it slowly fades away and disappears.

5. **Whizz back in time to when you would have been born.**

   Go to your parents' house and put your mind's eye replay on fast forward and see how you were never a baby or infant. Note all the different things your family do as a consequence. See how you never went to school or made or played with friends.

6. **Look hard at the world as it goes by.**

   Realise that all the pictures you drew as a child never existed, all the joy you gave to your parents is gone; the laughs and companionship you gave to your friends never happened.

7. **Continue the alternative reality replay in your later life.**

   See how things are different because you never completed your education or got a job, never met any life partners, never had an apartment or house, and never worked with colleagues or made any friends. See how empty the world is without you in it?

8. **Let the alternative reality fade away and disappear as your consciousness slips back into your physical body.**

   Breathe a deep sigh of relief.

9. **Spend the next couple of minutes reflecting on just how much impact you've had on so many other people.**

   Allow the realisation to come rushing into your mind, filling the vacuum of the imaginary world without you in it.

You're an important person and are in this world for many reasons. You have your right and proper place in it and bring many valuable things with you. Because of your existence, other people's lives are enriched, and they live a far more fulfilling life than if you'd never been born.

Reconsidering how others perceive you

Studies in which participants are asked to rate themselves and others on a variety of factors, such as beauty, honesty, integrity, charm, wit, kindness, intelligence, and so on, consistently show that people rate themselves about 20 per cent lower than other people do. This insight immediately informs you that if you have a low feeling of self-worth, you can immediately adjust it upwards by 20 per cent, just to match the view that other people hold of you. The truth is that people often perceive you better than you think!

Here's a simple visualization exercise to help you readjust your internal feeling of self-worth to match the higher worth that other people hold of you:

1. **Imagine that you're looking at a gauge registering your current feeling of self-worth out of a hundred, as depicted in Figure 13-1 (for example, you may believe it to be 50 per cent).**

2. **Think of a few people you know well and accept that on average they may perceive your 'worth' to be 70 per cent.**

3. **Adjust the gauge upwards by 20 points and fix firmly in your mind that this result is probably the opinion others have of you.**

The exact value that shows on your gauge during this visualization isn't important. The object of this exercise is simply to show you and your unconscious mind that you may be substantially undervaluing yourself.

You can also try using this exercise to go back in your memory to periods of low self-esteem and re-evaluate them upwards by (at least) 20 per cent, so that you can now feel the higher sense of self-esteem you ought to have felt at the time. Doing this will help you to deconstruct any old patterns of self-loathing you may be carrying.

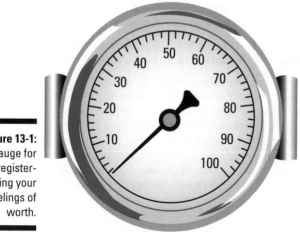

Figure 13-1:
A gauge for register- ing your feelings of worth.

Valuing yourself as equal to others

You're a human being fulfilling your role in society. Your views, opinions, and actions are of equal value to other people's. Your rights under the law are the same as others. You are, therefore, of equal worth to anyone else.

To further your equality in the world and begin to adjust the way you feel about yourself to a higher, more reasonable level, practise the following exercise:

1. **Recall the value of worth gauge from Figure 13-1 in the preceding section.**

2. **Think of someone for whom you don't have a great deal of respect, such as an international terrorist, and align how you feel about this person to the far left of the scale. This serves to set a value in your mind for the lowest possible level.**

3. **Think of someone you greatly admire to set a value for the highest level: perhaps a great leader such as Winston Churchill, Abraham Lincoln, or Mahatma Gandhi.**

4. **Think briefly about a few of your family, friends, and colleagues, and note the corresponding value that you imagine the gauge displays when you do so.**

5. **Add the totals in step 4 together and divide this figure by the number of people you thought about to obtain the average.**

   This figure (or somewhere thereabouts) is the setting to use when assigning your own feeling of self-worth to the gauge. Suppose that the figure you came to was 80 per cent.

6. **Reconfigure the gauge so that it displays only your own feeling of worth, which may be, for example, 20 per cent.**

7. **Mentally increase the reading of the gauge as required until the meter shows 80 per cent; hold it there and sense how you feel.**

Doesn't this higher level of self-worth feel good, and somehow just right? You're now valuing yourself as equivalent to most other people, and your level of confidence begins to adjust accordingly as your unconscious mind readjusts to your realisation that you do have a higher worth than you previously believed.

Considering other people as being important and of the upmost value is vital, because if you don't value others you can never value yourself highly.

Remembering the importance of integrity

Daily life constantly confronts you with choices that test your integrity, such as opportunities to hide taxable earnings, the chance to get promoted by putting down a colleague, being inadvertently given too much change by a shop assistant, and so on. How you react to this type of situation depends on your integrity.

A major part of maintaining a high level of belief in yourself is being able to base this belief on the way you behave: for example, thieves can't base a personal healthy self-esteem on their honesty when they're clearly behaving dishonestly. You can only go so far by deceiving yourself that you have integrity if you don't, and the more frequently you make selfish choices or act against the good of others, the less you find that you believe in yourself, because deep inside you know that you're not an honest person, and you find it hard to reconcile this fact with feeling good about yourself.

Imagine the following scenario that tests your integrity. You see a £20 note on the floor at the grocery checkout, and an elderly lady in front of you just putting away her purse. Some people would be tempted to pick up and pocket the note while nobody's looking, but perhaps that would result in the lady going hungry at the end of the week. Now she may or may not have dropped the money, but you know that you're going to feel much better if you offer it to her – the course of action that I'm sure most people would end up taking.

By being considerate towards other people and helping them where help is needed (even if your action means making a sacrifice of some kind), your personal level of integrity blossoms and your self-belief shoots up.

Considering the Dunning–Kruger Effect

As if to throw a spanner in the works, the psychological phenomenon of the Dunning–Kruger Effect shows that the more people know, the less confident they are, whereas the less people know, the more they overestimate their abilities.

This bias occurs when unskilled people make incorrect conclusions about their abilities, because their lack of skill and experience denies them the ability to appreciate what they don't know and can't do. Unskilled people therefore tend to rate their ability as above average (and much higher than it actually is), whereas

skilled people often underrate their own abilities. The result can be situations in which less competent people rate their own abilities higher than more competent people do!

You often see this effect on TV talent shows such as *American Idol* and *X-Factor* in which the weaker contestants consistently rate their musical ability far higher than it really is, while many talented performers are often overly modest about their skills. This phenomenon illustrates how competence may actually weaken self-confidence.

To help strengthen your resolve when tempted, and your overall approach to opportunity, greed, and other people, the following affirmations can be used:

- ✔ I'm an honest and reliable person.
- ✔ I value integrity in all people extremely highly.
- ✔ I choose always to act in an honourable manner.
- ✔ I'm a loyal and trustworthy friend.
- ✔ I always do my best to tell the truth.

Note that the final affirmation isn't 'I always tell the truth', because sometimes lies are unavoidable and recognising this reality is important. For example, you know that the correct answer to the question 'Do I look good in this?' is always 'Yes, you look great!'. I cover honesty in more detail in Chapter 12.

Speaking the Right Body Language

Before humans developed spoken language, they communicated through the use of the body – deliberately and directly with signs, and accidently and indirectly with involuntary facial and other movements.

You do a few things almost unconsciously that reveal a huge amount about how you're feeling and even about what you're thinking. Check these out:

✔ How you walk

✔ How you stand

✔ How you sit

✔ How you direct your limbs

✔ How you hold your head

✔ How you move your eyes

Most people can easily read basic body language without any training.

When you like someone, your pupils dilate, an effect that's very noticeable. You may also smile more broadly and mirror the actions of the other person, such as crossing or uncrossing your legs to match, or leaning forwards or backwards in harmony, scratching your nose at the same time, and so on.

Being aware of your body language allows you to control the image you portray to other people and perhaps appear more self-confident than you feel (helping lead to real confidence later). You can also use the same knowledge to better read other people in order to relate with them more fully.

By using techniques of Creative Visualization you can learn to modify your own body language to better control the impression that you give to others.

Mental flash cards for boosting your confidence

As well as the visualizations outlined in this chapter, when you have a few spare moments (or when you think you need to use them), to help with increasing your confidence levels you can use a few mental flash cards:

✔ **Shaking your hero's hand:** Choose a favourite hero of yours, one who you really look up to, and see yourself shaking hands with the person and feeling that he or she also respects you.

✔ **Viewing your wall of achievements:** Create a wall of achievements in your mind and whenever you think of a new one, attach an image representing it to the wall. When you feel low in confidence simply call up the image of the wall and view it for a quick boost.

✔ **Revelling in thunderous applause:** Imagine you've just given the performance of your life and you're standing centre stage with the entire audience up on their feet and applauding you.

✔ **Wearing a suit of armour:** Visualize the world's most advanced suit of armour. It's invisible, light, and protects you against any negative thoughts or opinions. Nothing can hurt you while you're wearing this suit.

✔ **Remember the Dunning–Kruger Effect (see the sidebar):** Understand that your confidence may be reduced simply because you're competent, and automatically readjust your feeling of confidence back up again to take this into account.

Practising good posture

People's postures can tell you a lot about them and what they may be feeling or thinking. Check out these examples of body language postures and what they often reveal:

- ✔ Slumped posture: Low-spirited or depressed
- ✔ Erect posture: High-spirited with energy and confidence
- ✔ Leaning away: Defensive and/or uninterested
- ✔ Leaning forward: Attentive and/or interested
- ✔ Crossed arms: Defensive or disapproving
- ✔ Uncrossed arms: Willing to listen

You can use creative visualization to focus on your posture by adopting a feeling of self-confidence and practise holding that feeling, so you get used to it. With continued practice, the feeling becomes natural to you in real-life situations.

Imagine that a ball of energy is pulsing right between your shoulder blades. The ball is warm and strong and radiates intense waves of confidence throughout your body. These waves travel up and down your spine like shivers, out along all your limbs to your fingers and toes, and up to your head, which tingles right at the back of your skull and sends its own shivers from there throughout your brain. When the energy is released, your body and mind are energised throughout with all the confidence you need for any task and this self-belief is evident in your posture.

Draw on this feeling of self-confidence to practise your composure (for example) in the following interview visualization:

1. **See yourself as you enter through the door, and close it behind you.**

2. **Imagine providing your details to a receptionist and being encouraged to take a seat while you wait.**

3. **Walk slowly to the indicated chair and sit down with your legs uncrossed and a little apart.**

4. **Raise your eyebrows and smile when the interviewer approaches you and firmly shake his hand.**

5. **Follow the interviewer slowly with your head held high and steady, while demonstrating a solid forward-pointing gaze.**

6. **Wait for him to sit down before you settle in your chair and calmly wait for the interview to commence.**

Try adapting this visualization to various different types of situations in which you need extra confidence, incorporating the specific body postures included.

Performing this exercise a few times imprints the sensation of being self-confident onto you and enables you to draw on it whenever necessary. Over time, a confident body posture comes to you naturally and is simply a part of who you are.

Making and holding eye contact

People with low self-esteem tend to have difficulty holding eye contact, which unfortunately people can misunderstand as shiftiness or deceit. Eye contact is one of the surest indicators of confidence and is therefore well worth practising.

Revisit the interview visualization outlined in the preceding section, and imagine that you've been asked a question and you want to answer it well. Take a moment to imagine constructing your answer and then look directly into the interviewer's eyes as you begin your answer, and hold your gaze for about five seconds as you speak. Now flick your gaze away as you consider your follow-up statement, before looking back to look into his eyes as you talk.

You don't need to invent an actual discussion. Simply picture yourself making and breaking eye contact as you talk. See yourself using it to emphasise important points, and then look away after the point is made. Make sure that when you want to appear properly attentive, you look into the interviewer's eyes when he talks or asks a question. If he describes something, look away as you imagine the object, and then back again to acknowledge the fact that you've done so.

For many people this kind of making and breaking of eye contact comes entirely naturally. If it doesn't to you, this exercise helps you to increase your level of eye contact for sensible durations and with appropriate breaks.

To exude greater self-confidence, watch the eye movements of people on television who you feel are confident and see how they fit into the patterns described in the exercise. Practise making the movements yourself while imagining talking with another person, tying the correct eye movements to what you're saying. Note that this exercise isn't about discovering how to lie, but about helping you to gain more conscious control of your eye movements in order to convey your message more confidently.

Looks can be deceiving

When talking, people use their eyes as they recall or invent details. For example, when asked to remember something visual, most people move their eyes up and to their left. But when inventing a visual image (or pretending to recall a real one), people generally look up and to their right. The same thing happens with auditory information except that people look to their left for remembered sounds or to their right for imagined or reconstructed sounds (roughly in the directions of their ears). When people talk under their breath or in their imagination, they tend to look down and to their left. People's eyes also reveal when they're feeling a sensation in their imagination by moving down and to the right.

These movements may be very tiny indeed and often are unobservable, but when you see them you can often get a good indication of what people are thinking or feeling, and whether they're being truthful. Never rely on this technique for anything more than an indication,

however, because these patterns of movement aren't always identical in everybody, and sometimes are even reversed.

Using this information, you can try to control your eyes and guard against revealing too much to other people such as the fact that you're nervous, or that you're attracted to someone (and wish not to let them know, maybe because you shouldn't be!), and so on. However, doing this isn't as easy as it sounds.

To acquaint yourself with how your eyes move, roll them around in a complete circle and notice how they try to settle in several spots. These positions are the natural ones where you frequently move your eyes when thinking or recalling. You can try experimenting with them by moving your eyes to these places and seeing what feelings or memories this elicits; in some people this practice can help inspire creativity when a block is encountered.

Mirroring the moves of other people

In recent years, scientists have discovered that many of the neurons in the human brain are *mirror* neurons. This term means that as well as triggering when you perform certain actions, they also go off when you see other people doing these actions, which explains why people are so keyed in to automatically mimicking others they like, due to the mirror neurons causing an emotional response. For more on neurons, take a look at Chapter 1.

Therefore, by mirroring some of the actions that other people do (in a non-obvious manner), you can help them unconsciously start to like you; this reaction is human nature and almost unpreventable.

Have you noticed that when you're with someone in a café or a pub and one of you takes a sip of a drink, the other frequently does so at the same time? If you haven't, try it next time you're out with one or more people. When you take a sip, keep your eyes alert and see who also drinks. That person is likely to be the one taking most interest in you at that moment.

To help build mirroring into your body language as a confidence-boosting technique, revisit the interview visualization from the earlier section 'Making and holding eye contact', but this time add in two or three instances of mirroring things the interviewer does, such as shifting weight from one thigh to the other, scratching an ear, pushing glasses back up your nose, and so on. Over time you can become used to the concept of mirroring and your body goes ahead and does it for you whenever you want to ensure that someone gains a good impression of you.

Don't make your mirrored movements too obvious because you're likely to cause the opposite effect. You don't want to look like you're playing a giant game of Follow My Leader!

Listening with more than your ears

Another way to increase the level of self-confidence you convey to others (and therefore your actual self-confidence too) is to pay full attention to what other people say. By this, I mean really listening to what's being said, taking it in, and understanding it, instead of listening dispassionately or simply hearing and forgetting.

Take an interest in the other person and use appropriate body and facial movements in response. When the other person pauses, clarify a point or ask a related question as evidence that you've listened and understood.

Interacting with people while listening to them demonstrates that you care about them and as a result they instinctively warm to you.

To help become a better listener, repeat the following affirmations, which when practised over time become part of the way you naturally listen to people:

- ✔ I'm interested in what others have to say.
- ✔ I enjoy listening to other people.
- ✔ I enrich my own life by listening and understanding other people.
- ✔ People who know that I'm going to listen are more inclined to listen to me.
- ✔ The world is a better place when people properly listen to each other.

Overcoming Public Speaking Nerves

Imagine that an important speaking appointment is fast looming and you've done everything you can to ensure a good session. You've carried out your homework, looked up your facts, written a few jokes, and generally put together a very good speech. But still you're scared stiff of giving the actual talk. Why is that?

The basic cause is down to your need for acceptance from your peers. On a one-to-one basis you can generally hold your own and manage putting your point across quite well. When delivering a speech to a group, however, the sheer quantity of people who may end up disapproving of you can be overwhelming and result in anything from mild nerves, through to panic and hysteria.

Time to be realistic! Deep down you know that the worst that can happen is people find you a bit boring and forget most of what you say. Or they may feel sympathy for you if you stutter or lose your train of thought. On the whole, most audiences want their speaker to be interesting and do well, and they offer applause and support when they get the chance. They know that public speaking isn't easy and probably don't like doing it themselves.

This section provides some practical tips and techniques to make public speaking easier, by reducing your nervousness to a manageable level so you can concentrate on giving a good performance.

Being properly prepared

When preparing to speak in public, be as sure as possible about what you're going to say: verify all facts; avoid offence by excluding any too near-the-knuckle jokes; and check that the content is appropriate for the particular audience you're addressing.

If question and answer sessions or group discussions are held after the talk, your thorough preparation ensures that you can confidently maintain your viewpoint. The last thing you want to be is dissuaded from your opinions in public before you've had an opportunity to reconsider and re-evaluate your viewpoint.

To help with your preparations for public speaking, repeat the following affirmations, starting from when you first know that you're going to be talking in public until right before you do so:

✔ I'll be fully prepared for this speaking appointment.

✔ I'll ensure that all my facts are verified.

✔ I'll consider my viewpoint and when it's developed stick to it.

✔ I'll consider any doubts about my position only after the engagement.

By regularly repeating these affirmations you approach your preparations for the speech according to them, so that you're completely ready when the big day comes.

Speaking with conviction

Speaking about your given subject with strong conviction helps you to get your point across and reduce your anxiety levels, because you know that you know what you're talking about.

When you're fired up about something, you speak more loudly and more vehemently, and as a result others take more notice. Tests have found that public speakers who use very mild expletives in a speech (but only one or two!) are consistently rated more interesting, informative, and compelling.

I'm by no means encouraging you to swear when talking in public; you don't want to offend your audience before they can take on board what you're saying. But the strength of feeling needs to be present – the feeling of how important your topic of discussion is, how strongly you feel about it, and the determination to get your point across – and you can help build these feelings through the following affirmations:

- ✔ I believe strongly in the content of my talk.
- ✔ I'm going to get my points across because they're important.
- ✔ I really want my listeners to understand my point of view.
- ✔ I'll speak with complete conviction.

Repeat these statements to yourself and you increase your self-confidence by re-affirming the important reasons for wanting to give your talk in the first place. Keeping these affirmations in mind makes your talk more interesting and memorable for your audience.

Pacing yourself

When you want to be (and appear) more confident, pace yourself and practise speaking slowly – much more slowly than you think is natural. In studies in which speeches have been rated for various qualities such as their content and also the confidence of the speaker, one of the key factors that resulted in a higher rating was how slowly the presenter spoke. Talking quickly indicates nervousness and the desire to hurry through a presentation, while a slower speed indicates authority and confidence.

To practise speaking more slowly, Google a famous speech or look up a well known passage from a book. Or (if you've already written it), practise with the contents of the talk you're going to give. Read the text out loud, not in a dramatic way, but in your own voice and, while speaking, keep visualizing an activity associated with calm and slowness; for example, swimming a gentle breaststroke or taking a very slow walk in the countryside. See yourself in a relaxed and comfortable setting as you read, and take a pause after each sentence, ensuring that you maintain your pace throughout.

Slowing it down: A royal remedy

In 2011, the Best Actor Oscar went to Colin Firth for the movie *The King's Speech*. Firth portrays King George VI of England who had a devastating stutter that may have prevented him from talking in public. However, with the aid of a speech therapist he was able (mostly) to overcome his disability and make some very commanding speeches.

Among a number of different techniques, he was advised to slow his speaking right down. You may never have noticed or thought about it, but when you're nervous you tend to talk more quickly, almost as if the quicker you finish the sooner the experience will be over. Not only does this cause difficulty for the audience trying to take in what you're saying, but also listening is very uncomfortable because your anxiety is so obvious. By slowing your speech right down, you become easier to follow.

Whenever King George VI felt a stutter rising he paused and waited for it to pass before speaking his next word. This technique gave him a unique and statesmanlike presentation, which the British public found endearing and perfectly acceptable.

Using this visualization when speaking in public helps you to better pace your talk so that it is understood and remembered, and you won't feel so much of an urge to rush through it and be done with the speech. When you feel you're getting better at speaking more slowly, ask a friend to listen and tell you how you're doing. Often you'll find speaking even more slowly would be better still. If in doubt… remember that you… can almost never… speak too slowly!

Managing Mistakes and Setbacks

Throughout life, everyone encounters setbacks and makes mistakes. The ability that separates achievers from non-achievers, however, is how they deal with them.

Successful people look on setbacks as challenges to be overcome, and also tend to learn from their mistakes and rarely repeat them. These people also share another quality: they tend to appear extremely self-confident.

In contrast, other people are always getting in trouble because they repeat the same mistakes over and over again. They also seem to have difficulty handling setbacks, which often prevents them overcoming them.

Most people are somewhere between these two extremes, which means that you're most likely to be reasonably confident, fairly good at avoiding repeating mistakes, and can sometimes overcome setbacks. But, with a little effort and the help of creative visualization, you can improve upon how you manage your mistakes and setbacks.

Facing up to your 'faux pas'

Only by admitting your mistakes do you have any chance of avoiding repeating them. If you simply ignore and forget about something foolish that you've done, you're surely destined to repeat it in the future. You need to face up to what happened in order to move on. Apologising to those affected by your mistake is always the best course of action and the first thing to consider.

When you decide to apologise for something, be totally sincere, intend never to repeat your mistake, and do your best to make amends wherever you can.

If your mistake affects only yourself, you may think that you can avoid the apology, but don't. Always apologise to whoever your mistakes affect, and if that happens to be yourself, make sure that you say sorry (check out the following section 'Forgiving yourself' for more details).

Saying 'sorry' sincerely

In a recent study, two groups of people were given a small amount of cash and told that if they handed that cash over to a third party (another researcher) it would be tripled and they would receive half of it (resulting in having 50% more than before). However, in all cases only half the *original* amount of cash was returned to both groups, who (quite rightly) felt that they'd been treated poorly.

Each member of one of the groups was then given an apology by the third party and afterwards asked to rate its effect on them out of 10. The average rating given was 3.5. In other words, the apologies were accepted but only begrudgingly. Instead of receiving an apology,

the other group were asked to imagine receiving one and rate how that would make them feel. This group's average was a value of 6, a much more satisfactory acceptance level.

This result shows that merely receiving an apology is insufficient unless people believe that the person offering it is sincere and, what's more, that they won't commit the transgression again. The group that received the real apologies only heard the words without any discernable contrition or apparent intent to do better or make amends. But the group that visualized the apologies imagined them to include these extra features and therefore rated them significantly more highly.

Forgiving yourself

Just as you need to apologise to others when you make a mistake that affects them, you also need to say sorry to yourself when you're the victim. When you forgive someone you're letting the matter go. In the same way, by forgiving yourself something you're closing a door on it and can move on. This can be an important step towards enabling your levels of self-confidence to rise. Using creative visualization, you can face up to your mistakes in your imagination, and go over them one final time before putting them to rest by forgiving them.

When you apologise to yourself for a serious mistake, forgive yourself just as you hope others have forgiven you. Say to yourself something like, 'I forgive you for the mistake you made and the problems it caused, because I know you didn't intend it and plan not to let it happen again.'

Don't worry if you think that talking to yourself is the first sign of madness – give it a go! Your unconscious mind appreciates the sincerity, understands that you don't want to repeat the mistake, and guides you where it can to help avoid it ever recurring. By closing something painful in your mind by forgiving yourself, you're able to break out of a pattern in which you may repeat that same thing another time. You're confirming to your unconscious mind that you don't wish for the mistake to be repeated, so your unconscious mind takes this on board and steers you away from similar situations in the future.

You have two parts to your mind: your conscious and unconscious. And in this situation you need to ensure that these two 'minds' communicate with each other because conflict between the two leads to anxiety, difficulty in decision making (because of two possibly opposing views), and inner conflict.

When you carry out this internal dialogue, you start to feel much better about yourself and your mistakes. You also find that moving on with your life is much easier. Trying to do this on your own without creative visualization isn't easy because you may simply say the word 'Sorry' to yourself and hope that it was sufficient. But it usually isn't. If you visualize your mistake and feel how bad it made you feel and your desire to not repeat it, and follow this with an apology to yourself (both you and your unconscious mind) and also express a sincere desire to never repeat it, then you will be much more likely to be able to put it in your past and properly move on.

Letting go of your mistakes by laughing about them

When you acknowledge a mistake and apologise for it, and make sufficient amends if necessary, the error can still somehow hang around in your mind, weigh you down, and hold you back. A good way of letting go of a mistake is to try and make light of it.

Of course, not all mistakes are small ones that can be laughed at, and so feel free to jump to the later section 'Living, learning, and moving on: Accepting mistakes as a part of life' for more ways of moving on from your mistakes.

In the late 1980s and early 1990s, when sales of microcomputers began to decline as PCs gained dominance, I read a report in which a reporter asked the director of a previously successful computer games company how the company's year had been. To this day, I vividly remember his reply: 'Well the first half was like sailing up s**t creek without a paddle, and the second half was like swimming all the way back again.' Not the type of humorously honest comment you expect from a prominent businessperson! He was evidently trying to come to terms with his company's difficulties and putting himself in the right frame of mind to move on. Subsequently, he picked himself up after this setback and is currently the director of a leading market research company.

So, if the mistake is of the kind that you can eventually laugh about, do so, as long as you take a lesson from it. Laughing at a past mistake is like saying 'Wow – that was a terrible time in my life, but I'm only human. Somehow I got through it, learned from it and I'm still here to tell the tale!' As the famous saying goes, 'Laughter is the best medicine'.

Supporting other people when they make a mistake

You want others to give you the benefit of the doubt when you make a mistake or are having difficulty attaining an objective, so try to offer the same latitude to others. It's only fair and does wonders for retaining your integrity and own feeling of self-worth. A good idea is to discover how to criticise other people constructively, by offering suggestions about how to improve a situation instead of just stating that it's not good.

At the same time, people appreciate a pat on the back when they do well, so always be ready to give praise and congratulate people when they deserve it.

Use the following affirmations to help improve your ability to criticise constructively and spontaneously offer due praise:

- ✔ I value the things that other people do.

- ✔ I enjoy it when others are creative.

- ✔ I'm going to provide helpful advice and suggestions where possible.

- ✔ I'm going to resist the urge to criticise without making suggestions.

- ✔ I like congratulating people when they achieve something good.

Practising these affirmations allows you to build closer and more fulfilling relationships, and helps your own levels of self-confidence to grow as a result.

Living, learning, and moving on: Accepting mistakes as a part of life

If no one ever made mistakes, everybody would run the risk of becoming over-confident and even arrogant. People would think that they were somehow perfect and incapable of error. Mistakes remind you that you are, after all, only human. When you fail, the experience hurts your pride, but taking on board lessons can help you become a more humble person, accept that you're prone to errors, and be more forgiving to others who also make mistakes.

This kind of empathy is developed mostly through making personal mistakes, so view your errors as important discovery milestones in your life. Mistakes and setbacks are valuable and lead you towards achieving goals, increasing your resolve, commitment, and determination to overcome problems, and enhancing your ability to understand the feelings of others.

Repeat the following affirmations from time to time, to help keep the mistakes you make in perspective:

- ✔ I'm only human and prone to making mistakes.
- ✔ I make mistakes only when trying to achieve things.
- ✔ I can only try my best to avoid making mistakes.
- ✔ I'll do everything in my power to make up for any mistakes I do make.
- ✔ I'll accept when I fail, learn from the experience, and move on.
- ✔ I'll remind myself that mistakes are valuable learning tools for personal development.
- ✔ I know how it feels when others fail and will sympathise with them.

Chapter 14

Succeeding in the Workplace: Creative Visualization as a Leg Up in Leadership

*T*o paraphrase a line from Shakespeare's play *Twelfth Night*, some people are born leaders, others naturally progress to positions of leadership, and some have leadership thrust upon them. But whether or not leading comes naturally to you, being a good leader isn't easy. You need to make difficult choices, assume responsibility for your team's successes and failures, accept the praise and the blame, and keep people motivated, in line, and working together.

Being aware of the specific leadership traits you want to develop allows you to use visualization effectively to become a good leader.

A number of different traits make for a good leader, of which these are probably the top five:

✔ **Confidence:** You have a high sense of confidence, in line with reality.

✔ **Consistency:** You maintain a core set of values and follow through on plans.

✔ **Priorities:** You ensure that group members know what needs to be done and when.

✔ **Purpose:** You have a strong vision that you share clearly with the group.

✔ **Relationships:** You're concerned about group members and their input.

In this chapter I describe how you can use creative visualization as a practical tool to address many of the challenges that leaders face.

Visualizing to Achieve Success as a Leader

A good leader is never satisfied with past achievements and is continually on the lookout for ways to do better. Without these characteristics you stand the risk of increased competition from other groups in the organisation and other organisations as a whole, who (if they haven't already) may surpass you in one or more areas such as research and development, creativity, turnover, profit, and so on. The world of business is highly competitive and good leadership is essential to maintaining a leading edge.

But even in less competitive industries, such as health care, education, and social work, room for improvement always exists and is often required. Faster response rates, higher qualifications and pass levels, and providing greater assistance are constantly demanded, especially in difficult economic climates in which more is expected from fewer financial resources.

The following visualization exercise helps you to stay on the lookout for ways to further improve your leadership skills:

1. **Imagine that you're a pole-vaulter.**

   The bar over which you need to vault is set at your current level of ability as a leader.

2. **Hold the pole alongside your body and start running towards the jump.**

   Lift the pole high above your head as you run.

3. **When you're close enough to the bar, thrust the foot of the pole into the receptacle.**

   Leap as it lifts you up and clear of the bar.

4. **Feel your sense of achievement as you sail over the bar.**

   Fall back down safely, and land on your back on the thick and spongy mat.

5. **Visualize that the bar is now raised an additional inch (indicating even greater leadership skills) and perform the whole exercise again.**

   Vault successfully over your new personal leadership best.

Each time you practise this exercise, you reinforce in your mind (and your unconscious mind) your desire to always improve yourself and become ever better at leading others well and effectively.

Aiming for excellence

Excellence is a talent or quality that's unusually good and so surpasses ordinary standards. So by aiming for excellence, you're trying to raise your standards that little bit higher.

You can't be the best at everything, but you can excel at one or two things by selecting a couple of goals at a time.

You may decide that your first excellence goal is customer satisfaction. Achieving such a rating requires dedication from all your customer-facing team members, with encouragement and support from you as their leader.

In order to provide your team members with the necessary reinforcement to achieve this (or any excellence-based) goal, repeat the following affirmations to yourself:

- ✔ I aim to rise to excellence wherever I see the potential.

- ✔ My quality of work will surpass ordinary standards.

- ✔ I have the ability to produce superb work.

- ✔ I will be the best that I can be.

- ✔ I'm proud of the excellent things I've done.

Repeating these affirmations holds the concept clearly in your mind that excellence is all about being better than ordinary, producing things that are better than the average, attaining higher marks than the mean, and in leadership, guiding your team always to produce better than expected results.

When you repeat these affirmations think of something superb that you like such as a great painting, a wonderful piece of music or a gripping novel and desire to be as good as that. This helps strengthen the effect of the affirmations.

With this notion of excellence at the forefront of your mind, you motivate your team as follows:

- ✔ You can explain to team members why providing truly excellent customer service is so important (repeat business, customer recommendations, fewer contract cancellations or product returns, and so on).

✔ You can outline how improving customer satisfaction affects team members on a personal level (a friendlier team, greater satisfaction with customer contacts because they complain far less, greater job security due to a strong business, and so on).

✔ You can demonstrate to team members successful ways of managing difficult customers.

These affirmations can be used with any excellence-related goal and help keep you focused on continually raising your standards in order to be a successful leader. As you read this chapter you may notice that some of the affirmations in it connect with or are similar to other affirmations in the chapter. That's to be expected because nothing is ever clearly defined and cut and dried, and much overlap exists between the various aspects of leadership

Maintaining high standards

Good leaders set consistently high standards because it encourages the entire team to aspire to a higher level of excellence. If less than high standards are set, usually only mediocre results are seen because the team members unconsciously (or even consciously) assume that not too much is expected of them.

Of course, the standards considered important vary between organisations, but some examples of keeping high standards in a business are as follows:

✔ Ensuring that reports are comprehensive and completed on time.

✔ Making research as accurate as possible and displaying it in a quality manner that's easy for all to understand.

✔ Being punctual for meetings and other events.

✔ Refusing to take sick days unless you're really unwell; normal colds and coughs are annoying but most people can still work despite having them.

✔ Maintaining a strong dress sense and always looking smart and neat.

To help keep striving for high standards, repeat the following affirmations every now and then:

✔ I enjoy aiming for and maintaining the highest standards.

✔ I'm the person to set the bar for high standards.

✔ I can more easily lead my team to success by maintaining the highest standards.

✔ I refuse to let my standards slip.

✔ I know that keeping up high standards can be hard, but doing so is absolutely worthwhile.

As you speak these affirmations (preferably out loud, but in your head if necessary) imagine yourself climbing up a ladder of which there are many, both to the left and right of you. See that some people are below you on their ladders, so you're already doing quite well, but a few others have reached a higher position than you. They have therefore set an example for you to do as well, so see yourself spurred on to match, and then pass them.

As you read each affirmation, in your imagination pull yourself another rung or two up your ladder of excellence and also note your subordinates below you as they follow your example.

This exercise may sometimes feel a little intense. Therefore, when you've finished, take a moment to relax before going about your day in a calmer manner.

Injecting a little innovation

The adoption of innovative practices, products, and ideas sets winners apart from losers, because innovation is something that drives you to the top.

Apple created the digital publishing revolution with Mac computers, seized the portable music throne from Sony with the iPod, stole a huge slice of the mobile phone pie with the iPhone, and single-handedly created the new field of tablet computing with the iPad.

How does one company keep beating the competition in this way? The simple answer is innovation. Apple consistently brings to market brand new products or ones that are demonstrably superior to those already in existence. Apple isn't a 'me-too' company. When releasing a product, Apple fully intends to become the market leader, and it does so through innovation.

Being innovative takes creativity and thought, which are two attributes that you can enhance using creative visualization. Use the following affirmations to keep the concept of innovation at the forefront of your consciousness:

✔ I'm a creative person who loves to come up with new ideas.

✔ I often pick up an item and instinctively know how it can be improved.

✔ I see ways of enhancing almost everything.

✔ I love the 'Eureka!' moment and the light that flashes in my mind when I have a great new idea.

✔ I'm becoming more and more innovative with each passing day.

As you repeat these affirmations visualize yourself – plucking great ideas out of thin air like little seeds blowing in the wind. Bring them close to your eyes and look at each one, noticing its shiny golden glow, then let it go again – because there are plenty more where they came from.

This helps strengthen your inner feeling that good ideas are everywhere and you simply have to find them to be more creative.

Turn to Chapter 17 for more exercises to develop your powers of creativity and innovation.

The LEADERSHIP mnemonic visualization

To help continuously improve your leadership skills, the word 'leadership' is a good *mnemonic* (memory-aiding technique) that sums up ten positive attributes a good leader needs, so that you can easily recall and work on them:

Level-headed — Staying calm at all times, no matter what happens.

Expectation — Fully expecting a positive outcome from your group.

Adaptability — Being able to change course according to new developments.

Demonstration — Showing each member of your team exactly what's required of them.

Enthusiasm — Possessing an overriding conviction in your team's ability and intense eagerness to succeed.

Reliability — Being reliable, sticking to your word, and coming up with the goods.

Sincerity — Speaking from the heart.

Honesty — Having integrity and never lying or cheating.

Innovation — Coming up with new ideas and ways of doing things.

Passion — Being completely committed to the team and its goals.

When aiming to improve your leadership skills in general, set aside the occasional ten minutes in which to visualize each of these attributes in turn, reflecting on how you relate to them, and how you're bringing each one more completely into your personal leadership style.

Outshining your competitors

One of the biggest indicators of your success as a leader is being able to beat your competition. You can measure your performance against others by comparing results of marketing a product in terms of units shipped, market penetration in different regions, consumer brand awareness, value of company by share price, and so on.

Use the range of all possible sets of data at your disposal to fire up your team, and from them pick the easiest target to achieve as the first goal, and move on when that's attained. When you've pinpointed a particular area in which you can beat at least one other competitor, such as product or service sales levels, try practising a visualization such as the following:

Think about the product or service your company provides: a very specialised product, a particular consulting service, a computer program, or anything. Focus on it clearly in your mind and run through all its features. Look at each feature and consider how functional it is. If within your control, change or improve that function or consider ways of doing so.

All the time think about the satisfaction of your customers and whether the feature is going to make them want to purchase more of your product or service. Consider the way your product or service is seen by the customer, such as the way it's presented, its colours, style, and design.

By performing this exercise you'll be able to think creatively about a product and more easily come up with ways in which you can increase its sales.

Using previous successes to inspire new ones

Nothing breeds success like success itself. For example, have you ever noticed how those people who do the most and obtain the best results are often given the most (and most interesting) things to do? That's because they're go-getters who thrive on success. They build a reputation for getting the job done and so end up being given increased responsibilities.

In contrast, less successful people are generally asked to do fewer tasks because they usually take much longer to finish them and always seem to have their plates so full they couldn't manage any more work. And that's just fine by many of them, because they'd often rather not have too much on their plates. But this tendency can lead to a downward spiral (of avoiding responsibility and so being offered less), which in the worst case can result in redundancy or being fired.

In a more mature organisation or team, a good idea is to remind everyone of the business's past successes to help engender feelings of pride and victory. Your team can then direct these feelings towards current projects.

Whether your team has one or one hundred past successes under its belt, I recommend providing your team members with a sheet of affirmations such as the following:

✔ Our team thrives on success.

✔ All our team projects are going to be successful.

✔ We all have the ability to bring all projects to a successful conclusion.

✔ We all play a valid part in creating success.

✔ We're all working hard towards a successful outcome.

When reading or saying these visualizations, suggest that your team members also think about a successful sporting team (or any other type of team) they support or admire, and how its members work together to achieve their results. Focusing on this role model team at the same time as reading or saying the affirmations helps to reinforce the team spirit in your staff.

You can alter these affirmations to fit in with your particular team or organisation and, in fact, ask the group members to come up with their own set of affirmations, and even use this process as an exercise in team building. In this way, everyone's part of the creation and formulation of the collective aspirations. If the team is small enough, why not ask team members to come up with one affirmation each? As your team grows, you can encourage new members to add their own affirmation to the list so that everybody's ideas are included.

I also recommend telling your team about the incredible results of writing down goals (as I describe in Chapter 4). Ask all members to take a few minutes to note down their own personal goals as they relate to the organisation. These goals don't need to be shared with the rest of the team, but are for your team members to refer to regularly in order to keep their goals at the forefront of their minds.

Gaining Respect as a Leader

Great leaders are respected because of who they are rather than the power they wield.

To be a leader you need only issue orders and ensure that they're followed, but to be a great leader who commands natural authority, you need to be respected for your confidence, reliability, trustworthiness, tolerance, and so on.

Good leaders acquire these traits through experience – the making of and learning from mistakes – and through practice. As a younger person thrust into a position of leadership, you can often face difficulties because people assume that you're too inexperienced. In which case your task is to set about earning respect as quickly as possible. But even as an experienced leader, you can keep working to maintain the level of respect your team holds for you by continuing to demonstrate characteristics that contribute to your success as a leader.

Conducting yourself with confidence

A leader needs to be (or at least needs to appear to be) extremely confident in order to earn respect. Without confidence you may appear weak and unsure of your role and strategy in the organisation, and people will then feel you have less authority over them and will be harder to motivate to properly perform the tasks you require of them. If you feel they aren't high enough you can repeat the following affirmations to help increase your confidence levels as a leader:

- ✔ I'm confident of my ability to lead people.
- ✔ I enjoy being a leader and feel extremely comfortable about it.
- ✔ I have this position of leadership because I'm the best suited for the job.
- ✔ I know that my skills and character are what make me a good leader.
- ✔ I'm a good leader and will become a great one.

To further enhance these affirmations you may wish to try standing upright and adopting a confident position as you say them. At the same time try to visualize yourself as a great leader – someone famous you admire, such as Winston Churchill, Abraham Lincoln, Mahatma Gandhi, Nelson Mandela, or perhaps an entrepreneur such as Richard Branson, and feel the sense of confident leadership that person engenders in your mind.

By combining the affirmations with your physical stance and visual imagery of a great leader, you provide lots of information to your unconscious as well as your conscious mind. The three techniques then work together to maximise their effectiveness in making you a much more confident leader.

Check out Chapter 13 for more confidence-building exercises.

Offering encouragement

One of your main tasks as a leader is to encourage the members of your team, to spur people on to do the best that they can and enjoy doing so. Your role as a leader is to explain the task at hand, describe how to accomplish it, ensure that team members have the skills required for their contribution, and encourage people to work together to complete the project – even when deadlines are ridiculously tight, money is a scarce resource, and job security isn't totally secure (even for you).

Some members of your team may struggle to motivate themselves and even those who are normally able to get started on their own may still require some encouragement. Be aware that everyone needs a bit of support now and then and people appreciate their leader taking the time to provide it.

You can encourage people in many different ways, and you're probably going to need to use different approaches for different people, as not everybody requires the same level of support. But hey, you're the boss and you know your team, so you should be able to figure out the best way to support each individual.

To develop your ability to encourage others, practise the following visualization exercise:

1. **See yourself standing in the middle of a circle of ten men and women of different ages.**

   You don't know any of them and you aren't their boss and none of them are yours. However, you know that they're all people who need a little encouragement in their lives.

2. **Visualize yourself shaking each person firmly by the hand and imagine an energy passing from you to each individual.**

   This energy contains strength, motivation, and encouragement, and it feels refreshing and healthy.

3. **Sense deeply that you want the person whose hand you're shaking to succeed in everything in life.**

   You want them to do as well as, or even surpass, you.

4. **Continue working your way around the circle until you get back to the start.**

   Pass the vital and powerful energy to each person.

5. **Go to the circumference of the circle and become the 11th person in the group.**

   All place your arms on each other's shoulders, and feel your unity and companionship.

Take this feeling with you as you go through your day at work and even throughout the rest of your life. Drawing on the feelings of comradeship and team membership generated from this exercise helps you to become more motivated to encourage other people, and makes it natural for you to bring people along with your vision.

All people are equal, even when they have authority over each other, and you're providing encouragement to others because you have the ability to do so, you want to do so, and you'd happily accept it from others – whether you're someone's boss or not.

Choosing to be trustworthy

As a leader, your team members need to trust you, otherwise it will be hard to get them on your side. Without trust, people feel little moral duty to comply with your requests and may only do so in order to keep their job or to achieve promotion, instead of because you asked them, and creative visualization can help you build this trusting relationship.

As a good leader your job is to be above reproach. To be a trustworthy leader you need to:

✔ Avoid the temptation to take shortcuts, lie, or steal.

✔ Refrain from talking about other people (peers, superiors, or team members) in a derogatory manner.

✔ Never stab others in the back.

✔ Keep to your word.

One of the major causes of upset in organisations is broken promises by the boss, leading to disappointment and grudges. If you promise something to an employee you need to stand by your word. Your word is your bond.

To help remind you of and emphasise your own honesty and trustworthiness, and to help resist temptations to get involved in corporate back-stabbing and other unpleasant things, repeat the following affirmations from time to time:

✔ I'm an honest person who's thoroughly trustworthy.

✔ I keep my promises.

✔ I refuse to use other people as simply a 'means to an end' for my own benefit.

✔ I don't talk negatively about people behind their back.

✔ I enjoy being known as an honest and trustworthy person.

Turn to Chapters 12 and 13 for more information and exercises to do with honesty and integrity.

We all know some highly successful people who get to the top using under-hand methods – but do you want to be one? I don't think so or I doubt that you'd be reading this book. Leaders who aren't trusted tend to be despised and are only tolerated as much as necessary. For example you would very soon lose respect for a boss who continually promises you a promotion or pay rise that never materialises. Neither would you trust a boss who talks badly about other employees behind their backs to speak well of you when you aren't there.

Temptation comes upon everyone and the immediate rewards can appear quite huge, but in the end an honest person regrets taking any such shortcuts.

Practising tolerance and respect

You're going come into conflict with things and people from time to time. When this situation arises, you can cope in one of two ways. On the one hand, you can tolerate and simply put up with it, albeit grudgingly. On the other hand, if you take into account why people do something or why a thing is the way it is and work on appreciating those things, people respect your behaviour. The latter respectful approach is more positive and makes for far better relations in the workplace.

As a leader, ensuring that all your team members are treated equally is important. Make sure that you fully respect all individuals' abilities, prac-tices, and beliefs, inside and outside of the workplace. When you establish a genuine sense of tolerance in your team, people are more likely to respect each other.

Creative visualization can help you practise being a tolerant and respectful leader, so that these qualities will clearly come through in your work life.

By respecting differences through understanding them (even if you disagree with them), you're better able to integrate your team, enjoy working with everyone, and pass your values of tolerance and respect on to others.

The following affirmations help you to keep tolerance and respect firmly in mind so that you always properly take into account the views, practices, and needs of everyone in your team.

✔ Tolerance is a worthy aim, but respect is far worthier.

✔ Even though I may not believe in something myself, I respect other people's rights to do so and their reasons.

✔ As a leader I want everyone working together as a team and won't exclude any member for any practice or belief.

✔ I understand that other people may not agree with my opinions but trust they'll respect my right to have them.

✔ My leadership philosophy is always inclusion over exclusion.

While repeating these affirmations, visualize that you're walking in the park when a thunderstorm suddenly blows in, and the rain begins pelting down. Fortunately you have an umbrella with you, which in your visualization is able to expand to any size you need. This is fortunate because you can now invite all the other park visitors nearby to shelter under it with you. There are people of both sexes, all ages and all religions, but all are welcome under your umbrella.

It's a slightly complex visualization to imagine while repeating affirmations, so just imagine one or two people coming under your umbrella at a time, before moving on to the next affirmation, so that by the time you've finished repeating them you have a motley collection of colourful characters all sharing the use of your umbrella.

By combining these affirmations with this visualization you experience what it is like to respect and provide a service to people simply because they are fellow humans.

Being reliable

When you're responsible for a team of people, you have to be thoroughly reliable, otherwise the team flounders and ultimately fails in its tasks. You're the oil in the works and the master clock by which others are set. To be an effective leader it is best to set a good example by attending all meetings where you're needed and producing your reports on time. When you say you're going to do something, it's important to ensure that you do it. And when a team member is stuck, you're the person to help them out if no one else can.

Your vision and leadership drive your team and if you can't be relied on in your tasks, your team members are likely to be unreliable as well. For a start they may be confused by mixed signals due to never knowing whether (or if) you'll turn up for meetings, or when you'll have your reports ready, and so on. And after a while you can lose control of the reins and find that another (more reliable) member of the team usurps your role.

Mental flash cards for better leadership

The following mental flash cards can help you with becoming a good leader:

Getting a deal or completing a project: See the deal completed or the project finished in your mind's eye. Note how good you feel and savour the satisfaction of success.

Noticing opportunity when it knocks: Imagine that you're in a corridor with hundreds of doors and behind each one is a wonderful opportunity. Approach any door and as you hear a quiet knocking, open it and feel pleasant surprise at what awaits behind.

Being a lighthouse: Visualize yourself as a lighthouse standing tall and proud, a beacon for your colleagues, lighting the way to a safe and successful navigation of the current project. Feel yourself as a strong protector of others.

Navigating a mental road map: In your mind's eye, create a map of your project, filling in all the roads, obstacles, stopovers, milestones, and so on. Keep the map updated and review it from time to time.

Playing tug of war: Imagine that your team is playing tug-of-war against your competitors. Each of you is pulling as hard as you can on the rope and you easily pull the competition over the line. Experience the pleasure you feel in being part of the winning team.

Here are some affirmations you can repeat to keep the concept of reliability uppermost in your mind. If you're prone to being disorganised, these phrases help you lead a much more manageable life:

- ✔ Punctuality is important to me.
- ✔ I'm never late for appointments.
- ✔ I do what I say I'm going to do.
- ✔ I always finish the things that I start.
- ✔ I can be relied on to help others in a fix.

As you repeat these affirmations imagine a large clock in your mind's eye, with the time set to 11:55 a.m. and a door under it behind which you're due to attend a meeting at 12:00 p.m. You're five minutes early and have therefore arrived in good time, just as you always do.

This single focus, combined with repeating the affirmations, will help embed your desire to be reliable more deeply, and will help you find the time you need to be punctual, the motivation to complete tasks that you start, and the willingness to help other people in need.

As with all visualizations and affirmations, try your best to feel an emotional response as you perform the exercise to further enhance its effectiveness. For example, feel a quiet pride in always being punctual and standing by your word, and feel compassion for others so that you have increased desire to help them.

Communicating Your Vision

People follow good leaders because the person displays something that others want to follow; usually, this 'something' is the leader's vision, which infects everyone else with its vitality.

As a good leader you have to be a good communicator and develop the ability to explain your own and your organisation's visions (which are closely inter-related, I hope). In other words you need to be a storyteller and an example setter, and show that your vision drives you and keeps you and your team motivated to complete a project successfully.

Using creative visualization you can practise passing on your vision to others so that when it comes to doing so in real life you're more effective at getting it across.

Sharing your enthusiasm

An enthusiastic leader is an infectious one, because nothing shows dedication and vision more than enthusiasm. As a leader, be as enthusiastic as you can about your organisation and its products or services so that you similarly enthuse your subordinates.

Being enthusiastic is a great benefit to you as well as your team, because the enthusiasm that you bring to a project helps to keep you fired up and focused.

To keep your enthusiasm strong, here's a visualization exercise you can practise:

1. **Imagine that you're somewhere outside, quiet and peaceful.**

   Perhaps you're by the seashore, or at a country campsite. The sun has gone down and the sky's a dark blue with just a few specks of stars starting to show.

2. **Hold your hands out in front of you forming a bowl and notice a small orange glow in it.**

   This glow is your enthusiasm for life.

3. **Gently blow onto the orange glow to feed the flames.**

   Watch the ball of fire grow as it writhes and flickers colours of red, yellow, orange, and sometimes blue and white.

4. **Remember how much you love life, love your friends and family, and all the things you do, at home, at work, and everywhere you go.**

   Feed that love into the fire and watch it grow to the size of a basketball. The love even has a little weight so you have to use your muscles to hold it up.

5. **Feel the warmth and energy coming back to you from your ball of enthusiasm.**

   Look around you and see how it lights the ground and other things nearby (such as rocks or trees) with a shimmering glow.

6. **Get ready to release the ball.**

   Tense your muscles, take a deep breath, and fling it high into the sky where it explodes like a magnificent firework, sending colourful sparks across the world to light up other people's lives.

7. **Watch the firework of enthusiasm fade away and then let your eyes get re-accustomed to the night sky.**

   Smell the fresh air, feel the gentle breeze, and sense that you're at one with the world.

Don't worry that your enthusiasm is now gone because you have plenty more where that came from – nothing is lost by doing this exercise; in fact it helps to substantially increase your enthusiasm.

By practising this exercise you increase your own levels of enthusiasm, which you outwardly express and are able to use to help motivate your team.

Demonstrating your commitment

Some projects or work environments are long-term and keeping up the necessary work can be difficult. In this situation you need *commitment*: the dedication to turn up day after day to complete a hard day's work and to stick with the project at hand and not quit.

As the team's leader, your job is to stay focused and lead from the front. Even if you have a really bad cold, try to turn up because you should have fewer sick days than any other team member. At those times when you find inspiration hard to come by and are tired, don't let yourself slack off. You're the leader and are expected to work the hardest of all.

Using creative visualization you can reinforce your level of commitment to such an extent that it is clearly obvious to the rest of your team or department.

Here are some affirmations you can use to keep yourself (and your team) going when you find the going gets tough:

- ✔ I always finish whatever I start.

- ✔ I'm not a quitter.

- ✔ I lead my team from the front and by example.

- ✔ I care deeply about this project, my organisation, and my team.

In America there was a very well-known series of TV advertisements for a mobile telephone company, in which an engineer was seen continuously testing the signal strength of the network in a variety of locations. And always behind him was his team of engineers carrying a range of different pieces of equipment, ready to work on any problem or make any necessary upgrades to the network, and so on.

As you repeat these affirmations, imagine you're like that engineer, and that your team is right behind you as you lead the way forwards. You provide leadership and direction, while your staff provide the support required to achieve the team's objectives.

'Painting the vista'

Victor Kiam was an entrepreneur who started his career as a salesman for the Playtex company. He became famous when, after his wife bought him a Remington shaver, he was so impressed that he 'bought the company'. Things aren't quite as simple as that, though, because he had amassed substantial savings and was looking for a good venture in which to invest – the shaver simply came along at the right time. But the incident made a great sales line that Kiam used in his television advertising.

In his autobiographical book _Going for it! The man who bought the company_, Kiam frequently tells how important 'painting the vista' is when trying to bring other people on board with your vision. He explains the process as being like painting a picture in front of someone, and this technique works remarkably well when you need to explain something to your team.

The unconscious mind loves imagery and responds well to it, so share your 'vistas' with others and discover a great communication tool.

Making decisions and justifying them

You're the boss, and your way is best. Of course you're open to the ideas and suggestions of other people and you're not saying that every idea you have is the only way that something can be done – but you're sure that your approach to the job in hand is the right one.

The following affirmations help you to evaluate your decisions in order to always try and make the best ones:

- ✔ I always try to examine things from all possible angles.
- ✔ I consider the effects of taking and of not taking a decision.
- ✔ I imagine implementing all the options to see which works best when more than one way of doing something is possible.
- ✔ I'm open to suggestions and if an idea is better than mine I'm happy to use it.
- ✔ I take care to make the right decisions so I can always explain my reasoning.

When repeating these affirmations, try bringing back to mind the sphere in the preceding section and visualize turning it to a variety of different angles, as you peek into different parts of your organisation to get yourself even better acquainted. This gives a visual enhancement to the affirmations that helps increase their effectiveness.

Your job as leader is not only to make the decisions, but also to communicate them to the team and quite often to persuade others to get on board with your ideas and plans of action.

Creative visualization can help you better justify your decisions to other people by analysing them in advance so that you have ready answers always available for even the trickiest of questions.

Here's a visualization technique that can help when you're presenting a new idea, strategy, or project to a group of people.

Visualize clearly in your mind's eye what you need to explain, as if you're looking at an actual painting. See all the parts that make up the whole and how they relate to each other. If you like, add some explanations or diagrams to the picture until it's complete and fully explanatory. (For more on creating pictures in this way, see the earlier sidebar 'Painting the vista'.)

When you're ready to make your explanation, recall the image you painted previously. As you talk, paint your picture again in your mind's eye in bright and vivid colours with broad and confident brushstrokes. Take your audience with you as you're painting, and when the picture's finished, everyone has a very clear idea of exactly what you want them to know.

Visualizing in order to Motivate Your Team

Whenever I think about motivation I'm reminded of a line in the song 'Motivation' by Steve Hillage from the album *Motivation Radio*: 'Motivation is the key'. The entire disc is a concept album (much loved by 'hippies') about getting up and doing something positive in your life. But the record also has a clear message for everyone in that motivation is the key to many things.

Without motivation in life, little would get done. Humans even have chemicals in their brains that make them feel good in order to motivate people to do all the necessary things for survival: for example, when you eat, you feel an enjoyable sensation. If these chemicals didn't exist, perhaps humans wouldn't have lasted very long as a species, because early humans would simply not have bothered to eat very much (assuming the negative motivator of hunger was also missing).

But humans have come a long way from being primitive creatures and now have a whole host of things that motivate them, such as money, possessions, arts, crafts, sports, and so on. The trouble is that with so many distractions nowadays, people can have difficulty choosing their motivators. Consequently some people give up and do very little.

But if, as a leader, you can guide your team members in the right direction and find the necessary motivators, you can steer your team wherever you need it to go, and by using creative visualization you can gain experience and practice in motivating your team in your mind, before doing so in real life, helping ensure that you do a great job.

Providing focus

When your team has a number of goals to achieve, keeping everyone working together with the same aim can be hard. But if you provide focus for your team, it more clearly sees where it needs to be heading and its members understand what's required of them.

You can provide focus for your team by using creative visualization. If you highlight single goals at any one time and let your team focus all its energies in that direction, you can ensure that the job gets done, and gets done well.

Here's a visualization technique you can use to refine the focus in your mind and help identify where focus needs to be directed within your team:

1. **Spend five minutes looking at all the things your team needs to achieve.**

   For example, trim overheads by 10 per cent, beat company X at selling units of product Y, increase the number of visitors to your website, and so on.

2. **Try and narrow in on the one most important task as your focus.**

   For example, perhaps you decide that beefing up the website is the most important task because Internet sales are cheaper to make than sales through distributors.

3. **Examine clearly in your mind: it's the focus point on which your team needs to concentrate.**

   For example, does your current website require a re-design? Do you have sufficient web servers to handle a lot of additional visitors? Can you negotiate a better commission for credit card sales from your card processor if sales do increase? Do you have enough customer support staff to handle the potential additional enquiries?

4. **Once you have all aspects of the task in your mind, decide which one to work on first.**

   For example, you may decide that a re-design is the first port of call, so you've found the most important priority.

Repeat this exercise from time to time. And if the focus point turns out to be the same as the last time you performed the exercise, that's fine – you just haven't quite completed that aspect of the project yet.

When you have this focus clearly in your mind, you can more easily convey it to others when guiding their progress and motivating them.

Setting challenges

One great way to motivate people is to give them challenges.

When my wife and I used to run public houses and restaurants, we frequently set contests in which employees attaining certain goals (such as serving a set number of customers or up-selling a fixed quantity of desserts) achieved a cash bonus or small prize, with an even greater incentive for the member of staff who performed the best. We kept a chart on the wall and the staff constantly tried to outdo each other, while behind the scenes staff in the kitchen had their own non-customer-facing targets and bonuses too.

All organisations are different and lend themselves better to different incentives, which means that you can have some fun coming up with your own challenges and incentives for your staff or team members.

Try this creative visualization exercise to focus on the challenges and incentives that motivate your team to perform to their highest capability.

Set aside some time to think about and visualize your team as an organic whole, rather than a collection of individuals. Think about the power they have as a team due to the ability to split large tasks into smaller parts and assign them to different people to undertake.

Concentrate on areas that can be improved in your organisation and imagine ways in which you can motivate your team to achieve these improvements. Work through these areas in your mind and use mind movies to see whether the incentives you think of seem to work.

For example, perhaps you operate a restaurant and have determined that the layout of the tables is slowing down service to the tables, due to waiting staff having to detour around certain sections. In this case, to save moving the tables about many times until you achieve a solution, visualize doing so and make a mind movie of your waiting staff using a new layout to see if it works. Now you need only to try out this smaller number of configurations that have worked in your imagination, and you'll have a solution far more quickly than through physically trying a large variety of different layouts.

Go to Chapter 2 for more on creating mind movies.

Implementing the challenges and incentives that you visualized can result in a more highly motivated team.

Meeting milestones

When your team is working on larger, long-term goals, a good idea is to set milestones at appropriate points in a project's overall time line, which can be treated as mini goals. When these milestones are checked off, they can work just as effectively for motivation purposes as main goals.

You can break the stages of any project down in the same way and creative visualization can help you.

Use the following visualization technique to help you identify appropriate milestones in your project for yourself or your team:

1. **Visualize your whole project, and everything required to complete it, as a movie that you can play through in your mind.**

   Visit Chapter 2 to discover how to make your own mind movie.

2. **Start the movie rolling and make notes of important landmarks.**

   For example, completing each of a number of different sections in a catalogue, receiving proofs of the catalogue for grammar and spell checking, and so on.

3. **Use your mental fast-forward button to skip past less relevant scenes.**

   For example, collecting proofs from the typesetting department and other essential administration but make sure that you see all the important ones.

4. **Run the movie backwards, because the backwards viewing provides a different viewpoint to forwards.**

   See if that brings up any scenes you'd forgotten about: you don't want to miss anything important, so double-checking is good practice.

5. **Get a pen and piece of paper.**

   Write down all the noteworthy events in order of occurrence.

6. **Decide which of the events need to be treated as milestones.**

   These will be things that have a clear end, such as completion of a section of a catalogue, taking the final photograph, and so on.

7. **Choose what reward to provide for the completion of each milestone.**

   Maybe allocate a budget from which to provide free cinema tickets, restaurant vouchers, and so on.

Using a spreadsheet program is an easy way to record your milestones and keep track of them when they're achieved.

Building camaraderie

If you want a productive team, you need a happy one. Camaraderie is more than simply friendship: it's the good natured and light-hearted rapport between people who spend a lot of time together.

Using creative visualization you can first get this camaraderie going in your own mind, before setting out to spread it around your team.

Repeat the following affirmations in order to keep camaraderie uppermost in your mind as something important to foster in your team:

- ✔ I want everyone working together towards a common goal.

- ✔ I always give praise where praise is due.

- ✔ I ask team members to take on greater responsibilities as and when they're ready.

- ✔ I require team members to rely on each other more and more as they become more capable.

- ✔ I always do my best to engender greater commitment from the team, to the project, and to each other.

As you read these affirmations, imagine that you're the captain of a sports team (in any type of sport such as soccer, volleyball, baseball, cricket and so on), and visualize that you're about to play a match and are giving a pep talk to your fellow team members. Feel how you're being your most encouraging and persuasive to motivate everyone to put in their best effort and work towards beating the other team. Feel the warmth of agreement and support from everyone as together you're all whipped up to a level of excitement ready to go out and win.

The combination of this visualization and the emotions accompanying it along with the affirmations will ensure that your commitment to building team camaraderie will remain high.

Encouraging growth

Just as you're continuing to grow in your personal and professional life, also assist the growth of your team members by encouraging them to try different tasks, take on new roles, attend training, and so on.

Their personal growth is important to you and to them, because as their skills improve so does the input they provide to your organisation. And, yes, some are going to grow wings and fly away to pastures new. But that's the nature of life; never hold anyone back just for your own benefit.

You may find the following affirmations helpful in increasing the amount of growth you encourage from your team members:

✔ I value each person as an important team member.

✔ I want all my team members to excel at what they do and always get better at it.

✔ I do everything in my power to help my team members fulfil their true abilities.

✔ I won't stand in the way of team members who are clearly heading for bigger and greater things, and I'll help them if I can.

✔ I want to grow in my life and so I encourage my team members to grow too.

A good visualization to accompany these affirmations is to imagine your team as a blackberry bramble. All right, they may be prickly plants but their fruit is delicious. See yourself and each of the team members as a leafless bramble at the start of spring. Some of you are roots, while others are branches and vines interconnected with each other. Then, as spring arrives, others of your team form leaves, while yet others blossom into flowers. As the season turns into summer, a few vines return to the earth and bury themselves to form new roots and whole new brambles, as the plant that is your team creates off-shoots (representing people leaving for other departments or companies).

Simply imagine a new stage of growth between each of the affirmations, and feel the sense of both your team and the bramble experiencing strong and healthy growth. Growth is the lifeblood of most businesses, and so this combination of visualization and affirmations helps you to embody growth as an important part of your personal management style.

If you encourage growth in those you lead (and everyone, in fact), you all grow together and keep experiencing bigger and better things as your group's input into your organisation (and life in general) increases.

Leadership For Dummies by John Marrin (John Wiley & Sons, Ltd.) is packed with lots more tips on how to be a successful leader.

Chapter 15

Attaining Sporting Excellence

. . . .

. . . .

*N*owadays, just about every professional sport incorporates creative visualization into the training process in one way or another. So take a leaf out of the professional sportsperson's book and use visualization for your own purposes, and those of your local sports team.

Time and time again research shows that visualizing yourself participating in a sport in advance allows you to increase your results. Of course, you also have to practise your skills physically and increase your strength, but when you visualize as well you improve those skills at a far greater rate.

Whether you actively compete in a team sport such as football, rugby, or cricket, an individual sport such as tennis, golf, or athletics, or you enjoy an informal game of pool or darts or participate in quiz nights (a form of mental sport), the visualization exercises in this chapter help you increase your ability and performance.

When you get the hang of the techniques in this chapter – and prove to yourself that they work (and work well) – you can pass your knowledge on to team members or fellow enthusiasts so that everyone benefits from the results.

Stretching Your Ability

The objective of all sports is to improve your performance continuously (even when at the peak of your sport), because world records are always getting broken as people push the barriers further and further and keep on raising the bar. Simply maintaining excellent skills isn't sufficient when your competitors begin to surpass you.

You can (and will) continue to improve your abilities. Keeping this perspective at the forefront of your mind ensures that you stay driven to push yourself ever harder to attain your goals.

Whether you're an amateur or a professional, or you simply play the odd game of ten-pin bowling for fun, you gain tremendous satisfaction each time you're a little bit better than in the last game. Or at least on average, your results tend to improve.

Going the extra mile

Whichever sporting activity you participate in, the long-distance running analogy of 'going an extra mile' works well. For example, pole-vaulters raise the bar, weight-lifters increase the weights, and runners decrease the length of time to cover a set distance. The following visualization exercise helps you when preparing to participate in a marathon race:

1. **Imagine that you're in your running clothes and standing on the starting line of a marathon race.**

   The race is just over 26 miles in length, and the average time to complete the distance is between 4½ and 5 hours, which works out at somewhere between 10 and 12 minutes a mile. However, for the purposes of this exercise, you're going to complete the entire course in only a couple of minutes.

2. **Hear the starting pistol fire and begin running.**

   Use a strong, solid, and regular pace that you intend to maintain for the marathon.

3. **Visualize passing the mile markers.**

   At this speeded up time, each 5 seconds or so represents a mile, so imagine passing the mile markers every few seconds, counting them from 1 to 26 and to the finish line.

4. **Keep going for another few seconds even when you pass the finish line so that you complete a 27th mile.**

   See how you took only a few seconds extra at this superfast speed, and then think that you'd still take less than 12 minutes more to complete that extra mile in a real marathon.

By seeing yourself completing a marathon and also going that bit farther, when you do run one for real this exercise helps to keep you psyched up through to the end, with energy to spare. Practised regularly, this visualization also instils in you the urge to always do that bit better.

Whatever your chosen sport, you can adapt this visualization to it. For example, you can imagine pole-vaulting higher, leaping farther, throwing a javelin a greater distance, climbing higher, swimming for longer, and so on – simply imagine completing an event and then doing that little bit extra.

Becoming stronger and faster every day

Every day that you train, the goal is to become better at your sport, which means that you need to be getting stronger and faster until you reach your peak; and even then you can often improve on that.

You can be sure that by putting in the hard work of exercising you're going to improve – the laws of physics say so, particularly when you follow tried and tested training regimes. And visualizing creatively allows you to speed up the process and achieve bigger and better results, because you're bringing your whole consciousness onboard with the programme – both your conscious and unconscious minds.

Use this visualization exercise to work on your physical strength:

1. **Imagine that you're in front of a fairground strength tester.**

   You need to smash the mallet as hard as you can onto the tester to send an indicator shooting up the device.

2. **Make your first attempt.**

   Pick up the heavy mallet, heave it up and over your shoulders down onto the tester, and watch the indicator fly up to the 80 mark. Not bad, for a first try.

3. **Make the second strike.**

   Hit even harder and send the indicator all the way up to 90, which is a great improvement; but you can do even better.

4. **Try one last time.**

   Visualize mustering all the energy you have until your body's pulsing with vitality, and then swing that mallet down as hard as you can so that the indicator shoots up the tester and smashes into the bell at the top with a loud ding.

Running faster involves not only the speed of your body but also your reflexes, and you work on both in the following visualization:

1. **Prepare to run a 100-metre race in your mind.**

   Get yourself ready at the line in your starting position with your feet on the blocks and begin building up all your energy reserves until you feel like a tightly wound spring.

2. **Go!**

   When you hear the starting pistol, explode all this energy into your initial dash from the starting line, and then keep your head down against the wind resistance as you move your legs faster than ever before, driving yourself quickly forwards.

3. **Push harder.**

   About halfway along the track, start straightening out your body ready for the final dash. Stay full of energy but also relaxed, knowing that you have more than enough energy reserves to finish the race at this speed. Continue running until the last few metres when you put every ounce of energy you have remaining into going even faster, so that as you thrust your chest forward and cross the line you're moving at your maximum speed.

Doing your best plus a little more

In this exercise you do your very best and then a little more, pushing yourself beyond your previous limits:

1. **Imagine yourself performing a pull-up – lift your body up until your chin touches the bar.**

   The first time isn't too hard, and is maybe even easy. But after just a few pull-ups, most people can't go on. So visualize that you're capable of exactly ten pull-ups before your arms are totally exhausted (unless you're already good at pull-ups, in which case just imagine the final ten pull-ups you can do before your arms give up).

2. **Pull your body up another nine times.**

   Each time you stretch your neck to get your chin to touch the bar, and each time you summon more and more strength to your arms, while the ache and pain of tired muscles creeps up, until you have only just managed to perform your tenth and final pull-up. That's it, your arms hurt far too much to go on, and so let your body back down until your toes touch the floor.

3. **Visualize that you have a reserve of fuel, just like in a car, and that just enough energy remains in your body to go for one final pull-up.**

   You know that doing so is going to hurt like mad, but you also know that you can do it.

4. **Lift up that one extra time, knowing that you can do it.**

   You can break through that pain barrier and your muscles are going to provide the strength to get your chin to touch the bar one final time, and as you see yourself doing this in your mind's eye, release a mental flow of painkillers into your arms as you let yourself back down. The pain is gone and you feel good. You achieved something you never thought possible: you passed the point that always held you back.

Now you know that, from time to time, you can beat your personal best. Doing so may take grit, determination, and some pain, but you *can* do it.

Cheering yourself on

The support of a crowd definitely helps when playing sport, which is one reason why teams win more often at home than away. But when you're practising, you often do so on your own (or with a few others) and with no one to cheer you on.

Using creative visualization, however, allows you to benefit from the positive energy that supporters bring even when you're training alone:

1. **Visualize that you're running a 1,600 metre race – very nearly a mile, exactly four laps of a standard track,. Or, if you're a runner, choose any distance you commonly run.**

   Now imagine and that you're into the final lap, with two runners just ahead of you. See how you're pacing them well but just can't quite get the speed up to overtake.

2. **Visualize a crowd of supporters cheering you on from the stands.**

   They're shouting your name and willing you to win. Just hearing this support gives you a boost of energy.

3. **Feel the energy flow through you as you pass one of your competitors and move into second place.**

   You hear a roar from the crowd who now know that you have a chance of winning, so they shout even louder.

4. **See yourself draw neck and neck with the leader with just 100 metres left to go.**

Again hear the crowd roar, spurring you to pull on just enough extra resources to inch ahead, and then take the lead by a metre as you pass the finishing line.

Seeing how you achieved a goal

By imagining that you've already achieved a goal, you can put yourself in the position of looking back to see how you managed it. This exercise creates the effect of making you think through and examine the steps necessary to attain a goal, and encourages you to try that bit harder in order to do so.

1. **Imagine that you want to win a pool tournament.**

   You're going to have to beat some really skilled players to do so.

2. **Think of the person who's the best pool player you're likely to be up against.**

   Imagine sinking the final ball in the final game to beat that person.

3. **Think about the other player's style of play.**

   Perhaps it comprises many straight shots but not sharply angled ones. Or maybe there are a few shots that bounce off a cushion rather than directly.

4. **Look back at the match and see how you managed to manoeuvre the balls in such a way as to make every shot as difficult as possible, taking into account your opponent's strengths and weaknesses.**

   See how your accuracy in potting the balls was excellent and that you hit all the shots that your opponent found hard.

Whatever competitive sport you participate in, you know something about your competitors and their abilities and failings, so use this information in your visualizations to see yourself beating them by using their weaknesses against them. Even in sports that aren't directly competitive, you can simply visualize looking back on a race you won or some weights you lifted (or any other success) as if you've already achieved it, and see the whole process of doing so in your mind.

This type of visualization is as good as an actual physical practice session in terms of developing your skills. It also has the advantage of demonstrating to your unconscious mind what attaining your desired goal feels like, and showing ways in which it can help you.

Being a Winner

No matter how often people say that taking part in sport is more important than winning, you can't get past the fact that winning feels wonderful. Unfortunately, having winners also means having losers; perhaps the fact that no one can win every time is all to the good, because others also therefore have a shot at winning. Winning spurs you on, and everyone wants to (and needs to) win from time to time.

But how do you get to win that very first time? The answer is to play against others of equal ability, which is why different leagues or divisions exist in many sports, with the best players moving on to the better teams. As you grow and improve you keep moving up until you reach your level of ability, racking up wins along the way.

Even in non-competitive sports (or physical activities that you can enjoy without competing), such as canoeing, surfing, hiking, cycling, jogging, and so on, you can still be a winner by playing against yourself and beating your previous records.

These achievements feel every bit as good as winning against a competitor, particularly because you always win when you participate in sport because you're making your heart healthier and your muscles stronger, and you're losing excess weight.

Breaking the ribbon

Many metaphors for winning exist, of which the most obvious is probably breaking the ribbon at the finishing line. Even if running isn't your sport, you can still use the following visualization to strengthen your desire to win and get your unconscious mind more fully on board with your sporting ambitions.

1. **Picture yourself running in the race that I introduce in the earlier 'Cheering yourself on' section.**

   You're at the halfway mark running with all the speed you can muster.

2. **Steal a quick look around you and notice that a couple of runners are close on your tail.**

   A few more are a little farther behind them, while in front of you are just two runners.

3. **As in the previous visualization of this race, pick up the pace until you pass one of the leaders.**

   You're now in second place.

4. **Move into first place.**

   You're leading by a metre.

5. **Cross the finishing line.**

   Break the ribbon as you win.

6. **Feel the paper tape snap and fall away.**

   You're number one. You've won!

Of course, actual ribbons haven't been widely used in professional track events for years (organisers now use infrared beams of light). Nevertheless, visualizing the physical nature of the ribbon works well for this exercise. If you do participate in track events and want something more realistic, however, imagine breaking a warm beam of energy-giving light instead. Even though the beams are harmless and don't convey any heat, imagining that they do is useful for the sake of the exercise.

Standing on the winner's podium

After you've won an event in any reasonably large competition, a prize-giving ceremony follows in which you normally get to stand on a podium. Many athletes aspire to this goal and doing so makes a powerful visualization.

1. **Imagine that you've won an event at the Olympic Games (perhaps the race in the exercise in the preceding section).**

   You're approaching the winner's podium.

2. **Look around you and see the audience in the stadium clapping and shouting wildly.**

   Camera flashes are glittering all around.

3. **Climb the steps to the top position on the podium.**

   Wait as the competitors you beat into second and third place join you.

4. **Watch the Olympic official approaching and bend forward to allow placing the medal cord over your head.**

   Shake hands, stand up straight, and wave to the cheering crowd.

5. **Revel in the fact that, right now, you're number one.**

   You are the champion.

When performing this exercise, maintain strong expectations that this occasion is going to happen to you one day (perhaps not the Olympics, but maybe another winner's podium). Keep firmly in your mind that through effort and dedication you're going to work your way to the point of being able to beat the other competitors at your level of your chosen sport. Firmly believe that winning is your destiny and not just an idle fantasy. Know that you have to work hard – probably harder than all your competitors if you're to win – and that winning isn't going to be easy, but that you *will* succeed.

Making the highest jump or longest leap

Winners go higher and farther than anyone else, which is why they win. And when participating in any sport, your objective always needs to be to try and do the same; go higher or farther than your previous best, or than the other competitors.

1. **Imagine that you're competing in a high jump contest and are to go last.**

   See the other contestants run up to and leap over the bar head first, some succeeding without knocking the bar down, others not so lucky.

2. **Take your turn.**

   Visualize a good approach, springing up high, easily soaring over the bar, and landing safely and smoothly on the padded mat.

3. **Watch as the bar is raised for the next round.**

   See all your competitors try to jump over it, with a couple of them almost making it, but none succeeding in doing so without knocking the bar off its rests.

4. **Take your turn again.**

   Know that you can clear this height. You've seen the other participants get close and can feel just where they went wrong. All you need is that extra half-inch of lift. So take your run up and jump the hardest you've ever jumped in your life.

5. **Switch the scene to slow motion and feel yourself gliding through the air, lifting your legs and body up high enough to clearly pass over the bar by at least an inch.**

   You made it and are the clear winner.

Similarly, you can try a visualization based on the long jump. Practise the same exercise but change the situation to a long jump and visualize landing in a soft sand pit. Practising these exercises allows you to strengthen your desire to win and your belief that you can do so.

You can easily change this exercise to almost any sport to better suit your personal sporting ambitions.

Hitting the bull's-eye

Some sports and activities require skill and accuracy rather than speed and stamina. These include archery, pool and snooker, darts, and shooting, or mental sports such as quizzes, card games, and so on. You also need to be accurate in team sports in which passing the ball without it being intercepted is critical, or when scoring a goal in football or a hoop in basketball.

To help psych yourself up for greater accuracy, imagine that you're in front of a dartboard, as shown in Figure 15-1:

1. **Visualize yourself throwing darts ever closer to the bull's-eye.**

   Each one is getting closer than the last.

2. **Start by aiming at anywhere on the board.**

   See the dart land in an outer segment.

3. **Throw more and more darts.**

   See each subsequent dart landing closer to the centre, until you get one into the outer of the two bull's-eye rings.

4. **Keep on throwing in this way.**

   Note the weight of the dart in your hand, the feel of your arm, and the action of your wrist as you throw; and hit the centre bull's-eye over and over again.

5. **Now visualize going round the board hitting sections of your choice at will.**

   Aim for all the larger outer sections in order from 1 to 20, and then the inner ones, and then all the small sections on the circumference (the double point areas) followed by the smaller ones farther in (treble point areas).

If you have access to a dartboard, try practising one of these exercises first for real and note down how you do. Then perform the visualization exercises, take a brief rest, and try throwing darts again for real. You may well see an improvement even after only one visualization session. And over time, by visualizing as well as practising, your aim steadily improves.

If archery is your sport, try this exercise with that equipment. Or take a basketball and practise shooting hoops from varying distances in real life and as a visualization. You can do the same with golf and many other sports involving accuracy.

Figure 15-1:
A dartboard
with 20
subdivided
sections
and an inner
and outer
bull's-eye.

Scoring the winning goal

If you like to participate in team sports, a great visualization exercise is to
imagine yourself scoring the winning goal in football, basketball, ice hockey,
or any team sport with a ball and a goal (or hoop or whatever).

1. **Visualize the last couple of minutes of a game in which the scores
   are level.**

   See yourself being passed a golden opportunity by a team member.

2. **Seize the day and make sure that you don't fumble.**

   Receive the ball and kick it into the back of the net, or toss the basketball into the hoop, or whack the ice-hockey puck into the back of
   the net.

3. **Hear the final whistle or bell sound.**

   See your team all run up to you to congratulate you. Your goal helped
   your team to victory.

If you don't play in a goal-scoring position in your team, modify the exercise to
where you make an essential last-ditch tackle or provide the perfect pass to a
team member who then scores that winning goal. Or you can save a goal in a
penalty shoot-out and lead your team to victory that way.

Enhancing Your Physique

The tone of your physique has an important bearing on how well you play
a sport. Even less obviously physical sports such as golf, darts, and pool
require trained and controlled muscles for maximum accuracy, and energetic
sports need a strong body with toned muscles and plenty of stamina.

But as well as focusing on specific limbs, sets of muscles, or other parts of the body you use for your sport, it also makes good sense to ensure that your whole body is in the best condition you can manage. The exercises in this section help you with this aim. You can then focus on the specific areas you want to target.

Feeling energy pulsing through you

Practise the following visualization exercise regularly whenever you're trying to build up your strength and stamina. You therefore prepare yourself for the work and exercise required to tone your body. And the exercise gives you the mental energy and endurance you need to stick with the task, when you may otherwise get too tired or distracted.

1. **Sit upright in your chair.**

   Imagine that your spine is an energy-receiving point for your body, acting like an antenna picking up cosmic vibrations from the universe.

2. **Relax and focus only on your spine.**

   Tune it into the most energetic vibrations, until you can feel your spine tingling from top to bottom.

3. **Feel shivers running up and down your back.**

   Wriggle your shoulder blades and hips as the energy starts to pulse into your arms and legs.

4. **Feel the energy push out along your limbs.**

   It's revitalising every muscle and nerve, relieving aches and pains, and replacing them with a warm feeling of vitality.

5. **Sense the energy also continuing up your spine and into your brain.**

   It feels warm and tingly too.

6. **Now the energy reaches your fingers and toes as it completes filling up every part of your body.**

   Like a battery you're fully charged, so tune out your energy receiver and go and practise your normal physical exercises.

Practise this visualization immediately before exercising or doing anything that requires you to use your muscles extensively; doing so psychs you up and gets you off to a great start. If you've read Chapter 13 you may have noticed that this exercise is similar to one I provide there for infusing yourself with confidence, because this type of exercise works well for empowering both mind and body.

Always warm up slowly when exercising, particularly if you're older and even if it doesn't seem to hurt. That way you avoid over-exerting yourself, your muscles, or your heart. And if you haven't exercised for some time, make sure that you consult a qualified professional first.

Striving to be ever stronger

The cornerstone of all strength training equipment is the bench press or free weight bench, in which you lie on your back and lift barbells up over your head. Although hard work, it really brings results and makes for a great visualization exercise:

1. **Imagine that you're lying on a bench press.**

   You have a stack of weights on both sides of you and the barbell above. You can see ten pairs of weights in total, and you're going to lift them all.

2. **Lift the first set of weights.**

   Visualize your personal trainer attaching the lightest pair of weights, and now lift the bar off its rest and up over your head. Hold it there. It's an effort to do but manageable.

3. **Lift the next heaviest weights.**

   Have your trainer swap the weights for the next heaviest pair and lift them. This time you have to strain more and you pull you face into a slight grimace as you do so, but you manage to lift the bar up and hold it for a few seconds. Feel how your muscles are acclimatising to the work and gaining in strength with each lift.

4. **Complete this exercise until you've lifted all ten sets of weights, each heaver than the previous set.**

   When you've returned the final pair to the rest, note how your muscles feel. They may be a bit tired (or even a lot), but they also feel more powerful than ever.

By practising this exercise regularly you help focus your body and unconscious mind to work with you on increasing your overall strength. Your belief that you can become stronger grows, and your desire to do so strengthens.

Imagining endless stamina

Having *stamina* means passing through pain barriers to keep going, retaining your focus, and not getting distracted or bored, and it requires physical and mental dedication. To help increase your stamina levels, repeat the following exercise from time to time:

1. **Think of somewhere relaxing you like to go.**

   Perhaps it's the beach, a forest, the cinema, or simply at home in front of the television.

2. **Imagine yourself jogging on a treadmill in that place.**

   Keep on running and enjoy the scenery (or the TV or film) as you do so. After a while, feel the first running pains shooting through your limbs; but stick with it and they soon disappear. Just concentrate on keeping your speed going and enjoying your location.

3. **Speed up time in your visualization.**

   Two minutes pass for each one in real life. Keep ramping up that speed slowly to three minutes for each one, and then four, until you get to a speed of ten times normal time.

4. **Watch yourself as you maintain the same jogging speed and work through several pain barriers.**

   A marathon run takes up to 5 hours to run, so even at this speeded-up time the visualization takes 30 minutes to complete. Therefore, speed up things to 15 times normal time, and then 20, 30, 40, 50, and 60 times faster than reality. Time is really whizzing by for you now, and in five minutes you've run the equivalent of a marathon.

5. **Keep the visualization going until five minutes have passed.**

   Realise that every minute is an hour of imaginary time and that all the time you're running, and running, and running – without stopping or becoming too tired. Every time you feel a pain barrier you know it's only temporary and pass through it. Imagine the endorphin release of pleasure as you do so, which makes the exercise even more enjoyable.

Exuding health and vitality

Although being *healthy* certainly means being free from illness or injury, according to the World Health Organization it's also a state of complete physical, mental, and social wellbeing.

To be a top athlete you need to be in the peak of good health and full of energy and vigour, but these aspects are beneficial to participants in all sports and at all levels, and are also essential for inactive people. Therefore, the following exercise is worth practising whether or not you participate in sport; everyone can benefit from repeating it from time to time:

It's all in your head. . .

Stamina is mostly in the mind. Many amateur runners (some of whom have never run great distances before) have managed to complete a full marathon a day for several days in a row. For example in 2009, at the age of 47, British comedian Eddie Izzard ran 43 marathons for charity over the course of 51 days (taking only Sundays off), covering a distance of over 1,100 miles. Without prior training, Izzard started by taking ten hours to complete each marathon. But as his body got into shape, that decreased to about five hours by the final marathons.

As your body adjusts to training, it copes better with physical demands; your muscles enlarge, your heart rate adapts and lowers, and your lung capacity and breathing improve. And that's exactly what happened for Izzard, who completely toned up his body during the course of the marathons. 'It changed my body,' he said afterwards.

If you want to follow through these marathons with Izzard, view his Twitter account (`http://twitter.com/#!/eddie izzard`) and start reading the posts beginning on 27 July 2009. He posted almost every day and you can see how pure grit and determination enabled him to complete the task, even through immense pain and discomfort.

Izzard took professional medical advice before embarking on this feat, and he also had medical assistance available at all times. So, to ensure your body is up to it, you should also get advice from a qualified professional before changing your level of physical activity.

1. **Sit comfortably with your arms resting by your sides facing palm up.**

   Close your eyes.

2. **Concentrate on the beating of your heart.**

   Sometimes you can feel the 'biddy-bum' of it beating, but if not, imagine that you can, and that it's repeating about 60 times a minute. Take a moment to tune into this regular rhythm and then move on to focus on your breathing, which is slow and regular at about a 12 breaths in and out per minute.

3. **Feel the life-giving oxygen entering through your lungs.**

   Imagine it entering your bloodstream, from where your heart pumps it around your body. Envision your industrious lungs endlessly incorporating oxygen from the atmosphere, pumping it around your body, and then collecting unwanted carbon dioxide, which you then exhale.

4. **Feel the life force pervading your entire body.**

   In your mind's eye see how all your cells are fed and nourished, with each new beat of your heart bringing a fresh load of energy.

Mental flash cards for sporting excellence

You can use the following mental flash cards to help with your sporting ambitions:

✔ **Carrying the world on your shoulders:** Before any exercise involving heavy lifting, imagine you're like the famous statue of Atlas carrying the entire world on his shoulders. Yes, you're *that* strong.

✔ **Leaping over a skyscraper:** Before any jumping exercise, imagine taking a short run-up and then jump and leap right over a tall building.

✔ **Scoring an almost impossible goal:** See yourself standing in your own football team's goal area and kick the ball high in the air and right down the pitch to the opponent's goal, where it shoots past the goalkeeper into the top corner of the net. Or imagine making a long run in American

football, wriggling and writhing past several defenders to plant an amazing touchdown.

✔ **Wearing an Olympic gold medal:** In your mind's eye, stand on the winning podium at the Olympic games as your national anthem plays and the crowd cheers you on, and then see yourself being presented with the gold medal.

✔ **Running around the world:** Picture the world like a sort of Google Earth Internet program, which displays a zoomable map of the entire world. Zoom right in to your current location (as if you're a spectator) until you can see yourself standing in running clothes on the road. Now follow yourself running fast from town to town, city to city, and country to country, as you whizz around the world faster than the speed of sound.

When you perform this exercise, visualize your body gently vibrating with an abundance of health and energy, like a racing car revving up before the start of a race. Feel the energy coursing through your entire body from your fingers and toes to the tip of your nose. Notice how you also feel at one with the world; calm and peaceful, but strong and capable. This feeling is health and vitality. Sense and savour it, and decide that you want to feel this way as frequently and for as long as possible.

Visualizing the perfect body

What exactly is the perfect body? Well, in my view no such thing exists because everyone's preference is different: tall people may want to be shorter and vice versa, and some may choose to be more or less muscular. And who's to say which is better?

The purpose of this exercise is to think of the perfect body as it applies to you and your body, and then imagine that you already have this body. Therefore, you're a little on your own in this visualization. Spend a few moments initially thinking about your own body and anything you want to change about it. When you've built up a picture of your ideal, you're ready for the creative part:

1. **Visualize yourself standing up and a realistic manikin of the body you want to have is placed beside you.**

   You're both wearing underwear or swimming clothes so that you can see your shapes and curves more clearly.

2. **Imagine your consciousness leaving your body like a sort of puff of smoke that you breathe out.**

   You are that consciousness, so go with it, and then turn around so that you can view your body and the manikin. You're an especially powerful spirit form who can change physical things as easily as moulding clay, simply by observing them.

3. **Use your skills to reshape your body until it has all the features of the manikin.**

   Lengthen or shorten limbs as necessary, maybe adjust tummy fat and abdominal muscles, and so on. Perhaps the easiest approach is to work from head to toe until you've transformed your body so that it's just like the manikin.

4. **Allow your spiritual form to be sucked back into your body in a big intake of breath**.

   Feel yourself slip into it, just like putting on a new suit and pair of shoes. Sense your muscles and other changed parts with your fingertips. Notice all the differences. If you're shorter or taller, note how the world appears differently at your new height. Jump and feel how heavy you are. Stretch and test your muscles. Do whatever occurs to you and use your imagination to the full to feel all the different sensations.

The point of this exercise isn't to try to get you to change to the new body shape physically. Instead, it helps your imagination understand what your body feels like in peak condition and gives your unconscious mind guidelines as to the directions it needs to move towards in your training. Therefore, if you prefer, in the exercise you can even visualize different bone structures and features that you'd never attain without surgery; for a few minutes, you can imagine having them.

Through repeating this exercise frequently, the perfect body image you imagine naturally drifts towards one that you can achieve in reality with normal exercise and healthy eating. If you then also put in the work, your body starts altering in that direction.

Being a Good Sport

In any sport you follow sets of rules (both written and unwritten). The written rules outline game play and what to do in certain eventualities, and the unwritten rules are the ones you're supposed to already know and apply to your sporting conduct and overall behaviour on and off the pitch, field, or track.

In this section, I concentrate on the unwritten rules of sport, also known as *good sportsmanship*. The following exercises allow you to cope better with the disappointment of defeat, to work more efficiently as a team player, and to handle winning with class.

Playing fair

Fairness means treating others the way you want to be treated, and fair-minded people play by the rules (in both life and sport) and don't take advantage of others. In both life and sport, the urge to win can be overwhelming but any victory gained by cheating is hollow, and if you achieve a win or obtain a promotion dishonestly, can you live well with yourself? The answer for most people is no, and therefore you try to play fair.

But the temptations can be strong, and sometimes the rules of a game are less than clear-cut; ways may be available to circumvent them that aren't technically against the rules but which may be considered unsporting.

For example, the way the ball is bowled in cricket is a controversial subject and over the course of the game's development many different styles have been invented for bowling hard-to-hit balls, several of which have been deemed to be cheating. But defining exactly how a bowler cheats was quite difficult until it was decided that when bowling, anything up to a 15 degree bend in the arm was allowed, but no more, encouraging players to get as close to that as possible.

Now 15 degrees is a hard thing to measure and may need several video replays to detect. So how close do you go to ensure that you don't cheat but still bowl difficult balls?

There again, in soccer there is a rule called the offside rule, which disallows forward passing of a ball while in the opponent team's half of the pitch. This is to prevent players from hanging around the opposing side's goal, waiting for long passes to kick into the net. But sometimes players can tell when the referee isn't looking in the right direction and may try to get away with such a pass. Would you?

The benefits of not getting caught when cheating in a sport can be great, with players and teams often given huge financial bonuses for wins. But when sports players are caught cheating, they lose the respect of their fans and are often given long bans that make returning to the sport later on very difficult.

For example, a cyclist caught blood doping at the Pro tour level receives a four-year ban, which effectively amounts to a lifetime ban. Cyclists at their peak are unlikely to return to that fitness after so many years, and probably can never compete at that level again.

You can cheat in sport in hundreds of different ways, but if you want to be known as a 'clean' player who's honest and fair, repeat the following positive affirmations from time to time. If you're ever tempted to cheat, you'll be less likely to do so:

- ✔ I value integrity and always try to play fair.

- ✔ I never try to beat someone else by cheating.

- ✔ I'd forever sully my beloved sport if I cheated.

- ✔ I'd be unable to live with myself if I cheated to win something unfairly.

- ✔ I want people to appreciate my achievements for what I do without cheating.

As you repeat these affirmations try to recall a solid feeling of love for your sport, the passion that makes you get up day after day and push your body to the limit so that you can participate in it. Think of how wonderful it is to be able to enjoy your sport and how great it makes you feel when you do so.

By bringing these emotions to mind while repeating the affirmations you'll convey a far greater depth of feeling to your unconscious mind, which will help you to keep building your inner desire for fairness, honesty and integrity.

Being a team player

Being a good team player isn't simply about doing your best as a player at each match; that's only part of the equation. A winning team is one in which the members share a range of common attributes and abilities, as follows:

- ✔ **Communication:** You need to be able to communicate well with your fellow team members so that, for example, you know when to pass or receive the ball.

- ✔ **Co-operation:** Put aside any differences you have with other team members and work with them to achieve your common goal of winning.

✔ **Listening:** Be a good listener, on and off the playing field. You need to understand and follow orders from the team captain or coach, and also listen to the discussion of your team mates.

✔ **Participation:** If you can, speak up in meetings and discussions and offer any suggestions you can think of. Don't just turn up at the matches and play.

✔ **Reliability:** Always arrive on time for training and stick to any agreed game plan during the game.

✔ **Sharing:** Share your advice and tips with other members on how to play, improve their skills, and so on.

✔ **Strategy:** Develop your ability to think on your feet and adopt the right strategy for the team as a whole when you encounter a situation you haven't practised.

You can find a lot more about teams and team-building in business (particularly from the leader's point of view) in Chapter 14, but the following affirmations help you specifically with regard to becoming a better team sport player:

✔ I value my team and want it to do as well as possible.

✔ I'm a valuable member of my team, equal with all other members.

✔ I do my best to help other members for the benefit of the team.

✔ I'm prepared to help other better-placed team members to score instead of chasing personal glory.

✔ I listen to what my team members have to say and give advice when asked.

As you repeat these affirmations, visualize that your team comprises ten people (even if it's more or less) and hold your hands out in front of you, palms facing out and fingers pointing upwards. Each of these fingers (thumbs count as fingers in this exercise) is a team member, and you're one of them. Reflect on how together your fingers can help you do many intricate things such as sewing, painting, and playing a musical instrument. Now close your fingers and feel how comparatively useless your hands are with your fingers in this position. They would have difficulty turning the pages of a book, typing, lifting objects, and performing everyday activities such as cooking, let alone the previously mentioned fiddly tasks.

So, as you say each affirmation, open up a couple of your fingers and feel how much more useful your hands are becoming, until you've said all five and your hands are fully open. Now, as a team, all your fingers can work together to the best ability of your hands. Associating these actions with the affirmations helps increase the underlying value your unconscious mind applies to teamwork.

Respecting coaches and officials

Referees, umpires, and other sports officials attain their positions of responsibility as a result of many years of training and are often highly skilled players themselves. They generally love the sport, want to play a significant role in it, and are usually motivated by a sense of fairness.

Therefore, when such an official makes a decision against you it has nothing to do with you as a person. The decision is based only on your game play and on how the official sees an incident. Good players accept all decisions from officials, even if they believe them to be completely incorrect.

The correct time to address bad decisions is after a game and through the relevant channels. Doing so can be extremely difficult in some sports in which live action replays aren't viewed by the referee, and as a result teams are mistakenly disqualified from competitions. But rules are rules and the best option is always to grin and bear it.

Show the same respect for your coach and team managers who also have a huge amount of experience and try to make decisions for the benefit of the team as a whole. If you're not picked for a certain game or to play in a particular position, by all means discuss the decision if you can, but don't let yourself get angry. Take the situation as a challenge to improve your skills. Maybe ask the coach what you need to do to get chosen next time.

Sports, although they can be a living for some people, are generally an amateur activity in which people participate for the fun. In team sports, the thrill of playing with other people is what drives a player on, and if you can win some important games, all the better. So try to respect the people who make possible your participation in this tremendously enjoyable activity.

If you've had issues with officials in the past, or think you may have in the future, use the following affirmations to help increase your respect for them, and give them a break. In the long run these affirmations help you to keep calm and collected, and improve your progress in your chosen sport:

- ✔ I acknowledge and understand that referees and other officials are highly skilled and rise to their position due to their ability.

- ✔ I'll bite my lip and keep quiet when I disagree with an official's decision.

- ✔ I'll co-operate with my coach and manager because they only want me to improve.

- ✔ I'll discuss any problems with someone off the playing field and use relevant procedures.

- ✔ I'll forgive officials who mistakenly make the wrong decision and accept that they're only human.

While repeating these affirmations hold images of any coaches, referees, managers, and team captains you know in your mind. Feel how they are real people just like yourself who love the sport you participate in, and who are always doing their best for the interests of the sport and the people in it. Understand that by being human they can make mistakes from time to time, just like you can. But feel an overall devotion to the sport from these people so that your emotional response to them is one of acceptance and gratitude for their input.

By building this emotion in your mind, and viewing examples of these types of official, at the same time as stating your affirmations, you bring all these things together in a way that'll strengthen your understanding of and willingness to work with them.

Losing gracefully

Everyone likes to win, and often the main reason for participating in a sport is because you want to be a winner, but the sad fact is that only one person or team can win. And yet, even the worst team in a league wins occasionally, so you get the chance to win something when you play against equally capable teams.

As an individual, you may win at a variety of events when up against people of similar ability. But the higher you aim, and the more skilled the people you compete against become, the harder winning is and the less likely you are to win.

But losing needn't (and usually doesn't) stop anyone from participating in a sport. In fact, it generally drives people on to try again, but the next time a bit harder. And that's the right spirit with which to approach each loss. Because like it or not, you're going to lose many times unless you're a remarkably skilled and gifted sportsperson.

An old saying goes, 'Success is getting up one more time than you fall down'. In fact, although you immediately understand what it means, the quote is illogical because you can only ever get up as many times as you fall down. But nitpicking aside, the moral is to keep on trying, or as Dory the fish keeps saying in the film *Finding Nemo*, 'Just keep swimming, just keep swimming. . . '.

To help circumvent the bitter feelings of defeat and get used to framing losses in a more positive and motivating way, repeat the following affirmations from time to time:

✔ Each occasion when I lose is a milestone on my road to eventual success.

✔ Winning is great, but playing or participating as well as I possibly can is more important, even when I lose.

✔ For me (or my team) to lose means that another wins and I feel happy for him or her – but I'll try to make it my (or our) turn next time.

✔ When I lose, I'll examine everything I can about the event to determine what I can do better next time.

✔ I always congratulate my opponents or competitors when they beat me, and try to enjoy their success rather than dwell too much on my loss.

As you repeat these affirmations imagine you've fallen down while running along a dry and dirty track. After each affirmation pick yourself up a little bit. Get up onto one knee and wipe any dirt off and attend to any cuts or grazes on the other. Stand up. Relax. Dust yourself down, and get ready to resume your running.

By feeling the emotion behind this metaphor while you repeat the affirmations, you enhance your ability to cope with defeat and simply pick yourself up and start again. Your mental and physical resilience improves and you manage defeat more easily.

Although trying to improve yourself is always a good thing, whatever you do in life and however you fare, you have value as a person. Losing (like winning) is a passing event that happens as you progress through life. Your worth is based on who you are and how you live your life, not on how you perform in certain areas, and your self-esteem needs to be based on this essential worth.

Winning with class

Every now and then (and more often the better you get), you win at a sporting event or game, and that's great – for both participants and supporters. A swell of serotonin and endorphins (natural feel-good chemicals) rushes through you when the final whistle blows, or as you cross the finish line first, which sweeps you up and can be one of the highest highs for many people.

But at the same time as exhibiting your pleasure at winning, always try to remember the losers and understand that you may lose next time. Apart from being rude, unpleasant, and unsportsmanlike, taunting losers and their supporters may end up giving you a broken nose! Far better to show humility during your win and wish your competitors better luck next time.

Here are some affirmations you can repeat to prepare yourself for having a good attitude when you win:

✔ I'll enjoy the experience of winning, but remember the losers too.

✔ I won't gloat over the failure of others I've beaten.

✔ I'll evaluate everything about my winning performance to try to win again next time.

✔ I'll be gracious in my acceptance of any cup or medal that I'm given for winning.

✔ I'll always congratulate my competitors for a good contest or game, whether I win or lose.

To further enhance these affirmations, and also to provide motivation at times when you don't win, feel the intense joy and pride of winning as you repeat each affirmation. Even if you haven't yet won anything you can still imagine how it'll feel, so experience it from imagination. Notice how feel-good chemicals flood your brain, and also feel slightly philosophical in that you know you can't always win, so you savour your win now to tide you through the times when you don't win, when you can recall this feeling to build you up to try again.

Chapter 16

Achieving Success in Education and the Workplace

In This Chapter

▶ Developing your willingness and ability to improve your skills

▶ Retaining knowledge to pass exams

▶ Obtaining the job you want

▶ Securing a promotion or pay rise

A large number of people spend over 20 per cent of their lives in education, generally between the ages of about 5 and 21 – although children in some countries start earlier, and college or university can last longer than three years. And this period is just to get a Bachelors degree. For those interested in an academic career, obtaining a Masters can take another couple of years and a research doctorate up to another eight years depending on the specialisation. So in the latter case, formal education continues into your fourth decade.

In addition, many businesses provide courses for employee training, some mandatory and some optional, that help lead to promotion. And the market for adult distance-learning is also booming in the current economic downturn, because more and more people are busy earning additional qualifications in order to obtain the job they want.

People who pursue a career spend up to a further 60 per cent of their lives in the professional world, which means that up to 80 per cent of the life of a paid employee (that is, other than free time, weekends, and holidays) may be spent in the two occupations of education and work.

With such a large amount of your life dedicated to education and/or work, you're bound frequently to come across problems to resolve and difficulties to overcome, such as challenging bosses, colleagues, or fellow students, uncomfortable situations, difficult exams, important deadlines, and so on. In this chapter I provide a selection of exercises and tips that you can use to help make the time you spend in these two endeavours as enjoyable and productive as possible.

Excelling in Education

No doubt about it: the days are long gone when a good college or university education was only for the elite rich, or for the few highly talented individuals who obtained scholarships. And not because tuition fees have come down – in fact, they're rising almost everywhere. What has happened, though, is that intense competition for good jobs has seen more and more people applying for degree courses, generally using student loans to fund them. The tuition is affordable only because it's paid back over many years of the student's future working life.

So education is both expensive and extremely important if you want to secure the best job with the maximum remuneration and greatest advancement prospects. Therefore, you need to make the most of your education to get the biggest return for your investment in money and time, which means achieving the best grades or highest pass you can to place yourself in the optimum position for the future.

Therefore, don't look on further education as a chore and something to put up with in order to get a job. The exercises in this section help you want to study because you enjoy it, rather than because you have to.

This section also increases your desire to pass on the things you discover, which is always a win-win situation because your knowledge spreads to others and your own memory is strengthened in the process. You also encourage in yourself a greater sense of curiosity, which stays with you after your education is complete, helping you to spot unusual situations and make innovative connections – possibly letting you take advantage of opportunities before your competitors.

Loving to learn

Generally, people love to discover new stuff. For example, one of the most popular programmes on the television is the news. Almost all stations cover the news (and some do only that), because people want to know what's going on in the world and how it may affect them. People also buy millions of copies of newspapers every day and read news on the Internet.

People also like to keep in touch with each other on social networking sites to find out what their friends are doing, and web surfing is now catching up with watching TV as a major pastime. People have a continuous thirst for new information.

Keeping up to date in this way is fun; you don't even realise that you're improving your knowledge while absorbing or interacting with the wide range of media that pervades your life. But then something strange happens: when you have to study for a specific reason, such as passing a test or taking an exam, you can get flustered. The material looks too complicated and seems far too much like hard work, and so you procrastinate and leave it until the last minute. As a result, at best you do only a just-good-enough job. And when you get away with that half-hearted approach, you tend to stick with it and treat studying as a chore to be left until you've no further option but to do it.

When you like something, however, you take the time to find out more about it: for example, the rules of a sport and the standing of teams and players in its leagues or divisions, the life of celebrities, the work of artists and musicians, and so on.

To help increase your desire to study and make the process more enjoyable, repeat the following affirmations while keeping the subject you're studying fully in mind:

- ✔ I want to broaden my outlook because knowledge deepens character.

- ✔ I want to know more about everything I study.

- ✔ I know that when I fully understand something, it adds to completing the puzzle that then lets me discover even more.

- ✔ I plan to apply what I find out in my future life, education, and career.

- ✔ I enjoy the experience of discovering new things.

As you repeat these affirmations try to feel a strong feeling of desire for the subject matter. Desire to have knowledge, and hunger after solving life's puzzles. Yearn to soak in as much information as you can, which you can then put to good use throughout your life. Feel this as an emotion, the way you may feel about someone you really miss, or the anticipation you may feel while waiting for a long-planned holiday to come around, or when you're waiting to move into the dream home you've always wanted.

By combining these feelings, imagery, and affirmations the strength of conviction behind them is overwhelming and helps to ensure that a desire to improve your knowledge is always high on your agenda.

Passing on the best things you find out

Do you ever get that 'Aha' moment when you discover something new? The experience is like a light bulb going off in your head, or suddenly spotting a jigsaw piece and where it fits. When you do, you often then get the urge to tell your friends about it. I certainly do, although I have to restrain myself so as not to be boorish, and so only pass on the really good information. This behaviour is natural; people love to share what they discover.

Similarly, I love somebody telling me something new as much as finding it out for myself. In fact, probably more so, because they tell me something in connection with the conversation we're having, and because it's related to a subject in which I'm already interested, I pay greater attention to the new piece of information. And I'm sure that you're pretty much the same and enjoy sharing news and ideas with others.

One of the best ways to find out about a subject is to instruct another person in it, because you can only do so successfully when you understand it yourself.

You can put this observation to positive use with a visualization.

1. **Imagine that you're with someone who knows absolutely nothing about the subject you need to study.**

   If it helps, imagine a real person such as your grandmother, otherwise it can be an imaginary person.

2. **See yourself explaining this topic to the other person.**

   Start from first principles and take it from there.

3. **Where you find a gap in your knowledge, pause the visualization.**

   Now look up the information you need from your course material, or in a dictionary, encyclopaedia, or on the Internet.

4. **Continue with the visualization.**

   Repeat the first three steps until you've explained everything needed to understand your current assignment.

You can make a mind movie (a process I describe in Chapter 9) of this visualization by saving it to your memory. In the same way as running a screen-recording program on a computer and saving it to disk, you find that you can recall your teaching session visualization at any time and watch it back, with all the facts intact. You can even fast-forward or skip to particular sections and retrieve information in this way.

After 'recording' each teaching visualization session, try taking yourself through a test (or ask a friend) to see if all the information you need is present. Where any is missing, look up the answer and do a mental video edit to insert that item of information into the correct place in the video.

If you're studying something that requires a lot of application, keep filming these visualizations for each part of the coursework. You can then build up a sort of video library to draw on when exam time comes around.

In the real world, now discuss your course with interested friends. Let them tell you informative snippets of information, and return the favour with your new knowledge. You soon get into the habit of sharing the best new things and enjoy studying so much more. You also find that papers you need to write on the subject come ready-formed in your mind (or at least populated with headings and some sections of text), based on what you know, instead of you having to face a daunting blank sheet of paper.

Standing on the shoulders of giants

The sum of all human knowledge has been gained over the centuries by thinkers and scientists pushing back boundaries to understand just a little bit more of the world around them; too much stuff exists in the universe for any one person to work everything out, not even in a million lifetimes.

But together, over the years, people slowly built up the bricks of the foundation of science. And not just science: people understand psychology much better than they ever did; they examined, took apart, and rebuilt the subjects of politics, economics, and mathematics in different ways; they developed culture with understanding, tolerance, and respect; and today they create art and music that would astonish geniuses such as Michelangelo or Mozart.

And yet, people don't really know much at all. The more people discover, the more they find out the huge amount that they don't know; and that the unknown is an ever-expanding window.

But if you want to see through that window, discover things that few other humans know, and make a mark in the world – that is, create a true difference that wouldn't exist without you, you need to climb on the giant shoulders of those who've gone before you.

Geniuses such as Newton (who first wrote about standing on the shoulders of giants) and Einstein certainly forged the way for us, but the majority of human knowledge is advanced by dedicated people like you and me, taking the information passed on by predecessors and then using, adapting, and improving it, before passing everything to the descendants.

So be grateful for all the study, work, and effort that so many people have undertaken to advance human knowledge to its current level, and choose to use it. The greatest tribute you can pay to all the great thinkers of the past (famous or not) is to pick up what they have to teach you, and then to take it even further.

You can use the following visualization exercise to emphasise the wealth of information that you already know thanks to the dedicated work of others, increase your keenness to discover more, and develop a desire to pass it on.

1. **Imagine you're standing at the top of a human pyramid.**

   The two people supporting you have passed on their knowledge to you; they are school-teachers or college professors, and the like. You decide who they should be.

2. **Look further down the pyramid.**

   Underneath them you see their teachers and professors, of which there are four. You may not know them, but you know they exist.

3. **Keep looking down even further.**

   Among the eight people below them you start to notice famous figures such as Isaac Newton and Albert Einstein. And as you look further and further down you see more and more of these great figures at strategic locations in the pyramid.

4. **Allow the human pyramid to grow upwards.**

   Now someone's standing on your shoulders, and those of the person next to you (someone from one of the classes you attend or have attended). This new person has picked up at least a few things from the pair of you.

5. **See the pyramid grow ever upwards.**

   Notice how the things you found out from your predecessors, and which you now teach, are passed on upwards, helping to build the massive pyramid that is the sum of human knowledge.

Being forever curious

I touch upon curiosity a little earlier in the 'Loving to study' section, but expanding on the subject is worthwhile because curiosity is at the root of all human progress. Just as Dee Dee always says to her brother in the *Dexter's Laboratory* cartoon, 'What does this button do?', so have people also wondered throughout the ages – perhaps beginning with questions such as, 'What happens if I bang these stones together?' prior to the discovery of making fire or, 'How can I keep dry outside of a cave?' leading to the invention of reed or mud houses, and so on. In modern life, many an invention has been made by someone thinking, 'How can I improve this device?'.

Opportunities for improvement are everywhere, whether in products and services, manufacturing processes, economics, politics, music, and (in fact) everything people put their mind to. I challenge anyone to say that something is 100 per cent perfect, because I doubt that such a thing is possible. Still, you can try to get ever closer to perfection, or simply make changes for the sake of variety, as in new fashions and styles of music.

Mental flash cards for work and education

Use the following mental flash cards to help with your educational and employment careers:

✔ **Answering the exam questions:** Imagine the exam paper in front of you and see that, although hard, you can answer all the questions. Be sure that you previously put in the work required so that you can genuinely create a positive expectation.

✔ **Receiving the qualification:** See yourself standing up on the stage being handed your degree with the audience clapping. Finally, you have your qualification.

✔ **Getting the job or pay rise:** Imagine that the position or rise you want has already been given to you. But make sure that you have a positive expectation that this situation can happen in reality.

✔ **Performing the job:** See yourself fulfilling the role or position for which you're applying. Imagine performing all the tasks and taking all the decisions the role requires.

✔ **Success is my ambition:** Repeat affirmations such as, 'I am not a quitter. I will achieve my goal. I will be successful'. Believe them and repeat them.

Being creative (which I cover in Chapter 17) means being curious enough to ask yourself 'what if?' questions about everything you can. Repeat the following affirmations to help spur your curiosity about the world around you:

> ✔ I enjoy being inquisitive and asking questions.
>
> ✔ I want to know why things are the way they are.
>
> ✔ I like to discover what motivates people.
>
> ✔ I'm curious about how things work or are put together.
>
> ✔ I love storing away unusual facts – I may be able to use them one day.

As you repeat these affirmations, imagine yourself to be Sherlock Holmes, the fictional detective. In your hand you're a holding a magnifying glass, which you use to examine more closely things that interest you. Or maybe you may prefer to visualize that you're Jessica Fletcher, another fictional crime solver, or perhaps Lt. Columbo, or whoever your most favourite sleuth may be. The thing that unites them all, though, is an insatiable desire to get to the truth; to unearth new information, and solve mysteries.

Passing Exams with Flying Colours

To prove to teachers, employers, and society in general that you've learned what you're supposed to in your education, you need to pass exams. These tests begin at a very early age and continue on all the way through college or university, culminating in one or more exams or a thesis in order to obtain a degree.

And the testing doesn't end there, because throughout your working life you're often required to attend training courses in most types of occupation, whether on health and safety, being a better manager, quality control, and so on. Fortunately, many training courses provide a certificate for merely attending, regardless of how much you understand, but not always.

Restaurant workers in many countries are required to attend regular hygiene training in which they must achieve a pass mark before being allowed to work (or continue working) in the industry.

Like it or not, tests and exams are an important part of modern life and how well you do in them can affect your career deeply in terms of salary and promotion prospects. But if you practise the visualizations in this section (and do the required studying, of course), you can overcome any nerves or anxiety that may affect your performance in an exam. The exercises also help you to store what you find out in more easily accessible ways so that you can quickly recall the answers you need.

Accessing your mind library to retrieve information easily

Quite often when you sit an exam, the answers to some questions elude you, even though you're quite sure that you know them or they're on the tip of your tongue (or pen). And then, after the exam when you're given the correct answers to look through, you say, 'of course, I knew that!' – but you were simply unable to recollect the answer at the time.

This situation occurs when you cram your head full of facts in a short space of time, perhaps during revision, and they haven't had a chance to settle into their own locations in your brain, from where you can easily recall them. If this happens to you, instead of trying to remember stuff as you revise, try actively assigning the material a holding place in your mind. The following exercise can help:

1. **In your mind, visualize yourself in the middle of the largest library in the world.**

   The building is huge and circular with a ceiling many storeys above you and steps leading up to balconies that wrap around the circumference of the library. More steps then lead to the next storey, and so on.

2. **Think of all the things that you're studying in your course and assign each major part to one of the balcony levels.**

   For example, if you're studying computer programming, make the first storey the section on computer hardware. The next one may be for device drivers (small apps that interface between programs and peripherals such as printers, monitors, and keyboards). The third level can be reserved for applications programming (creating software such as web browsers or word processors), and so on.

   Now, subdivide each storey. So, the first storey has different sections for Desktop PC architecture, another for Apple smart phones and tablets, another for Google Android devices, and so on. To help with this assigning process, consult your curriculum to ensure that you don't forget any sections.

3. **Fill your mind library.**

   You can do this part during revision or, even better, from the very first lectures you attend. Whenever you discover a piece of information that you think may require recalling later, locate the place where it belongs and save it in your mind library, imagining the fact as a book with a vivid picture on the cover representing the fact. Then place the book on the shelf in the right location.

Because you take the time to classify information according to the way you think, when the exam comes you can use the same process to retrieve it. Simply decide which section you stored the information in and fetch it.

Looking things up in your mental encyclopaedia

Whatever your age, you have a multitude of fascinating facts and interesting ideas locked away inside your skull, and the older you are the more of them you possess. Although they may seem to be stored in a random order with no logic or reasoning, your brain knows what it's doing when it saves memories. Your brain associates memories, facts, and ideas with what you were doing when you discovered them, where you were, what you were thinking and feeling, what you smelt and felt, and so on.

All these memories are stored holographically. In other words they occupy thousands of different neurons in many different parts of your brain (rather than being all bunched together in the same location), all interrelated with other memories that are similar or are in some way connected. The problem is how to browse through your vast repository of knowledge in any kind of logical manner. The answer may surprise you. All you have to do is choose to recall it logically. For example, try the following exercise:

1. **Think of everything you know about Africa.**

   Whether that's a great deal or not a lot, simply think about it.

2. **Imagine opening up your mental encyclopaedia at the chapter entitled 'Everything I know about Africa'.**

   Go on, take a look, and you find that the information's there.

3. **Flick through the pages.**

   See the headings and subheadings such as 'Some of the countries I know that are in Africa', 'Some famous Africans I've heard of', and so on.

4. **Spend some time looking through the subheadings.**

   For example, 'What I know about Nelson Mandela'.

5. **Browse through the rest of this mental encyclopaedia.**

   View things you've seen people say or seen on television, photographs, drawings, and all the other odds and ends about Africa that you've filed away over the years. Amazing isn't it? All the information is there.

This mental encyclopaedia isn't like a normal one (thoroughly researched and classified with huge quantities of facts). Instead, this 'book' is your own personal encyclopaedia, which is why the headings and chapters use the words 'I know' in them, because only things you know about are featured, and things you don't know aren't (but can be added at any time).

By rummaging through your mental encyclopaedia, you can often recall things you need to know that are related to a project you're working on. Just flick through the pages in your mind, link ideas together, and connect them.

Creating mental mnemonics

Instead of (or, indeed, as well as) using the mind library that I describe in the earlier section 'Accessing your mind library to retrieve information easily', you can use an ancient technique to store information for the long term and then easily recall it at any time. The method is called *mnemonics* and an example is the phrase 'Every good boy deserves favour' – the first letter of each word represents the lines on the treble clef stave when writing or reading music, for the notes E, G, B, D and F.

If you can come up with a mnemonic for a chemical compound, physical equation, or other fact using this method, you can easily recall it later. Simply apply the first letter of each word in the fact to another word in a sentence you create. Now all you need to do is remember that sentence. Oh, and the stranger or crazier the sentence, the better you recall it.

You can also use linked mnemonics to remember lists. This is the main technique used by eight times world memory champion Dominic O'Brien, author of several books on the subject and owner of the Guinness world record for memorising the order of 54 packs of playing cards by viewing each card only once (with just eight mistakes).

There are a number of different ways to link items in a list together, but there's an easy one you can test for yourself by seeing how well you can memorise a list of words without using a memory aid, and then another, similar list using the simplest form of linked mnemonic, a visual storyboard. Just follow these steps:

1. **Read and spend a minute or so trying to memorise this list of words:**

   – Hammer

   – Mouse

   – Sneeze

   – Skateboard

   – Shampoo

   – Cloud

   – Acrobat

   – Sponge

   – Window

   – Spark

2. **Close this book and write down the words in order.**

   See how well you did by returning here. Try to avoid reading any farther until you've done this step. How did you do? If you recalled them all, well done! But if not, carry on to Step 3 to almost guarantee perfect recall.

3. **Now read this list of words.**

   – Cat

   – Television

   – Clown

   – Potato

   – Motorbike

   – Chocolate

   – Clock

   – Tree

   – Shoe

   – Egg

4. **Take the words and put them into a sequence of interconnected events, like a storyboard.**

   For example, think of a huge **cat** sitting in front of you grinning. Absorb this image until you can clearly see it, and then see the cat opening its mouth wider and wider into a huge yawn, out of which pops a bright pink **television** set, which lands with a thud right in front of you and explodes into a thousand pieces that fly out.

   Let this image sink in then see how, as if on the end of elastic bands, these pieces come shooting back and form themselves into a brightly coloured **clown**.

   Take a moment to be sure that you've clearly seen this sequence of events so far (you must see everything, not just think it). Now notice how the clown is about the same size as you but is juggling a single **potato** just as big as he is, which then splits in two revealing it to be hollow and containing a **motorbike**, which you notice is made out of brown, sticky **chocolate** that's melting and re-forming itself into a grand-father **clock**.

   Take a moment to be sure you've visualized all of this very clearly. Now, looking closer at the hands of the clock, you see that they're tree branches growing out with twigs and leaves extending from them. The whole clock has become a **tree** – a very strange tree wearing a giant **shoe**.

   Suddenly the tree makes a weird clucking noise and flies away, so you peer down into the shoe to see a large **egg** resting there. Finally, let the entire chain of images stay in your mind for a moment.

5. **Close this book and again write the words down in order.**

   Come back and see how you did. I bet you got all 10, and may easily have handled 20, 50, or even 100 items with some practice.

Whenever you have a list to remember, such as a collection of chemicals required for a particular reaction, or a group of precedents that apply under law in a particular circumstance, link them all together in a mnemonic chain storyboard. And make the symbolism as exaggerated and ridiculous as you can so that the links don't blur into the background when trying to follow them.

Viewing your revision pin board

Revision is a crucial part of taking exams; get it right and the exam can seem like a breeze. The exercise in this section helps you to revise by creating a difference between everything you studied in your coursework and what you study (or study again) in your revision. The result is that you can use your standard powers of recall to remember things you picked up as you progressed through the course, but you also have a second repository of information for everything you covered during revision.

1. **Imagine that you have in front of you an expandable pin board.**

   You can attach various facts, figures, and items of information to it.

2. **Choose something you're revising that you want to remember.**

   Pin it up on the board.

3. **Visualize the item as a piece of paper.**

   Perform the action of affixing it to the board, maybe with a brightly coloured pin.

4. **Look closely at what you've pinned up.**

   Ensure that you know what it is, and remember where you placed it.

5. **Add further revision notes to your pin board.**

   Place related ones together and, from time to time, peruse the board to see what you've pinned up.

6. **Drag the pin board frames in your mind.**

   As it fills up, expand it and create more space.

When the exam arrives, and if all else fails, you can recall elusive facts by viewing this revision board in your mind. Look at all the related items you posted to it and think about them and how they're connected to the information you need to recall. Now move on to the next question and, like an idea on the tip of your tongue, the answer may suddenly come back to you in a few minutes, after your unconscious mind has had a good rummage. You can then go back and complete the previous question.

Landing a Superb Job

When you're ambitious and looking for a new job – whether it's your first or a step up in your career plans – you want to be sure that you achieve the best for you in terms of salary, benefits, and your future. You also need to be able to shine in your new job so that you can progress further up the corporate ladder, or perhaps be head-hunted. If possible, you want a position that you enjoy, in which the work's stimulating and challenging. Even if you're less ambitious, you're going to want rewarding employment that pays your bills and allows you to live comfortably.

Whatever your requirements, you can be sure of one thing: plenty of other candidates have their eyes on the same opportunities as you. Therefore, you need to stand out from the crowd and beat the competition. You can strive for this aim in many different ways: some are risky and can backfire (such as gimmicky résumés or CVs, which aren't advised unless you're very clever or lucky) and others (such as impressive track records) take a lot of work and effort.

Fortunately, though, creative visualization can help you to land the perfect job, because you can better prepare for interviews, write more impressive applications and CVs, and present yourself in the most appropriate and job-winning manner.

Being the perfect candidate

After you've identified a position that fits all your criteria for the perfect job and are called for interview, you need to ensure that you're the perfect candidate. You're off to a good start by having matched yourself accurately against the job requirements and being invited for an interview. But how do you make sure that you come over to the company as being the ideal fit for their organisation?

Well, the first thing you do is undertake some basic homework and find out as much as you can about the company. Everything you want to know is probably available on the Internet, so set aside plenty of time to peruse the company website. Find out all the subsidiaries there are, then look for the companies with which they partner, have strategic deals with, sell to or purchase from. Perhaps draw a pie chart representing the areas in which the company makes its money, the larger slices of the pie being the ones you need to investigate more thoroughly.

This visual aspect is important as it builds a picture in your mind ready for visualizing your way to getting the job. So if the company is small or such a pie chart doesn't really apply, at least try to view a range of the company's products or imagine their services in application, so that you have pictures in your mind to draw on.

Your aim is to be able to show the interviewer that your goal in life is to work for the company, and you can demonstrate that by displaying in-depth knowledge of the organisation and by having prepared insightful questions about it. You need the confidence to stand out from the other candidates, and to get this you need to know as much about your prospective employer as possible. And you need to see in your mind through visualizing that you know that you know.

By gathering this information, in your mind you may even be able to put your interviewer on slightly unsteady ground by taking a more assertive and questioning role, almost interviewing them to see if their company is suitable for your talents. Don't visualize being pushy, but rather see yourself as extremely interested and excited about being granted an interview.

By the time the interview is over, you want your interviewer to be so overwhelmed with your knowledge and motivation that the other candidates will pale in comparison. You want it to be clear to this person that the rest of the interview process with other candidates is now going to be more or less a formality, as it would be almost impossible to find anyone better suited than you. See this in your mind to be the case, but base it on facts, not fantasy. Creative visualization works best when you have a positive expectation of success, which therefore must be backed up by facts. Once you have these facts behind you, you can't help but be keen and excited.

1. **Sit back and picture yourself performing the job you're after.**

   Visualize yourself interacting with other employees, attending meetings, putting together plans, organising events, or whatever the post requires.

2. **Think about positions higher up the ladder.**

   See yourself getting promoted and eventually taking on these roles.

3. **Feel how this company is the right one for you.**

   Understand how working for this company fits totally into your life plan.

4. **See you and the company as an organic entity.**

   Each of you needs the other to progress well.

Knowing that you have the ideal qualifications

When identifying an appropriate position you want, of course you take into account your experience and qualifications. But remember that although you know that you have the skills required, your interviewer doesn't. All the interviewer has seen is what you put on your CV, which you may have exaggerated (for want of a less polite word).

So before attending interview, take thorough stock of everything you know and how you've used this knowledge. If you're a recent school-leaver or graduate, you aren't going to have much experience yet, so concentrate on your knowledge from education. But if you've already been employed, think hard about all the ways in which you applied your skills in previous positions, especially in cases where you were particularly successful. With that in mind try the following visualization exercise:

1. **Run through all your skills and experience in your mind.**

   See how you've put them to good use. You're going to be asked about this at interview, so you want to have the information clear in your mind beforehand.

2. **Decide what are you particularly good at.**

   You want to be ready to demonstrate that your education was thorough and that you have (or can) successfully apply it in a work environment.

3. **Think about your other abilities that may not be quite so developed.**

   Be sure of what they are, and imagine ways in which you can further improve them, until they also become skills.

4. **Visualize the company and the products or service it provides.**

   Locate areas where what the company does and your abilities and skills match well. Dwell on these and see yourself already applying your skills and abilities productively in the company.

By doing this exercise, you've performed more preparation than most of your competitors, who only assume that they already know exactly what they know. But when the questions are asked, they have to sit back and think of good examples to illustrate their abilities, whereas you don't because instances spring immediately to mind. You've also imagined ways to use your skills at the new company and, if the conversation leads that way (and you can often help it do so), you can talk about how your skills exactly match the company's requirements.

Taking the long-term view

Many highly successful people start right at the bottom of their organisations, some without any qualifications (although doing so these days isn't easy). If you're having difficulty securing the position you want, therefore, you may decide to apply for one a little further down the ladder – as long as a ladder is definitely in place to climb.

Any large company worth its salt promotes from within where possible, and ways of progression to the top can be determined by performing Internet searches on the company and people who have been promoted within it over the last year. By a process of deduction you're able to discover the positions these people held and the departments in which they worked (and moved to), and you'll be able to see some of the internal corporate ladder structure – even as a complete outsider.

Once you've located a potential area within a company, you may decide that it could benefit you to begin with a smaller salary and a lower position than you'd prefer (as long as you consider yourself a go-getter and are prepared to demonstrate hard work and actual results), because you can then progress through the ranks and, within a year or two, attain the job you initially wanted. Also, by then you'll know the business inside out, your confidence will be high, and future opportunities will come more quickly than if you'd simply been given the job in the first place.

If this approach sounds like your type of thing, here's an exercise you can repeat to help focus on having the patience and motivation to slowly progress upwards (or quickly if you get lucky, or work extra hard) to obtain the post you initially desired:

1. **Stand up or sit upright.**

   Feel the inner strength that you have, both in your body and your mind.

2. **Rotate your shoulders.**

   First your left, then your right shoulder. Then repeat a few times.

3. **Rotate your head left and right a few times.**

   And move it into a variety of different positions that stretch your neck muscles.

4. **Now do both the neck and shoulder exercise at the same time.**

   Try to work a shiver up, so that one runs up and down your spine, and then relax. If you can't cause a real shiver, imagine one.

5. **Relax and visualize yourself standing on a hill-top.**

   Lift a hand to shield your eyes from the light and notice that in the far, far distance the fine wisps of a steam train trail can be seen.

6. **Know that this train will take you to the goal you're patiently waiting for.**

   This train is the key to your long-awaited promotion. When it arrives it will take you to your destination. All you must do is keep busy, do a good job, and wait.

7. **Look at all the land between where you are and where the train is now.**

   It's a long and windy road, covering a variety of terrains. But the track does lead to the foot of the hill – directly to your location.

8. **Imagine leaping forward in time.**

   Jump about a quarter of the time towards the date when you anticipate your goal being accomplished (in this case getting the promotion), and see the train that much closer to you. It's coming. Reflect on that and relax.

9. **Leap ahead three more times in the same way.**

   Each time the train is closer still. On the third of these time leaps see that the train is now down at the station below you. It's arrived.

10. **Calmly see yourself walking down the hill to meet the train.**

    It doesn't take long. End your visualization with you getting on the train to take you to your new position.

All the time you're visualizing, remember the neck and shoulder movements you made at the start. Then, whenever you feel things are progressing too slowly for your liking, recall that feeling and realise that your train is getting ever closer. You can even do a quick shoulder shrug and neck turn to recall the feeling from the exercise and relax, and then return to the job in hand, happy to get on with your work because you know your goal is on its way.

Never giving up

Perhaps you've applied for a few positions and been unsuccessful so far. No doubt you're up against strong competitors (many of whom may have read books such as this one), and so pick yourself up, dust yourself down, and find another position. Even in a sharp economic downturn, good jobs are available, just fewer of them – and they're tougher to land. But that's no reason to falter.

Getting what you want quickly and easily is extremely rare. Usually, these things take time and effort, and you may have to try many times before you're successful.

In the highly competitive field of book writing, almost without exception every great author suffered rejection after rejection before finally getting their break, many of them waiting many years. But the key thing they all have in common is that they stuck with it and never gave up.

Job hunting is the same. Remember that more than one great job exists for you; probably there are dozens or hundreds of possibilities, particularly if you're prepared to travel.

To build your resolve and strengthen your motivation in your job-hunting, try repeating the following affirmations from time to time:

- ✔ I will never, ever give up until I have the job I want.
- ✔ I refuse to let any setback prevent me from getting the right job.
- ✔ I know that the ideal job is out there for me, and I'm going to land it.
- ✔ I will get the perfect job for me.
- ✔ I can do it. I can do it. I can do it.

As you repeat these affirmations, visualize that the job you want is right in the centre of a target on a futuristic firing range, with your hand being like a laser gun. Imagine holding your arm out straight and viewing along it with your pointing finger indicating straight ahead too, and your thumb jutting up a little like a sighting device. Now imagine shooting laser beams from your finger that light up the target with a flash where they hit.

To get your job you simply have to be as accurate as possible and send your laser beams straight at the centre of the target. A steady aim, focus, and accuracy is what you need. Hold these thoughts uppermost in your mind, visualize the target, and take another shot between repeating each affirmation.

By combining this visualization with your affirmations you emphasise your determination to stay on focus, keep your target in your sights, and head exactly for your goal.

Getting a Promotion or Rise

If you already have the job you want and you're completely happy with the position, your responsibilities, and the rewards and compensation, that's excellent. But if you're ready to move on within the organisation, or you feel that the amount of work you do deserves an increase in salary, you need to start thinking about how you're going to achieve this goal.

Requesting a promotion or pay rise carelessly and without the correct planning, attention to detail, and supporting experience, ability, and strength of character, is likely to receive a firm 'no'. The attempt can even count against you if you give the impression that you're trying to get ahead without deserving it.

But you can use creative visualization exercises to evaluate where you stand and psych yourself up ready to make the moves and requests required for advancement or greater pay.

Knowing your value

Before you can put yourself forward for promotion to a more responsible position and/or a pay rise, you need to be pretty sure that you're worth it to your organisation. What's more, even if you know that you're worth a promotion or rise, you need to ensure that you superiors do too.

If you're ambitious, simply doing your job well isn't sufficient. Instead, you must do it superbly and with flair so that your abilities are obvious to all, and promoting you or increasing your pay seems an obvious thing to do. Now that's the ideal world, but company politics and the regular back-stabbing and in-fighting can make it difficult for an honest person to rise to the top. But you can; you just have to be smarter and work harder than the people that climb over or make use of others for personal gain.

You need to be totally sure of your own value and exude this belief all the time with confidence, so that others respect you and you become less of a target. Your superiors must see you as an achiever who never shirks responsibility and is thoroughly dedicated to the organisation. And your colleagues should see you as a hard worker and a great co-worker who always helps the team towards success. Don't forget that when you're promoted, these former colleagues become your subordinates, and your further progress is helped tremendously if they trust and respect you.

Therefore, prepare for your promotion or pay rise long before you approach anyone with your request. And to get you started, repeat the following affirmations when you believe that you've made sufficient progress in your organisation and wish to start preparing the proposal you're going to make:

- ✔ I am sure that this organisation is the right one for me to further my career.

- ✔ I will make my input, which is already highly valuable to this organisation, even more so.

- ✔ I will work (and be seen to work) harder than my colleagues.

- ✔ I will do my best to produce greater results than my colleagues.

- ✔ I will also work with my colleagues to help them to success.

These affirmations are all about certainty. So to help strengthen their effect, before you say them think of some certainties such as 'One and one equals two', 'Mixing yellow and blue paint creates the colour green', and 'I am alive'. Now feel that strength of feeling, the absolute knowledge of certain facts, and extend it to the affirmations as you repeat them.

In your heart of hearts feel how everything you say is absolutely true, and know that you'll succeed in it. Feel the quiet strength that this knowledge brings you, and the assured peace and determination that arises within you. At the same time feel love and compassion for everything and everyone around you, and know that you'll succeed because you'll use your success for the benefit of all, not just yourself.

This combination of determination, emotions, and feelings, mixed with the affirmations, presents a solid vision to your unconscious mind, which will respond by strengthening your grit and resolve to do what is needed to achieve your goals.

The last affirmation may seem strange or out of place. Why would you want to help out others when you want to progress yourself? Well, the answer is in the question. In life, people tend to achieve the most when they help others. They have a more enjoyable time and are rewarded for it.

When you have greater responsibility, don't prevent high flyers who work for you from being promoted to their level of ability (even one above your position) – being able to spot and promote good people is a sign of a great leader and, in fact, helps with your own progression. That's how good organisations grow; ability and achievement is spotted and rewarded – after all, that's what you want to happen to you right now.

Thriving on responsibility

If you want better pay or a promotion, you're going to have to earn it by taking on more responsibility. And if you're the type of person who generally shies away from responsibility, doing so may not be easy. In which case you need to start working on your mindset and begin to enjoy having the responsibilities you have now, and generate a desire to take on more.

Without the desire and urge to thrive on responsibility, you don't make a good manager, because your decision-making ability is affected and you're seen as weak and ineffectual. To help increase your ability to take more control and make more decisions, even in your current capacity, repeat the following affirmations from time to time:

- ✔ I like to be in a position where I have to make important decisions.
- ✔ I don't see responsibility as a burden, but as a wonderful opportunity to progress.
- ✔ I enjoy being challenged and having to find a solution.
- ✔ I'm prepared to take both the blame and the praise for my actions.
- ✔ I grab the reins where possible and lead my co-workers to success.

When talking about responsibility you may be reminded of phrases such as 'I have to *bear* the responsibility for this', or 'The responsibility was *weighing* on my mind'. This shows how being responsible requires strength in order to carry a weight – only the strength is mental, not physical. So to help emphasise these affirmations, as you repeat them imagine that you're a strong man or woman lifting up a not-too-heavy pair of bar bells, representing all your responsibilities.

Visualize lifting them up to about waist height. Then after each affirmation feel how the bar bells are heavy but you're managing to support them without difficulty. Yes, they are weighing you down and making you use your muscles, but you can do it; you have the strength and determination to hold them for as long as necessary.

By combining the imagined physical effort (which is controlled and sustainable) with the spirit behind the affirmations, you increase your desire for and ability to handle more responsibility.

Again, notice that in the final affirmation you choose to take your colleagues with you and let them share in your successes. You're choosing to be responsible for helping them to do better and achieve more, and if you can pull this aim off, you're management material for sure.

Being ready to expand

When getting ready to move on or to believe that you're worth more pay, visualizing this goal creatively can help, so that you start to embody your belief and exude it. When you do so, after a while the belief becomes a part of your psyche and you truly are what you believe.

Whatever field you work in, think of a living being that you can imagine yourself to be. If you're in a highly aggressive environment such as buying and selling stocks and shares among the bulls and bears of stock exchange, you may want to see yourself as a tiger cub growing into a fast and dangerous tiger. If you work in a creative field such as advertising, perhaps visualize yourself as a young painter such as Van Gogh or Picasso and then watch yourself grow into a great artist.

Following is a general visualization that you can use as is, regardless of your occupation, or you can adapt the exercise to make it your own, and therefore even more effective:

1. **Imagine that right now you're a small acorn buried a couple of inches down in the earth under a grassy field.**

   Visualize that one morning spring arrives and you need to stretch.

2. **Feel yourself yawn as if waking up after a very long sleep and spread your arms up high as you do so.**

   Imagine that you've sprouted a shoot that's rises up through the soil and pops out into the morning sunlight.

3. **Feel that shoot grow until it becomes a twig and then a trunk, at which point much of you is now above the ground.**

   Sense as well your roots starting to grow deeper and wider as they seek out water and nourishment and dig in solidly to hold up the massive weight that you eventually have.

4. **Visualize that by noon you're a small oak tree with a long trunk, and plenty of branches and twigs all covered with leaves.**

   You're young and strong and have much further to grow. Bed yourself in for the night.

5. **Stretch your roots to a sufficient length and width, and ensure that they're deep enough to drink in sufficient water and obtain all the nutrients you're going to need.**

   Grow taller, reach out your branches, and increase the number of branches and twigs you extend into the world.

Whichever metaphor you choose for this exercise, repeat it regularly. But don't grow yourself too far the first time you practise it. Instead, each time you repeat the exercise grow a little taller, become a little bigger, and extend your reach a little further. That way you're always expanding in the exercise, just as you grow in your working life. And as you go through that life, your natural self-image becomes similar to that in the exercise.

Imagining you've already achieved what you desire

As with many creative visualization exercises, if you can see the desired outcome as if it's already been achieved, you show your unconscious mind exactly what you want and it does everything in its power to help you to achieve that objective.

The golden proviso is that creative visualization only works well when you have a truly positive and realistic expectation of success, based on the sound knowledge that you possess the abilities required to succeed in your goal. So don't idly daydream about your fantasies. Instead, visualize your goals as achievements that you've already made.

This vision then pervades your psyche in such a way that you're prepared for and keen to take the necessary measures. Success doesn't come out of thin air – you have to work at it. But visualization allows the motivation needed for this hard work to materialise, accompanied by the required stamina to stick with the programme. You're also on the alert for any and all opportunities that come your way and ready to pounce and act on them.

By visualizing creatively, you wire your brain so that your goals are the main things uppermost in your mind, interacting with everything that you do, and so you naturally find ways to move forwards in the right direction. And inspiration for new ideas arises where none was before, usually because your unconscious mind (which never sleeps) is beavering away in the background, trying to come up with all the things you need. Like you, it wants what's best for you and for you to feel good. And if achieving your goals makes you feel better, that's what your unconscious strives for.

For example, say that you believe you're ready for promotion and you hear that your current boss is soon moving to another division. The move is some weeks away and the job hasn't been announced yet, but you think you can do it, and so you do the following:

1. **Visualize yourself as already having gained the job.**

   You've moved into the office that your boss used to occupy. See your computer on the desk, your family photos around it, along with your other personal belongings. Perhaps your name is inscribed on the door name plate and you now have a nicer company car.

2. **See yourself working.**

   Think about the decisions and choices you need to make in this job and imagine making some. Then see yourself writing up a report or attending a meeting with your new (higher-up) superiors. See how they respect your ability and that you're doing a good job.

3. **Look back and see how you obtained the promotion.**

   Visualize how you ensured that even before the job was officially posted you made sure that you were the ideal candidate. You worked even harder than ever and ensured that your bosses knew about it. Perhaps you had 'chance' encounters in the lift with one or two members of senior management and were able to mention how well a project you're working on is going, or how sales in your department are up 15 per cent thanks to an initiative you took, or whatever. Note how you took every opportunity to shine and made absolutely certain that nothing negative was available to report, even when you had to go into work when you had terrible flu.

   Then see the job posting on the corporate website and see yourself responding to it with an immaculate CV detailing all the things you've achieved so far for your organisation. Now fast-forward to the interview process and sense your enthusiasm in front of the panel and how you were able to show in-depth knowledge of the organisation and its current strategies, and even came up with a couple of positive suggestions when prompted. All in all, feel pleased and thankful that you were able to present yourself so well, and that you were granted the opportunity of taking over your former boss's role.

4. **Go backwards and forwards in your mind, examining every aspect of the process.**

   With the efforts of you and your unconscious mind, when the time comes to prepare and apply for the position in reality, you've covered every angle and are the ideal candidate for this job.

Overcoming obstacles and objections

Sometimes your requests for promotion or a pay rise are turned down, but that's fine because if you've done your homework right you've indicated to your superiors that you're aware of your abilities, that you believe you have a track record, and that you're looking for greater responsibilities and/or rewards. These things are noted and your chances of success next time are increased.

Sometimes, however, you may encounter a boss who's afraid of you and who does everything possible to block your progress. This situation is difficult because going over the head of a superior is generally bad etiquette. In such cases, you need to find ways to get around this obstruction without breaking any 'rules', which means that you need to be creative.

To help, try the following visualization exercise, which gets your unconscious grey matter pondering on ways to help you. Eventually, you can discover just the right way to get past the roadblock and progress on up the ladder.

1. **Imagine that you're driving along some winding mountain roads.**

   Suddenly you encounter your obstructive boss blocking the road in front of you in the form of a huge mudslide.

2. **Notice that other roads are available.**

   However you would have to either reverse back the way you came (give up), or take a very long detour (the equivalent of leaving to join another company).

3. **Also see that there's some rough wasteland down in the valley.**

   But it may not be suitable for vehicles and it's dangerous (the equivalent of trying to go over your boss's head).

4. **Realise that somehow you *are* going to have to get past this roadblock.**

   Notice that upon realising this the weather suddenly changes and it starts raining heavily.

5. **Watch the pile of mud slowly dissolving and sliding off the road and down to the valley below.**

   After a few minutes the roadblock is all but gone and you're able to pass by.

When you perform this exercise, you're not meaning any harm to your boss (even though you may be infuriated). Instead, you simply visualize the person as becoming irrelevant to your progress. In your mind the roadblock disappears.

Chapter 17

Becoming More Creative

· ·

· ·

Creativity is the force that drives new music, art, and inventions; it seems to well up from deep within you and often suddenly spills out when you least expect it. Creativity is an elusive beast that you can't tame and subjugate to your will, and thank goodness you can't, because tamed creativity would probably end up rather bland and uninspiring.

Some people find that drawing on creativity is difficult, whereas others appear to have an ever-flowing abundance. Why is that? Where does creativity come from, and if you aren't very creative, what can you do to become more so?

Creativity is all about: taking something and changing it into something new. But to be able to carry out this re-creation, you need to have a wide range of source material from which to draw, and therefore no substitute exists for reading all you can about the things you like, viewing as much art as you can (including paintings, photography, sculpture, and so on), listening to plenty of music, and generally immersing yourself in culture.

By soaking up the creative work of other people, you expand your outlook on the world and start the process of innovation stirring deep within you. And before long you find that you have no choice but to express that creativity in your own ways, perhaps through writing stories, poems, or songs, or maybe by creating computer programs or designing new gadgets. As long as you keep introducing yourself to other people's work and ideas, your unconscious mind welcomes them in and enjoys them, and begins to mix and change them into new ideas and concepts. This process gives you the raw material to draw on.

To help bring your creativity to life, therefore, practise the techniques in this chapter to draw on the thoughts welling within you, and give birth to inspiration.

Coming Up with New Ideas

If you've immersed yourself in art and culture, read an abundance of books, and watched a myriad of movies, but you still seem unable to come up with fresh ideas, what can you do next? You need to find a way to unearth all the creativity that's surely going on deep inside your mind. Like an oil company, you need to drill a well that releases your creative juices in a flood of usable ideas.

As the name suggests, *creative* visualization is clearly a great way to encourage creativity. Using the tools of your imagination itself, you can unlock all the wonderful ideas and imagery seething around in your unconscious mind (or as some would say, within your soul), and turn them into usable concepts in the form of works of art or music.

The more you practise the techniques and exercises in this chapter, the more you become spontaneously creative. You build the neural pathways required to keep absorbing, transforming, and mixing up new ideas you come across, and you can also quickly release your own new creations from your unconscious to your conscious mind.

Seeing yourself as a source of creativity

To start becoming more creative you need to believe that you are creative. In fact, you need to know for certain that you're a great source of creativity. To help you become aware of this fact and start building the pathways that allow your creativity to flow, practise the following visualization:

1. **Imagine that you're an artist standing in a great hall in a museum of art.**

   All around you are bare, white walls, stunning marble pillars, and arched ceilings that soar several storeys high. You're preparing for an exhibition of your work, which is wide and varied.

2. **Raise your arms like an orchestral conductor, and from deep within you pull up gorgeous painting after painting.**

   They can be portraits, still lifes, abstracts, or anything at all, with each one materialising in its chosen place on the wall as you point to it.

3. **Start to populate the great hall with your sculptures.**

   Again, bring them up quickly and easily: marble busts of people and animals, strange and hypnotic shapes, weird and wonderful structures. Some are monochrome, others shimmer all the colours of the rainbow as one by one you point to where they need to be located.

4. **Now create some music for the exhibition visitors.**

   Feel it shoot out of your fingers like musical notes on a stave, and then dance around the room as if in a Disney animated film. The sound is the most touching music you can muster, full of fire and fury, yet subtle and moving – better than any film soundtrack.

5. **Let your arms fall to your sides and walk around the exhibition, viewing all that you've just created.**

   See the sculptures and paintings from different viewpoints, and listen to how the music changes depending on the acoustics of the part of the hall you're in. Wonder at how all this beauty has arisen from within you, and think to yourself, 'Yes, this is what I want to show to the world'.

After performing this exercise you may feel quite surprised at the things you saw and heard, because everyone is creative but many people suppress it. However, in this exercise you release the blocks you normally place on your unconscious mind, which finding itself free, delivers a joyful abundance of creativity.

Take a moment to appreciate what your unconscious was able to do, thank it, and let it know that you'd really appreciate more (much more) of the same. Promise to do your best to keep feeding it with new ideas, sensations, sounds, and whatever else it desires.

Mixing and merging your ideas

Although coming up with anything entirely new is impossible, don't let that hinder your creativity in any way.

For example, there are only a little over a hundred known elements in the universe, but they make up everything that exists by being combined in different ways. Hydrogen (an explosive gas) and oxygen (a corrosive gas) can be combined to become harmless water, and sodium (a highly reactive metal) and chlorine (a toxic substance often used for bleaching and sterilising) can be brought together to form common salt. In fact, looking even more closely, each element is simply a construction of protons, neutrons, and electrons, which means that just *three* fundamental building blocks are used to construct everything there is, has been, or ever will be!

By contemplating this you can realise how the limitations you may think apply to your circumstances are purely imaginary. If the universe can be built up from just three types of building block, what can you create with all the elements at your disposal?

Consider also music, which consists purely of vibrations. Faster vibrations create higher sounds, and slower vibrations make lower ones, but the underlying cause of a musical note is simply a single wave form. A stranger to music might at first think music would be rather plain and boring due to being constructed only of a simple wave. But the richness of music that surrounds us every day is a witness to what creativity can achieve with something as simple as a vibrating wave.

Or how about light? The human eye can see an infinite number of colours, but uses receptors of only three primary colours to do this. By combining red, green, and blue in varying ratios, you can create any other colour and shade from black all the way to white, and everything in between. What's more, light is just a wave like sound, but it vibrates much faster. Again, one simple building block leads to infinite potential.

By drawing on the wealth of creativity of other people and from everything you see, hear, and feel, you can create something new; and even though it may comprise a bit of this and a touch of that, it's new. If sufficiently different from anything that has gone before, you can even copyright or patent your work to protect it. Here's an exercise that integrates these different types of building blocks together with creative visualization:

1. **Visualize that you're going to create something new.**

   It will combine a variety of elements.

2. **First think of its physical nature.**

   Just like the building blocks of matter, bring together a few basic elements. Perhaps a liquid such as water or mercury, combined with something organic like wood or rope, and a solid like glass or stone. Just choose a few things you would like to work with.

3. **Now think of its colours.**

   Imagine either a single colour or a combination of different colours that you would like to combine. Also choose whether to use dark or light shades, or both.

4. **Think about the sound it makes.**

   Does it make a sound when you hit it, or scrape your fingernail against it, or wave it in the wind? If so hear that sound in your head. And if you want it to make more than one sound imagine how you'll do this using the elements you chose to work with.

5. **Now close your eyes and start to see the object forming in front of you.**

   Visualize the various elements coming together one at a time and form-ing a new whole. Look at the colours and reflections, and listen to any sound the creation makes. Smell it too and see what that's like. And try playing with the device by moving it. If it's small enough you can imag-ine manipulating it in your hands and feeling its fine textures.

When you practise this exercise don't worry about the thing you create nec-essarily having to do anything or have a purpose. Just allow it to exist and be new. In my case I just imagined an hourglass shape looking like two brains instead of a pair of bulbs, in which a thick, orange liquid drips from one to the other (representing thoughts going from one mind to another) instead of sand. I also imagined it resting on a finely carved and lightly varnished wooden base. But the last time I practised this exercise the resulting creation was a xylophone made of coloured glass and wood (I like these two things at the moment).

If you're an arty type of person, you may even like the thing you just created enough to paint it in real life, or perhaps create a sculpture of it or build it as a model, or even full scale. If so, do it. Realise that creative urge. Let this new thing become a reality. I intend to do so with some of the objects I have invented this way, and have already started the process by amassing a collec-tion of materials I enjoy the look and feel of.

Following random thoughts

Free association – the following of random thoughts – is a well-known means of getting your creative juices flowing. The idea is not to impose a set idea; simply let your mind wander until you come up with something useful. When used inexpertly, this technique results in nothing more than daydreams, but if you bring creative visualization into the equation you increase your chances of coming up with the goods.

For the best results when using free association start off with a seed thought or idea, preferably one totally unrelated to the task at hand (to ensure that you begin with a fresh perspective).

1. **Think of the first thing that comes into your mind.**

   It can be a squirrel, a kettle, or anything.

2. **Hold that new thought in the front of your mind.**

   Examine it thoroughly.

3. **Is it an object?**

   If so look at it, touch it, feel it, smell it, and listen to it.

4. **Is it an idea, word, or anything else?**

If so interact with the thought in any way you can.

5. **Combine it with the subject about which you're being creative.**

Somehow find a way to merge the thing about which you are being creative with this new thought or object. Try fitting them together in many different ways and see what you can come up with that's new.

For example, assume that you're a designer and are trying to come up with a new design of a compact camera, and the thought you came up with was a banana. When you link the two together, you can imagine the inner fruit of a banana being like the zoom lens of a camera. Most people peel bananas in three strips, and so envision a safety shutter with three parts that fold in and out.

After going round a few times and writing down all your ideas as you have them, you may well surprise yourself by discovering the seeds of a great idea right in front of you.

Going on hunting expeditions through your mind

As Elmer Fudd in the Bugs Bunny cartoons is fond of saying, 'Be vewy, vewy quiet, we're hunting wabbits'. But here, rather than rabbits, you're going to hunt for ideas. That's right, put on your imaginary hunting hat, hang your binoculars around your neck, and prepare for a cerebral safari in which you're going to discover just the idea you need:

1. **Imagine that you're driving a truck painted in camouflage colours, with your hunting hat on, navigating on a safari through your mind.**

The scene looks very much like Africa or the Australian outback with wide open spaces interspersed with trees, bushes, and dense thickets, within which are lurking great ideas hiding from you. You drive past the undergrowth and greenery and spot glimpses of things that you can't quite make out, but which seem interesting.

2. **Keep going until you come across an idea.**

You're in a dense oasis of trees, with a waterhole in the middle, and standing there, right on the waterside, is a brilliant idea. You don't know what it is but you're going to collect it. You're not the type of hunter that kills its prey; instead you leap out with a big canvas bag and quickly push the idea into it and drive back to camp.

3. **Start thinking about the true nature of the idea.**

   What did it look like in the brief glimpse you caught? Did it make any noise? What was its shape? Did it have any meaning or relate to anything? Is it maybe a clue to another thing? What is that idea you have in the back of the truck.

4. **Arrive back at the camp and prepare to open the sack.**

   Ideas in your mind don't bite. They don't hurt you and you don't hurt them, and so let the idea out and see exactly what it is.

If you're lucky, today was a good hunting expedition because you landed just the idea you wanted. If not, that's still okay because your unconscious mind was with you all the way and keeps on searching for you until it finds the idea you're looking for.

Riding the idea train

If you don't travel much by train or bus, you're really missing out on a treasure chest of potential seeds for good ideas. Flying on a plane simply can't match it, because all you get to see (even with a window seat) are clouds, the horizon, and a slowly changing patchwork quilt far below. But on a train or a bus the scenery whizzes by rapidly, particularly in towns and cities, but also in the country.

1. **Next time you take a bus or train ride and have some creative thinking to do, try to sit by the window.**

   With every new thing you see, word you read, unusual building you spot, or anything else that attracts your attention, think about it and how it relates to your current project.

2. **Run the ideas together.**

   Mix and match them, turn them inside out and upside down.

3. **Merge them with other ideas you've already had about the project.**

   Also invert them and see that brings a new perspective.

Using this technique you'll get an endless supply of random thoughts you can use in much the same way as the exercise in the earlier 'Following random thoughts' section. And don't forget, although you need to keep your full attention on the road when driving, you can also try this exercise when travelling as a passenger in a car.

Thinking on Your Feet

The thing with being creative is that you can't simply call up a ready-made creation out of thin air, you have to construct it on the fly. So the answer is to have quick and easy access to your creativity resources so that, when pressed, you have the chance to draw on related concepts, mix them together, and maybe, just maybe, surprise yourself (and everyone else) with a really great idea. So to prepare for when you find yourself in a situation in which you have to think creatively on your feet, try some of the exercises in this section.

Turning an idea on its head

Sometimes all you need to do to an idea to change it into something different and usable is view it from another angle by, for example, turning it upside down.

In 1970, Spencer Silver, a chemist working in the 3M research laboratory, was trying to come up with an extra strong adhesive. One of the formulas he produced was noted for being even weaker than any 3M had previously manufactured, but being a good scientist he didn't discard it and instead stored the formula with many other currently unusable discoveries and inventions.

A few years later, this policy paid off big time because another scientist at 3M, Arthur Fry, who enjoyed singing in his church's choir, wanted to find a way to prevent all his bookmarks from falling out of his hymn book. Luckily Silvers' formula was still stored away, so Fry applied some to his bookmarks and found that the glue was sufficiently strong to keep them in place, but weak enough to allow him to easily remove them again. And so 3M had a huge success with one of the most popular office products of all time: Post-it notes.

You can help to release your creativity by turning the weakness in an idea into a strength using the following exercise:

1. **Visualize something that has an inherent weakness.**

   For example, take an incandescent light bulb, which gives off a lot of heat as a side effect of producing light, causing it to be much less efficient than a fluorescent or LED bulb.

2. **Imagine a use to which you can put this weakness.**

   Heat can be useful. Is there a way you can harness it? Think about what you can use this heat for.

3. **Imagine that you are short-sighted, have to type a lot, and your hands are often cold.**

   Instead of turning the central heating up, maybe you can place a gentle fan behind a desk lamp to blow its heat at your fingers, as well as lighting up your keyboard for greater visibility.

4. **Or imagine that you've invented an ornament of glass containing coloured waxes and dyes that move about when heated.**

   By placing this above a light bulb not only can you add light to the ornament, you can also provide its heating power – and you'll have (re-) invented the lava lamp.

5. **Try to think of any other uses for the weakness (in this case excess heat).**

   Continue thinking of ideas until you begin to draw blanks.

By simply turning the product's weakness on its head, and changing it into a strength, a great idea can be born. For example, in this age of digital books some artists are now taking old printed books and turning them into works of art by cutting out or reshaping sections. The weakness here is that the book is unwanted and might otherwise go for recycling, but instead it is turned into a thing of beauty.

Playing inverse snap

You know the card game in which players have a pack of cards face down and they take turns revealing cards, and the first one to shout 'snap!' when the cards match keeps the pile? Well, you can play the inverse of this game when you're in a meeting or brainstorming session and need to come up with some quick ideas.

Every time someone else comes up with an idea, immediately think of the inverse of it and then consider what that means and how it may be applied. Come up not with that idea but with one it brings to mind – one that isn't the exact inverse of the idea, but is a useful concept that adds to the discussion.

Don't worry if you can't think of an idea to add to the group discussion every time, but at least try to do so in your head, so that you have a collection of inverse and adapted ideas, probably all different to those your colleagues are creating. Now and then these notions may well help you to produce a great idea of your own. And, hey presto, you're a valid member of the brainstorming team.

You can also play this game on your own as a visualization.

1. **Imagine that you need to come up with a new idea for a dating service called Forever Together.**

   Now make a list of all the things you can think about that apply to such a service, such as, friendship, love, expression, attitude, character, forever, together, and so on.

2. **Work through each of these ideas in turn, and think of its opposite.**

   For example, friendship may make you think of hatred. Maybe there's a concept along the lines of 'Go on, be a devil', but that's not really very strong, so try the next idea, love. Again that returns hate – too similar. How about expression? That makes you think of impression, and then you may associate that to the phrase 'first impressions'. This looks a little meatier, so move on to the next step.

3. **Now take the current concept and turn that on its head.**

   OK, then, the opposite of 'first impressions' may be 'last impressions'. Hold on a minute, that's not bad... 'First impressions last'. This is starting to look like it has potential, so you can move on to the next step. Otherwise, if no other good idea occurs, return to step 2.

4. **You now have something that's really caught your attention, so work it through to possible completion.**

   The phrase 'First impressions last' may remind you a little of the L'Oréal slogan 'Because you're worth it', so you put the two together to come up with 'Forever Together – Because first impressions last'.

5. **If you need further ideas, keep working through steps 2 to 4.**

   With any luck you'll come up with a handful of ideas of which, hopefully, at least one may be just what you were looking for.

All right, maybe the phrase in this exercise (or one close to it) has been used before, but this exercise illustrates a powerful process you can use for coming up with creative ideas using opposites.

Getting Really Creative

In this section I present exercises that may seem somewhat left field, but then again, that's the point. Only by thinking completely differently to the norm can you be innovative.

Imagining colour blindness (or the opposite)

Do you have perfect colour vision? If so, you're lucky because approximately 8 per cent of men and 1 per cent of women are colour blind, which usually means they have difficulty distinguishing certain shades of red, brown, and green, although many different types of colour blindness exist, including being able to see only in shades of grey, like a black and white television.

1. **Imagine that the colours you know are not fixed and can swap with each other.**

   For example, red can be purple, yellow can be blue, and so on.

2. **Imagine that sounds and thoughts are colours.**

   If your project isn't in any way related to colour, that doesn't matter; simply imagine that shapes or sounds and so on are associated with colours. Indeed for some people with synaesthesia (in which senses can be processed by the wrong parts of the brain) they can be. For them certain words, numbers, musical notes, events, days of the week, and so on vividly create impressions of colour and shade (or other sensations).

3. **Imagine things and shapes as colours too.**

   For example, square things are red, circular ones are blue, and so on.

4. **Also mess with this situation by changing your type of colour vision.**

   If you are colour blind imagine having normal colour vision (perhaps reds and greens will be stronger and more vivid), otherwise imagine being colour blind (possibly confusing your reds, greens, and browns), and think what the world would look like.

5. **Now reconstruct your project as a colourful modern abstract painting.**

   In the previous steps you turned each part of your project into a different colour; now paint with them to create a wonderful canvas.

6. **Analyse your creation.**

   Now interpret your painting and see what it tells you or reveals about your project. You can help with this by turning colours back into thoughts, shapes, and objects, and so on.

Through this restructuring of the project, bringing all your senses together and integrating them into your colour awareness, you use your creativity in a number of different ways. Along the way it should help to release any hidden creative ideas floating just below your consciousness.

By using this technique your view of the world, your current project, and anything you think about becomes substantially different (almost alien, in fact), enabling you to see things that perhaps you previously missed, and come up with new ideas relating to them.

Reshaping 'the box'

I avoid advising you to 'think outside the box' in this chapter because that's now such an over-used concept that it's no longer all that helpful. The analogy was a clever idea at first, but the time has come to amend the box to create new ways of being creative that really get you thinking. So re-shape that box!

Instead of thinking 'outside the box', change the box into something else. Maybe it's a plain and simple cardboard box, but maybe it isn't. Perhaps it's a long cylinder like a garden hose, or a crystal ball, or a musical instrument.

If that doesn't help with your visualization of new ideas, try taking things further. Maybe the box is a concept – a pure thought. Or perhaps it's a frame of mind, an emotion, or even a scientific theory. What if the box was this universe itself and you had to think outside of that? How crazy would that be, and what would it be like?

So there's still life in that old box yet, as long as you turn it into something else first.

Using synonym strings

One useful way to explore a concept is to use a *thesaurus*, which is like a dictionary of words except that it lists words of similar meaning next to each other. For example, the word *creativity* brings up all the following synonyms: artistry, cleverness, genius, imagination, imaginativeness, ingenuity, inspiration, inventiveness, originality, resourcefulness, talent, and vision. And the word *artistry* has these synonyms: ability, accomplishment, artfulness, brilliance, craftsmanship, creativity, finesse, flair, genius, mastery, proficiency, style, talent, taste, touch, virtuosity, and workmanship, and so on.

Using this concept, here's an exercise you can use traverse a linked chain of ideas, until you find a new one you can use.

1. **Find all the words that are similar to or relate to a word to do with your current project.**

   You can use a printed thesaurus or an online one (such as www. thesaurus.com). If neither is at hand, come up with synonyms in your mind. Whatever source you use, write down all the words.

2. **Go through the words, using each one in turn as a new source word, and write down all the associated words you can find for that word.**

   Often the same words keep cropping up and you may find that drawing lines between the most common ones is useful (so that you can see whether a common theme exists).

3. **Sit back and see whether the paper is telling you something.**

   Is a new thought or idea embedded somewhere in one of the words, or can you infer one from some of the connections you've made?

4. **Soak in the contents of the sheet of paper.**

   Now close your eyes and try to visualize all the words on the paper turning into real things. The word car becomes a car, love becomes a beating heart, power becomes a little, buzzing nuclear power station, and so on.

5. **Let all these animated things interact with one another.**

   The heart and car may combine to form a vehicle looking like Herbie from the Disney film *The Love Bug*, or the car and power station may merge to create a power source on wheels or a nuclear powered vehicle, and so on.

More often than not, something of value is lurking on that sheet of paper, even if only to lead you in a another direction of research. And occasionally you hit the jackpot and just the idea you want pops right off the page.

Surfing through your mind

These days, more information than you can ever consume in a thousand lifetimes is available at the touch of a button on the Internet. And, with hundreds of channels of digital television available, you're used to surfing through it all looking for the good stuff that you like.

Well, you can use this surfing technique on the vast amount of data that you've sequestered away in your mind, and at about the same speed too – less than five seconds per channel:

1. **Think about your current project for five seconds and then immediately visualize pressing the channel change button (or your imaginary web-surfing button) and think about something else.**

   You don't know what that something else is yet, but as soon as you make the decision to flick channels it comes to you.

2. **Keep on channel/website surfing just as you normally do until something of interest catches your mind's eye.**

   Stop and spend a little time thinking about why it interests you, and try to get any information or ideas from it.

3. **Repeat this process until you feel tired and then write down every-thing you find interesting.**

   In fact, as soon as you find a good channel or website, start taking notes so that you don't later forget.

By forcing your imagination to instantly come up with something at each channel change you bypass the conscious filtering that you normally perform all the time, allowing your unconscious mind to send ideas straight into your head. This is similar to how hypnotised people are so quickly able to act in imaginary ways that they would be hesitant to do in normal life. It happens because the conscious mind is placed in a resting state by the hypnotist, allowing the unconscious mind to come to the surface.

Holding that thought

Here's a visualization technique you can use that returns good results but which takes a little while, because it requires you to hold a single related idea in your mind all day long.

1. **Start off thinking about your current project.**

   Choose an idea or subject area that's related to it and which you think may be worth contemplating.

2. **For the rest of the day, whenever you think about your project or any-thing else, consider how it relates to your idea of the day.**

   Ponder connections and differences, follow potential ideas, and dismiss ones that don't work. You have a full day in which to examine both your project and your seed idea and you may well be amazed at what you can come up with.

   First of all you have plenty of thoughts which after a while start to dry up. Then, generally by around midday, you find yourself out of new ideas, but that's when you redouble your efforts and the good material comes, because you now have to get really creative to come up with anything new.

   So stick with that seed thought and work on it as hard as possible, and each time a potential new idea springs to mind write it down.

3. **At the end of the day or the start of the next day if you're too tired, review your notes.**

   Remove any that seemed to get you nowhere so that you can focus on the better ideas, some of which may even be good seeds for another day's contemplation.

Mental flash cards for being more creative

Here are a few mental flash cards to help you come up with the creative ideas:

- ✔ **Seeing life as a painting:** Look around you, remember what you see, and close your eyes. Now re-paint the view with brushstrokes. Use an Impressionist or any other painting style to change the way the world looks and provide a new viewpoint.

- ✔ **Moulding your vision:** Take the project that you're working on and place it into your imagination. Now use imaginary hands to shape and mould it like modelling clay until it's how you want it.

- ✔ **Creating a firework fountain:** Imagine a fountain full of great ideas. Pour some more in from a big container if you like. Then set light to the top of the fountain because, unlike a water fountain, this one shoots out sparkling ideas. Watch them as they flash and sparkle and feel the good ones beaming themselves into your mind.

- ✔ **Visiting the universe next door:** Take a deep breath and imagine a white chalk line on the floor in front of you. Step over it and into the universe next door. The laws of physics are all different and everything's strange. What do you see?

- ✔ **Riding in a time machine:** Climb into your mental time machine and set it for one year ahead. When you arrive in the future, look at anything in the world related to your project and see how it developed over that time. Then get back in and go forward another year, followed maybe by another two or five more years. How different is the world in relation to your project now?

This technique works best when you have a few key thoughts that you think may bear fruit. Work through one a day until you've examined them all and then put all your notes together and see how they relate to each other. Somewhere in there you may find a diamond in the rough.

Overcoming Creative Blocks

When you've tried everything you can (including all the techniques I outline in the earlier sections 'Coming Up with New Ideas', 'Thinking on Your Feet', and 'Getting Really Creative') and you're still having trouble producing with the creativity you need, don't give up just yet. Your unconscious mind is full of all manner of things you aren't aware of, simply because it chooses not to let you know. This allows you to concentrate on using your consciousness for your day-to-day living, without getting bogged down in strange and dreamlike stuff that goes on in your unconscious mind.

But what if you want to access this unconscious material? What can you do if you've been wracking your brains for days, or maybe even weeks, and time's running out and you *really* need to come up with the goods – such as a great new name for your latest product, a title for a book, or the perfect marketing angle for launching a new product?

The answer is to start talking more closely with your unconscious mind – the part of you that's ever watchful and never sleeps. The unconscious doesn't have a consciousness that can say things like, 'I think therefore I am'. But it's a major part of you and works hard at pleasing you. Like a loyal dog it loves you and is faithful to you, and does anything it can to please you. But unlike a pet, it *is* you. Check out Chapter 6 for more on understanding and using your unconscious mind.

Some people think of the unconscious mind like a soul and you often hear people say things like their 'soul was moved' by a stirring piece of music. And those uncontrollable feelings that well up within, seemingly from nowhere, come from your unconscious mind. In fact, it provides a wide range of thoughts, emotions, and feelings to you, from which your conscious mind picks and chooses what and how to act upon, using your powers of consciousness and reasoning.

Deep within your unconscious mind, though, things are seriously strange. And yet they're totally familiar; just as familiar as a car turning into a hat in a dream. It makes perfect sense at the time – completely logical. But this place is the logic of the unconscious, which communicates using symbolism and emotions. And now you want to communicate with your unconscious to really come up with the creative idea you need. But you're going to have to use its language of symbols, images, and emotions.

So the exercises in this section help you to encourage your unconscious mind to share anything it can with you that may be helpful in coming up with just the idea that you need, even if your unconscious isn't sure whether that's a good idea or not.

Climbing the mental mountain to see over the other side

The following exercise is intended to explain to your unconscious that you know that the ideas you're looking for exist, and that you also know that your unconscious mind knows them, but that your unconscious doesn't necessarily always know which are the right ideas, and which ones may not be that good. Therefore you want to let it know that (just for now) you don't need your unconscious filtering everything for you, and that you don't mind being given a brain blast, even if it would normally be overwhelming.

Remain confident that you're happy to consider whatever ideas come forth, and that you take responsibility for dismissing the bad ones yourself. With this concept firmly in your mind, try following this exercise:

1. **Imagine that you're climbing a high mountain and at the end of your quest is the thing you desire to see, the one good idea.**

   Where you are, deep in the valley, it's a little misty and you can't see all that much. But in the valley beyond is a cornucopia of weird and wonderful things. It's a magical valley and you're not expecting to see conventional plants and trees. In fact, you don't know what you're going to see. You suspect that the valley contains a whole range of pictures, movies, smells, objects, sayings, and phrases, and it may be all a jumble. Some of it's going to be amazing and some of it unpleasant. But that's okay because you know that the good idea or ideas you're seeking are going to stand out like a campfire at night.

2. **Feel how close you're getting.**

   You continue up the mountain path, which is now so steep that you sometimes have to grab onto rocks at the side of the path to help pull your body up. And every now and then you need to take a rest to catch your breath. But you're near . . . you can sense it. The thing you desire is over the mountain and you're going to see it soon. As you think this thought, acknowledge to your unconscious mind that opening up the valley of wonders for you to see is fine. You desire seeing the valley more than anything and your unconscious need hold nothing back.

3. **Just as you reach the summit of the mountain, pause and gather your thoughts.**

   Feel calm, yet excited. Breathe deeply a couple of times and take those remaining steps over the top of the mountain and gaze down into the valley of weird and wonderful ideas.

What you see now is up to you; it can be anything at all. Or nothing. And what you see is going to be different each time you practise this exercise. But when it works, the thing you need (in this case a new idea) stands out from all the other things and you have that 'Aha' moment. If it doesn't seem to work, it still has. You just don't know it yet. That idea will come soon.

Flying over your mindscape like a bird

In the earlier section 'Riding the idea train', I suggest that a train or bus ride is a better way to find inspiration than a plane ride. But sometimes flying in a plane and looking over the landscape can be a rich source of creative ideas, especially when that landscape happens to be your unconscious mind:

1. **Imagine that you're the only passenger in a very special plane that flies over your mindscape.**

   The plane has the ability to fly through all the tucks and folds in your brain as if it's flying over a flat surface, similar to travelling in a real plane.

2. **Look down as you fly and see your emotions everywhere.**

   For example, love isn't just located in one place. Perhaps it's a reddish sort of pinky colour that appears in blobs with strands connecting lumps of it to each other, and surrounding other emotions and thoughts.

   Your mindscape is different to everyone else's and so you have to see it for yourself. For example, when you notice bright sparkly and frequently changing shapes that flit about, perhaps they're dreams or dream fragments. The deep red lakes may be pools of desire, and the two-mile-high pointy spikes are surges of motivation. Be creative. Decide what your dreamscape looks like and map it to your personality.

3. **Locate people you know and see where you find them.**

   Look into your memory for places you've been, things you like, enjoyable foods (and distasteful ones). Create a crazy world from your mind until you can fly over it and spot all the major landmarks.

4. **Find your current project.**

   Is it in one place, or spread out over many? What colour and shape is it? Does it move? If so what does it do and where does it go? What is it connected to elsewhere in your mindscape. Try to understand everything you can about it.

   Examine your project further and try to look for anything unusual, or any unexpected connections. If you find any, dig deeper. Somewhere in there you may uncover the seed of creativity the project needs.

I know that these visualizations are getting more and more abstract and can seem quite crazy. But this book is about creative visualization and this type of imagery is bread and butter to your unconscious mind. Feed it and it responds.

Being a fly on the wall in an idea factory

Here's a visualization that's very abstract but it may help retrieve that elusive creative idea from within you. The exercise assumes that the idea definitely exists and is waiting to be found, but you need to discover a way to retrieve it, using a little subterfuge:

Turning the ordinary into the extraordinary

Sometimes the thing that bogs you down when trying to be creative is the normality of a project, which somehow doesn't seem to lend itself to creative ideas and which therefore makes them hard to come by.

For example, Victor Kiam, the man who bought the Remington shaver company after trying one of its electric shavers, tells the story of when he was at Lever Brothers and was tasked with representing one of their brands of toothpaste to a gathering of high-profile buyers from top stores.

He was up against a number of other presentations from competing firms and his problem was that toothpaste is a very common household item in that, other than a few variations in colours, it has more or less the same stuff in it, regardless of the brand you buy. Scratching his head over what to do the day before the presentation, Kiam decided to take a walk downtown for inspiration and came across a pet shop. Inside was a rather mischievous monkey for sale.

Without any hesitation he purchased the monkey and the next day took it to the presentation with a cloth over the cage. After a number of other salespeople had made their presentations, Kiam took the monkey out of the cage, placed it on his back, entered the room, and said 'Ladies and gentlemen. It seems I have a monkey on my back and it's time I got him off!' At which point, he placed the monkey on the desk, whereupon it proceeded to kick over all the coffee cups, throw the pens and sheets of paper about, and generally cause as much mayhem as possible.

The whole meeting was in uproar and it took a quarter of an hour to catch the monkey and put it back in the cage. Now, aside from whether you think that this prank was cruel to the animal (I tend to think not, and that it had the time of its life), the end result was that Kiam substantially increased sales of his toothpaste brand in all the accounts that had been present, with all the major buyers talking about nothing but Kiam and his monkey for months (if not years) afterwards.

So, if you desperately need to come up with a creative idea, maybe you can take the project you're working on and do something extraordinary with it; something that's completely unconnected and unexpected. Consider the wild and wonderful and see whether you can maybe use that as your great idea. Sometimes wild and wonderful is just the answer you need.

A word of warning, though. Use spectacular or extraordinary ideas only sparingly or their power wears thin. Save them for when you're really stuck and nothing else comes to mind. But when push comes to shove, when you release the bounds of your imagination and choose the right project, you can be amazed at how creative you suddenly become.

1. **Imagine a factory somewhere in the world in which ideas of all manner are generated.**

   Not just your average run-of-the-mill ideas. Oh no, these notions are genuine industrial-strength ideas that knock your socks off. In fact, they're so good that the factory has a high level of security and unauthorised people can't get in or out. But for you that's no problem as you. . .

2. **Transform yourself into the body of a fly and enter through an open window.**

   Inside you can see hundreds of different strange machines stamping and forming every idea you can think of (only the good ones though). You can hear a tremendous clanking and whirring with wonderful ideas being dropped onto conveyor belts, from where they're whisked off to packing bays, neatly wrapped, and placed into boxes. Fly around the factory, looking, listening, and smelling, until you come across a machine making an idea that really interests you.

3. **Steal the idea.**

   Check that no one's looking, turn back into a human, and pick the idea up. Then, as the alarm bells start to ring, quickly change back into a fly. With the idea resized like you, take it and fly back out of the open window to safety.

   As you fly away, remember that the factory is actually in a land inside your brain, and therefore a part of yourself, so you haven't actually stolen anything, but you did come back with a great idea (of your own).

This exercise promotes the bringing forth of a great idea. You may not get a glimpse of what the idea is from the exercise, but over the next few days you may well find that your creativity levels are raised.

This chapter on creativity is the last one before the 'Part of Tens' sections, but creativity is the first thing you need in order to use creative visualization effectively. So now that you've learned all the techniques in this chapter you're really set to go out and start, change, or improve whatever you set your heart on – with creative visualization the world is in your hands.

Part V
The Part of Tens

The 5th Wave   By Rich Tennant

In this part . . .

The essentials of creative visualization are presented for you in bite-sized chunks. We provide you with advice on a number of elements that creative visualization can help you with, along with plenty of instant visualizations you can call upon as the need arises. We also offer you suggestions on good places to practice visualizing as well as a collection of great books and websites you can refer to for taking your visualizing to the next level.

Chapter 18

Ten Instant Visualizations to Promote Your Wellbeing

In This Chapter

▶ Uplifting your spirits

▶ Filtering negative and positive thoughts

▶ Having a sense of purpose

▶ Developing a positive attitude

*I*n this chapter I provide you with several instant visualizations, which I call mental flash cards. You can prepare these quick exercises in advance, store them in your memory, and call upon them in times of stress or when you need motivation, inspiration, or encouragement.

All you need to do is recall the visualization and spend a few seconds viewing it in your mind to bring back feelings and thoughts that are helpful for managing the task at hand.

When using mental flash cards, be as imaginative as you can when you apply them – really paint the picture that comes to mind as you read them. Then, when you've imprinted the picture in your mind, simply reviewing the visualization instantly recalls the images, emotions, and feelings it originally evoked.

Remembering to Laugh and Smile

Here's a simple yet highly effective flash card visualization you can use to lift your spirits. Simply imagine that you're smiling a big wide grin, beaming across your face. At the same time imagine that something really funny tickled your fancy, causing you to burst out laughing.

Notice how you feel as you do this visualization: your body becomes lighter and any aches and pains are forgotten; your outlook brightens; and your attitude to your current situation and other people is positive and happy.

Increasing Your Love of Life

Imagine that you love everything around you (even if you don't feel that way in reality). Feel good about being alive. Smell the air and love the fact that you can breathe. Listen to the sounds coming in your ears and love the fact that you can hear them. Look at everything around you and the wonderful colours you can see.

Now take a look at the people around you, whether they're friends or family, colleagues or strangers. Then wish them well, each and every one, as if they're brothers and sisters; see them all as fellow inhabitants of the same universe. This visualization takes only a moment, but each time you practise it you increase your enjoyment of life and your empathy towards other people.

Dismissing Your Negative Thoughts

If bad thoughts are bothering you – for example, someone was rude to you this morning, or you're angry about a difficult situation – remind yourself that you don't have to feel bad all day long. You have a life to lead and things to get on with and you don't need these negative distractions.

Choose to take time out from the stressful thoughts and decide that you're going to deal with them at a later date; no point letting them bog you down. Whenever a negative thought arises in your mind, visualize blowing it out of your mouth into an invisible balloon, and follow it with a puff of air to send it on its way floating away from you.

Encouraging Positive Thoughts

Hold on to all the positive thoughts that occur to you. In your imagination hug these thoughts because they make you feel good and you want more of them. Cherish the fact that you have such positivity within you.

To nurture your positive thoughts, and to encourage more of them, visualize watering a positive thought and putting it in a plant pot near the window of your mind, where the sun can gently warm and grow it.

Being Thankful

Get into the habit of expressing gratitude whenever something good happens to you. You can simply be thankful to the universe at large, or if you're religious, thank God. You may be surprised how good simply saying 'thank you' feels.

Expressing your gratefulness for being alive also allows your positive emotions to grow, such as love, happiness, compassion, and generosity. In your mind's eye visualize yourself simply saying 'thank you' to who or whatever has pleased you, and feel yourself sincerely meaning it.

Having Purpose in Your Life

In times of difficulty or doubt, think to yourself that your life does have a purpose, even though you may not know what it is. To help instil this feeling, visualize a galaxy. Picture the hundreds of billions of stars in it, and the hundred billion other galaxies that lie outside it.

Allow your mind to boggle over the fact that among all this incredible amount of matter, you are present and have been given the chance of being a part of this universe. Perhaps your purpose is as simple as living, sharing, laughing, loving, and learning with others. Whatever you think your purpose may be, remind yourself of it often to increase your level of fulfilment with life.

Feeling Needed

At times, you may feel unneeded, particularly when someone you love hurts or ignores you. But the fact is that the world would be a vastly different place without you in it. The following mental flash card focuses on all the good things you bring to the world so that you can call upon feelings of self-worth whenever you need to.

Consider the impact that you've had on the world: your relationships with other people; things you've made; people you've helped; children you've raised; ideas you've shared; and so on. Understand that you're an important person and are absolutely needed, even if others sometimes don't show it. Imagine all the people you've interacted with, and particularly those you've helped in even the smallest of ways, such as holding a door open for them. Then focus on those closer to you, such as acquaintances, colleagues and friends, and then think about your relatives, and then your close family. Even the little things you've done for these people amount and add up to your making a big difference in the world.

Being at One with the Universe

Sometimes you may feel a little uncertain of your place in the world, and where it is that you fit in. Physicists and mystics agree that everything in the universe is interconnected at some level, and you're definitely a part of it. To help you feel more grounded, visualize that the universe is your home and you're an essential part of it.

To envisage yourself as being at one with the universe, imagine holding your hand underwater with your fingers pointing upwards. Slowly raise your hand and visualize your four fingers and thumb appearing above the water. See how they look as if they're separate objects even though you know that they're connected under the water.

In the same way, think about yourself and everyone and everything else, and consider how you, they, and everything in existence are one, and feel at peace with the universe, because it's not you against the world – it's you *with* the world.

Striving to Improve Yourself

Resting on your laurels is never a good idea. As they say in Hollywood: 'You're only as good as your last movie'. In life, you achieve the most when you strive continuously to improve yourself and become a better person, which can be anything you want it to be according to what you perceive as being better. You may desire to become more moral, more skilled, more sociable, or any of a large number of other quality attributes – you pick the one(s) you wish to concentrate on.

Spend some time considering that, although you've achieved many things, you can still do so much more. Know in your heart of hearts that you're going to continue to improve, and that day by day you'll become a better person and achieve more things than the day before. Really feel this by visualizing yourself doing something you enjoy and getting better at it. For example see yourself playing a guitar and with every note or chord you play you get better and better.

Saying 'Yes, I Can'

When visualizing, you need to be positive. Psychologists who study creative visualization report that it works best when the person visualizing holds a positive expectation of success.

Therefore, treat the word 'no' as being outside your vocabulary and get used (even if only in your mind) to saying 'yes' to everything. Think of yourself as a can-do person, and you become a did-do person. Simply visualize yourself in a variety of situations in which you may say 'no', perhaps out of fear. For example, imagine saying 'yes' when invited to participate in a parachute jump, or when asked to speak at a conference, or anything else you normally would decline. Get used to the feeling of being a 'Yes, I can' person.

Chapter 19

Ten Great Settings for Creative Visualization

In This Chapter

▶ Incorporating visualization into your everyday life

▶ Practising creative visualization on your travels

▶ Visualizing in your professional life

▶ Calling upon your visualization skills anytime, anywhere

*W*hen visualizing creatively, choosing the most conducive time and place for the exercise is important.

Initially, you may prefer to seek out quiet and comfortable places where you're less likely to be distracted. As your visualization skills grow, you can start to visualize while listening to relaxing or atmospheric soundscape music.

When visualizing starts to come pretty easily to you, however, you can perform your exercises in most places and situations (with the exception of those requiring you to concentrate on something else – while driving, for example!). This chapter suggests ten top places for quality visualization and can be used in conjunction with Chapter 6, which contains loads more suggestions on this subject.

Finding Somewhere Quiet and Comfortable

The best location for beginner visualizers is at home, where everything is comfortable and familiar, and during the daytime so that you're not too tired and don't drift off to sleep in the middle of a visualization. A comfortable arm-chair or, in good weather, a suitable seat in the garden are ideal.

Settle upon a place and time where you can be alone and uninterrupted so that you can properly practise visualizing creatively and get the best results from it early on. In a busy household, especially one with children running around, this ideal may not be easy, but try if at all possible.

Listening to the Radio or an Audio Player

I recommend that you practise your first visualizations in silence for optimum concentration. When you're comfortable with silent visualization, perhaps add a little music to the mix, which can help due to its ability to relax you and help induce a trance-like state of mind in which you can more easily visualize. Classical, light ambient, or chill-out music is best, and try to avoid anything with words because they can impinge on your exercises. Vocal music without words, or in a foreign language that you don't speak, is often fine though.

Loads of ambient music and/or sound-effect CDs and downloadable digital files are available via the Internet. These products have been specially mixed to enhance meditative-type practices, so they can be worth purchasing.

I've also recorded a free guided audio exercise to help you get relaxed and prepared to visualize, which you can access on the Internet. You can play it by visiting tinyurl.com/guidedrelaxation.

Doing the Housework

As you begin to get used to visualizing, you may find that you can do it while performing simple tasks such as watering flowers, dusting, using a vacuum cleaner, or mowing the lawn. You know, the types of thing you do almost instinctively that require little concentration.

Some of the best visualizations to use in these circumstances are the auditory ones in which you repeat positive affirmations (which are spread throughout this book), because they don't interrupt your vision while you perform your household chores.

Travelling from A to B

Riding as a passenger – whether in a car, train, bus, or plane – is a wonderful time for visualizing. The surroundings change so quickly that you have a constant stream of new things to look at and think about.

You can let your surroundings blur into the background and use them as an animated backdrop to visualizations, or you can use the passing objects and people as seed ideas for coming up with creative visualizations.

Don't visualize while you're driving or operating machinery. Only visualize in situations where you can allow your concentration levels to drop safely.

On Holiday or a Day Trip

While spending recreational time – such as on a day out at the beach or on a holiday – you're very receptive to creative visualizations because you tend to be relaxed and calm. So why not spend a few minutes practising your visualizations or affirmations?

You may well find that you return from your trip feeling even more refreshed and energised than normal.

Participating in Meetings or Talking on the Phone

As you become more skilled at visualizing, you can call up the exercises on demand, especially the mental flash cards that are designed specifically for this purpose (such as those in Chapter 18).

So, for example, when you need an idea, extra energy, or some inspiration while on the phone or in an important meeting, run an appropriate flash card through your mind to bring up the feeling, response, or the creative idea you need.

Attending an Event

You can visualize creatively while attending special events such as pop or rock concerts and sporting events. Doing so can heighten the effect of a visualization due to the fact that many of your senses are involved when you practise it, including hearing, seeing, and even smell.

Don't feel as if you're depriving yourself of enjoyment; you need to spend only a few minutes visualizing at events to see useful results.

Taking a Walk

Walking is one of my favourite times for visualizing. It works best when I'm on my own, but even when walking with my wife I often sneak in quick visualizations in the quiet spaces between chatting.

While out on your walk take a note of the smells and sounds around you, and touch and feel things as you pass them. Providing multiple inputs to your brain during visualizing helps to increase the effectiveness of your visualizations by storing them in a variety of different memory areas.

Lying in Bed

Your bed is a great place to visualize. At night time, practise the sort of less-structured visualizations during which you can safely drop off to sleep without adversely affecting them. I prefer to do my 'thankfulness' and 'oneness with the universe' visualizations (which I describe in Chapter 18) at this time.

If you're the type of person who wakes up bright and breezy in the morning, run a quick visualization through your mind before getting out of bed. At this time of day you may prefer to focus on exercises intended to promote energy and motivation, such as those in Chapter 9.

Visualizing Anywhere

As your visualization experience and skills increase, you may well find that you can visualize absolutely anywhere. You're ready to do so when you discover that you've fully incorporated creative visualization into your everyday life and find yourself drawing on it regularly.

When you reach this point, you're well on the way to becoming the person you want to be. You've mastered the creative visualization technique and as you progress further through life, you can put your mind to, and be successful at, almost anything you desire.

Chapter 20

Ten Places to Discover More about Creative Visualization

● ●

In This Chapter

▶ Discovering respected creative visualization books

▶ Tracking down video- and audio-guided visualizations online

▶ Using social network sites to find new exercises and techniques

▶ Exploring useful blogs and websites

● ●

*T*he Internet contains a wealth of information on creative visualization, particularly in the form of websites, blogs, Facebook pages, and videos. The subject is also well covered from a range of perspectives in a number of books which discuss creative visualization for healing, sporting ability, finances, and so on.

This chapter features ten of the best places to continue your exploration of creative visualization, and each includes further recommendations you may like to follow.

Creative Visualization by Shakti Gawain

This book from New World Library – which shows you how to use your imagination to manifest your deepest desires – was first published in 1978 and is now considered a classic. The book was the first of its type and sparked the modern resurgence in creative visualization. This book is written in a simple and direct manner that is easy to follow and which explores creative visualization from a more spiritual angle, frequently discussing God, your higher self and the soul, although not from any orthodox religious point of view. But even if you're not a particularly spiritual person you'll still find this book highly motivating and enriching.

The Art of True Healing by Israel Regardie

First published in 1932, this book from New World Library contains practical techniques for holistic healing, such as rhythmic breathing and meditation. At the book's core is a meditation exercise called the Middle Pillar. Through this exercise, the reader discovers how to focus energy to improve health and bring success. This book focuses more on the mystical side of visualization than on the psychological or even spiritual, and also includes aspects of astrology.

The Mental Edge by Kenneth Baum

In this 1999 book from Perigee Trade, Kenneth Baum offers advice on maximising sporting potential, showing how athletes in any sport can benefit from performance cues, appropriate visualization, and other mental focusing techniques. If your main interest in self-improvement is to become better at sports, this book is packed with useful advice and visualization exercises.

Think and Grow Rich by Napoleon Hill

First published in 1937, this book from Tribeca Books was founded on Hill's earlier 1928 work *The Law of Success*, which was commissioned by Andrew Carnegie (a firm proponent of writing down goals) and based on interviews with more than 500 American millionaires over 20 years. One of the book's 16 creeds is: 'You must have imagination in creating your definite purpose and in building the plans with which to transform that purpose into reality and put your plans into action.' Although simply called *imagination*, in this book you can already see the beginnings of what we now call creative visualization.

Creative Visualization Blog

This blog (at www.creativevisualizationblog.com) is dedicated to helping you create your reality and understand how your beliefs and feeling enter into it. The blog is maintained by Dino Delano, who started teaching in 1972 and created a holistic centre called The Center For Mind Ecology. Regularly updated, the blog features commentary and videos on all aspects of creative visualization. It provides a great resource for keeping up to date with the latest developments in the field of creative visualization.

Guided Meditation and Visualization YouTube Video

This exercise contains an audio meditation and visualization that you play via YouTube (www.youtube.com/watch?v=1GnB3w80b8M). French-American author and video blogger Lilou Mace helps you to tune into 'an infinite source of wisdom that is within you'. Using this guided visualization, all you have to do is sit back, relax, listen, and follow the instructions. Because of this it makes a great introduction to creative visualization, particularly if you initially find it difficult to concentrate.

Making Creative Visualization Part of Your Life YouTube Video

This practical video (at www.youtube.com/watch?v=xQlmZfGIZ-o) gives you advice on making creative visualization part of your life, covering the importance of, and how to start, practising creative visualization on a daily basis. This video helps you to find ways in which to apply the techniques of creative visualization in all areas of your life, and offers advice on tailoring visualizations to your individual needs.

1 Create Everything, Visualize Self Healing YouTube Video

From the 'Spirit of Self Healing' collection, this video (at www.youtube.com/watch?v=sXKROcd6yMs) is an affirmation and visualization tool to help you self-heal. As the author states, 'We create everything in consciousness, and this meditation video can help you to create your amazing and abundant life.' By watching it you'll be inspired and energised to become more creative, and also discover how to become more relaxed and peaceful, and increase your sense of fulfilment.

Empowering Personal Development Website

This website, at www.empowering-personal-development.com, focuses on strategies and techniques for your personal growth and self-improvement, featuring a range of excellent personal growth and development resources. On each page you find encouragement, techniques, and tips to enhance your life and yourself with affirmations, meditations, visualizations, and more. The website offers free web seminars, radio shows, and audio downloads to help encourage you and keep you motivated to continue your personal development.

Success Consciousness Website

This website (www.successconsciousness.com) is maintained by Remez Sasson, the author of several books including *Peace of Mind in Daily Life*, *Willpower and Self Discipline*, *Visualize and Achieve*, and *Affirmations – Words of Power*. In the website, Sasson teaches and writes about self-improvement, positive thinking, creative visualization, motivation, willpower and self-discipline, spiritual growth, peace of mind, and meditation, all subjects he studied and practised from an early age. Using this website as a resource you're be able to take your practice of creative visualization and your own personal development programme to a more advanced level.

Chapter 21

Ten Goals that Creative Visualization Can Help You Achieve

Creative visualization provides you with a powerful range of techniques for dealing with real-life problems, and for making the changes you want in your life. These techniques existed for thousands of years, but became better known only when creative visualization developed into a major personal improvement tool.

By harnessing the power of your unconscious mind and visualizing the type of person you want to be, and the things you desire, you can break through the barriers holding you back, overcome anxiety and phobias, increase your creativity, and become more skilled at doing the things you enjoy. This chapter contains ten ways in which creative visualization can help you.

Alleviating Anxiety

By visualizing yourself as calm, and using the creative visualization techniques covered in this book to relax, you can remove nagging anxiety, lower your blood pressure, and overcome fears and phobias. Check out Chapter 11 for all the details.

Becoming Healthier

Using creative visualization helps you to focus on positive things and discover how to overcome aches and pains. You can also use it to improve your muscle tone, overall fitness, and self-healing ability. Chapters 3, 10, and 15 contain more information on using creative visualization to benefit your physical health.

Enhancing Your Creativity

A central element of creative visualization is that it's, well, creative! By using your creativity and imagination as part of the exercises, you discover how to become more creative generally. This helps you when needing to come up with new ideas at work, to enjoy hobbies such as art and music, and also to improve your use of creative visualization itself. Take a look at Chapter 17 for more information.

Strengthening Your Self-belief

When you lack self-belief and, for example, feel incapable of passing exams or overcoming obstacles in your life, call on creative visualization to strengthen your belief in yourself. As your belief increases, you naturally achieve more of the things you previously thought were impossible (as I explain in Chapter 13).

Building Confidence

Like everyone, you need confidence to present yourself successfully to other people and become an effective communicator. The creative visualization techniques in this book help you to assume a realistic, positive, and confident approach to life, helping you to take on more responsibilities, become a better leader, and enjoy life more fully by relieving yourself of doubt and insecurity. Turn to Chapter 13 for more on increasing your self-confidence, and Chapter 14 for more on leadership skills.

Achieving Goals

Setting goals and sticking to a commitment, such as quitting smoking or saving an amount of money, is never easy. But visualizing the goals and the results they're going to bring you strengthens your willpower and the determination to help you succeed. Flip to Chapter 10 for info on conquering bad habits.

Providing Focus

Amid all the fuss and hubbub of modern life, sometimes you can have difficulty seeing clearly what's important. Practising creative visualization, however, helps you to narrow in on the things that matter the most to you. This new-found focus then makes the process of obtaining your goals a whole lot easier, and understanding the things and people that matter in your life. Check out Chapter 2 for advice on how to focus on the important things to visualize about, and Chapter 12 for more information on building strong relationships.

Improving Your Body Language

With creative visualization you can review or assess yourself objectively, and certainly get a lot closer to the way you come across to other people. These insights allow you actively to evaluate and change your body language in order to convey exactly the impression you want others to have about you (Chapter 13 contains loads more on body language).

Increasing Your Energy

When you lack energy, drive, or motivation, getting on with (or even getting started on) a project can be difficult. But through creative visualization, you can create the energy and motivation you need, and use it to kick start your imagination and fire up your enthusiasm to get started on, work through, and complete a project, as I describe in Chapter 9.

Finding Fulfilment

One of the most important characteristics that creative visualization can help develop within you is a sense of joy and happiness – a contented feeling of fulfilment that leads to a peaceful sense of oneness with the world and the quiet knowledge of the importance of your place within it. Read Chapter 7 for all about using creative visualization to find contentment.

Index

FOR DUMMIES®

Making Everything Easier!™

UK editions

BUSINESS

Bookkeeping For Dummies
978-0-470-97626-5

Leadership For Dummies
978-0-470-97211-3

Project Management For Dummies
978-0-470-71119-4

Asperger's Syndrome For Dummies
978-0-470-66087-4

Boosting Self-Esteem For Dummies
978-0-470-74193-1

British Sign Language
For Dummies
978-0-470-69477-0

Coaching with NLP For Dummies
978-0-470-97226-7

Cricket For Dummies
978-0-470-03454-5

Diabetes For Dummies, 3rd Edition
978-0-470-97711-8

REFERENCE

British Politics For Dummies
978-0-470-68637-9

DIY For Dummies
978-0-470-97450-6

Researching Your Family History Online For Dummies
978-0-470-74535-9

English Grammar For Dummies
978-0-470-05752-0

Flirting For Dummies
978-0-470-74259-4

Football For Dummies
978-0-470-68837-3

IBS For Dummies
978-0-470-51737-6

Improving Your Relationship
For Dummies
978-0-470-68472-6

Lean Six Sigma For Dummies
978-0-470-75626-3

Life Coaching For Dummies,
2nd Edition
978-0-470-66554-1

HOBBIES

Growing Your Own Fruit & Veg For Dummies
978-0-470-69960-7

Allotment Gardening For Dummies
978-0-470-68641-6

Electronics For Dummies
978-0-470-68178-7

Management For Dummies,
2nd Edition
978-0-470-97769-9

Nutrition For Dummies, 2nd Edition
978-0-470-97276-2

30093 (p1)

FOR DUMMIES®

A world of resources to help you grow

UK editions

FOR DUMMIES®

The easy way to get more done and have more fun

LANGUAGES

Spanish For Dummies
978-0-470-68815-1
UK Edition

French For Dummies
978-1-118-00464-7

German For Dummies
978-0-470-90101-4

MUSIC

Ukulele For Dummies
978-0-470-97799-6
UK Edition

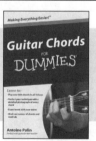

Guitar Chords For Dummies
978-0-470-66603-6
Lay-flat, UK Edition

DJing For Dummies
978-0-470-66372-1
UK Edition

SCIENCE & MATHS

Biology For Dummies
978-0-470-59875-7

Algebra I For Dummies
978-0-470-55964-2

Genetics For Dummies
978-0-470-55174-5

Art For Dummies
978-0-7645-5104-8

Bass Guitar For Dummies, 2nd Edition
978-0-470-53961-3

Criminology For Dummies
978-0-470-39696-4

Currency Trading For Dummies
978-0-470-12763-6

Drawing For Dummies, 2nd Edition
978-0-470-61842-4

Forensics For Dummies
978-0-7645-5580-0

Guitar For Dummies, 2nd Edition
978-0-7645-9904-0

Index Investing For Dummies
978-0-470-29406-2

Knitting For Dummies, 2nd Edition
978-0-470-28747-7

Music Theory For Dummies
978-0-7645-7838-0

Piano For Dummies, 2nd Edition
978-0-470-49644-2

Physics For Dummies, 2nd Edition
978-0-470-90324-7

Schizophrenia For Dummies
978-0-470-25927-6

Sex For Dummies, 3rd Edition
978-0-470-04523-7

Sherlock Holmes For Dummies
978-0-470-48444-9

Solar Power Your Home For Dummies, 2nd Edition
978-0-470-59678-4

The Koran For Dummies
978-0-7645-5581-7

FOR DUMMIES®

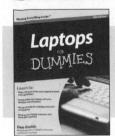

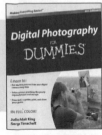
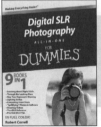

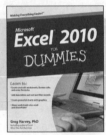